D1598129

SCOOP

SCOOP

The Life and Politics of
Henry M. Jackson

by PETER J. OGNIBENE

STEIN AND DAY/*Publishers*/New York

First published in 1975

Designed by Ed Kaplin
Printed in the United States of America
Stein and Day/*Publishers*/Scarborough House,
Briarcliff Manor, N.Y. 10510

Library of Congress Cataloging in Publication Data

Ognibene, Peter J.
Scoop: the life and politics of
Henry M. Jackson.

1. Jackson, Henry Martin, 1912- I. Title.
E748.J22045 328.73'092'4 [B] 75-28238
ISBN 0-8128-1884-9

To My Parents

ACKNOWLEDGMENTS

Although writing a book is solitary work, the research which goes into a manuscript and the production of those pages into a bound volume require the help of many. I feel a special sense of indebtedness to my literary agent, Julian Bach, for his valuable guidance from conception to publication; the book would not have come into being without him.

A number of *New Republic* colleagues were especially helpful. Doris Grumbach, former literary editor, gave me useful advice on the completed manuscript. Stanley Karnow, former foreign editor, graciously shared important research material with me. Paul Wieck, a fellow contributing editor, read and commented on several chapters and improved my perspective.

Terence Finn probably knows more about the legislative wrangles which culminated in the National Environmental Policy Act than any person alive, and I found his Ph.D. dissertation of immense value in writing Chapter 10. Arthur Hadley and Lindsay McKelvey had valuable insight and advice on the several chapters they read.

George Caldwell and Eve Tulipan of Stein and Day had good suggestions on the final manuscript. Margaret Cheney, as copy editor, came to the rescue of the English language more times than I would care to count.

Those whom I interviewed provided me with recollections and anecdotes which had heretofore been recorded only in their memories.

Although I did not directly use Bill Prochnau and Dick Larsen's book, *A Certain Democrat,* in writing this biography, their work suggested several areas for research that I might otherwise have missed.

The advice, information and ideas of these individuals as well as those I interviewed guided me in ways great and small. Of course, the text, conclusions and any errors are mine alone.

Contents

1. The Making of a Debacle, 1972 *13*

BASE

2. The City of Smokestacks *29*
3. The Other Washington *46*
4. Grass Roots: The Thirty-nine Counties of Washington State *63*
5. The Klickitat Shuffle: Screwing the "Radiclibs" Back Home *80*

AMBITION

6. The Early Senate Years *95*
7. Scoop and Maggie *101*
8. Chance Missed: JFK and the Vice-Presidency *113*
9. Oh! Henry! An Innocent Among Women *122*

ISSUES

10. The Land *133*
11. Generalissimo Jackson *150*
12. Vietnam: "We Must Pay the Price" *169*
13. Is He Good for the Jews? *182*

POWER

14. The Purge *199*
15. The Roots of Power *217*

Index *235*

Preface

THE ROLE of a political journalist ought to be that of an adversary, and I have written this book from that point of view. Senator Henry M. Jackson believes he should be the next President of the United States, and that alone is sufficient reason for giving his life and politics the closest possible scrutiny.

Jackson has more than one hundred people working for him among his Senate office, committee, and campaign staffs. Their role, like that of all political assistants, is to help their boss achieve his political ambition, which in Jackson's case means the Presidency. With their help, the senator will make speeches, issue press releases, hold news conferences, and conduct committee hearings to attract the "straight news" coverage which will transmit to the American public what he wants them to see and hear. But Scoop Jackson as presented by Scoop Jackson will inevitably be a distorted image. The ready corrective—imperfect though it is—is the lens of interpretive journalism.

Political journalists ought not be cheerleaders. Charm is a politician's stock in trade, and the reporter who gets too close to a politician does his readers and ultimately himself a disservice. There are many worthy men in public life and much of what they do springs from decent motives. On the other hand, certain men at times disserve those who put them in office. If the people are to judge their public servants, they need to learn not only what these men have done that is good, they need to know the bad as well. Because the politician and his staff will gladly tell the public the former, it falls to the political journalist to ferret out, report, and analyze the latter. Indeed, if he does not, no one else will.

Because this book attempts to zero in on aspects of Jackson's political past he might prefer to forget, his partisans will probably complain that this is not a "balanced" account. Were this the only source of information about the man, their point might be well taken; that, however, is not the case. Jackson and his hundred assistants have been telling, and will continue to tell, the public about the senator's good works, which are many. That is a legitimate function in our political system, but their hagiology must necessarily be a biased account. The antidote, again, is interpretive journalism.

The mind tends to telescope events, and those most close to us in time naturally stand out. Powerful senators such as Jackson are regularly in the news, and we understandably tend to perceive these individuals in the light of recent events. Jackson's public career, however, goes back nearly forty years, and no understanding of the man is possible without a comprehensive look at his extensive record. Because television, newspapers, and magazines have familiarized the attentive public with the senator's more recent deeds, I have not dwelled on them at length but have tried instead to incorporate them into the broader patterns discernible in his public life. Jefferson once said, "Whenever a man has cast a longing eye on offices, a rottenness begins in his conduct." We cannot assess whether this dictum applies to Jackson's longing for the White House unless we can determine whether his present positions arise from sincere motives or are calculated postures designed to get campaign funds and votes. To make such a determination we must scrutinize his past in detail.

Speeches and legislation leave a public record which is readily available to the political journalist. Equally important but considerably harder to research are the memories of individuals. So, in addition to reading most of Jackson's public record, I interviewed 120 people—about evenly divided between the City and State of Washington—to learn what I could of the man and his work. I have attributed these recollections when I could, but because many individuals for various reasons would speak freely only if guaranteed anonymity, I am obliged to omit their names in certain instances. I also interviewed Jackson and found him pleasant, if not very candid. At some point, however, he or his staff apparently decided that these interviews were not in the senator's interest. I had had two "sessions" with Jackson and had reached 1945 in my questions about his public career when my access to him was ended. My phone calls to his press secretary to inquire when these interviews might be resumed were rarely returned.

Because Jackson is only dimly perceived in the light of the electron tube or through the lines of newspaper and magazine articles, I have tried to organize this book into sections in each of which a particular facet of his career is examined and developed. While I would have preferred to write a flowing, chronological narrative which integrated all these facets, there are simply not as many sources of information about Jackson as there are about former presidents or famous statesmen long since dead. Such books about Jackson, should they be necessary, will be written many years from now.

This book is largely a study of power: how it is acquired, maintained, used, and misused. After the opening chapter about Jackson's abortive effort to capture the supreme political prize in 1972, there is a section titled "Base," which looks at his rise to power in Washington State and how he keeps it. The second section, "Ambition," examines in an eclectic way his transition from provincial to national politician. In the third section, "Issues," I have attempted to trace the evolution of Jackson's thinking in four important areas of public policy with which he is identified. The fourth section, "Power," is limited to an analysis of Jackson's present-day influence in government.

PETER J. OGNIBENE

July 1975
Silver Spring, Maryland

CHAPTER

1

The Making of a Debacle, 1972

ON PAPER he was the perfect candidate of "the real majority": a liberal on domestic programs eager to spend federal dollars on those he calls "the little people" and a hard-liner on the Soviet Union and the Vietnam War. AFL-CIO charts showed him with the best labor voting record in the Senate, and Republican businessmen found him a congenial ally in their pursuit of government contracts and subsidies. There was enough money to plaster the Florida peninsula with "Scoop for President" billboards, and no other candidate stumped that state from dawn to midnight with greater vigor. Yet, when the presidential preference vote was tallied there, Jackson found himself a distant third with just 14 percent of the vote. (Alabama Governor George Wallace got 42 percent and Senator Hubert Humphrey got 19 percent.) It was, he would learn many painful months later, the high-water mark of his first presidential race.

The symbol of Jackson's abortive campaign was a UPI photo of him standing on a park bench in Winter Haven, Florida, talking into a microphone before an apparent audience of two: an elderly woman and a young boy on a bicycle. When that picture was published throughout the country, Jackson was outraged and not without cause. A second UPI photo taken from a different angle showed there were considerably more people in the crowd, perhaps as many as two hundred. Nonetheless, the first photo perfectly symbolized Jackson's problem in 1972: when he talked, few listened. For a man who had spent three decades in Congress, it was a cruel blow. "He was disillusioned," says Stanley Golub, his close friend and 1972 campaign treasurer, "to find he was not well known or that people who recognized him didn't know his background in civil liberties and civil rights."

Another person might have looked into himself to learn the cause of his failure, but Jackson shuns introspection. He is uncomfortable probing his own psyche; his staff know this and carefully avoid telling their boss about his faults. (One who tried during the campaign found his access to the inner circle at an end.) Yet the *fact* that Jackson's presidential effort had ended in debacle could not be denied; hence, there had to be a reason for it, and to be acceptable to Jackson it would have to be one which would not further wound his injured pride. Several were suggested by his friends and staff, but the culprit ultimately convicted was "low recognition factor."

The term is a pollster's abstraction. "Have you ever heard of Senator Henry M. (Scoop) Jackson?" is the question, and in early 1972 perhaps two or three voters in ten were able to say yes. As Golub pointed out, Jackson was "disillusioned" to find that he was a cipher to some 70 to 80 percent of his countrymen, but that statistic also provided him a handy excuse. If people do not know who you are, they cannot know what you stand for. If they do not know what you stand for, they will not vote for you. It was an appealing rationalization, and one still hears variations of this syllogism when Jackson's most loyal aides talk about what went wrong in 1972. The people did not reject Jackson or his message, they assert; we simply did not have enough time or money to present the man and his record to the electorate.

The fallacy in this argument is the assumption that Jackson's low recognition factor simply meant that he was unknown and not that he or his message had been rejected. It does not take into account the tens of millions of people who had seen him on television or read about him in a newspaper and simply forgot who he was because he did not strike them as important enough to remember. Try, for instance, to recall the last TV commercial you saw. Most likely, you cannot because you either mentally tuned it out or quickly forgot it. People often treat campaigning politicians the same way, and I suspect many simply tuned out Jackson. After all, there are TV sets in 95 percent of the homes in America, and Jackson has been featured on local and network programs since the early 1950s. The chances of an adult viewer's not having seen him are about as great as his not having seen a commercial for milk of magnesia.

People tune out Jackson, I believe, because his appeal is largely a *negative* one. He talks about what is wrong rather than what the nation should do to set matters right. He looks back to the good old days of Democratic prosperity but offers no vision of the future. He lectures the electorate on the ills of the world but then offers a simplistic military solution which would probably exacerbate matters. He does not try to lift the spirit: he aims for the gut. Instead of appealing to what Lincoln called "the better angels of our nature," he takes us as we are and tries to exploit our anxieties or prejudices to win votes. In short, he seems like dozens of other politicians: not worth remembering.

Understanding Jackson's negativism is, in my view, the key to understanding why he failed in 1972. Two incidents which occurred during the Wisconsin primary, in which Jackson was fifth with 8 percent of the vote, reveal much about the way he thinks and operates.

A Seattle physician, active in politics, offered to help Jackson on health care, one of the more pressing concerns of the average American. He drafted a proposal which Jackson reportedly liked and arranged for the senator to present it before a hospital association in Wisconsin. The progressive electorate of that state would probably have responded favorably to a positive effort to provide better health care for the nation, but Jackson, unaccountably, decided against presenting this or any other health proposal and spurned the opportunity to speak to the hospital group. He preferred to exploit the more divisive "social issue." (Read crime, blacks, hippies, or conjure up a new abomination.)

A question-and-answer session with students at the Oshkosh campus of the University of Wisconsin was arranged for Jackson. A reporter, who accompanied him, recalls the scene: "Jackson kept using his 1954-vintage understanding of the issues, and when one student asked him a question about Indian affairs, the one defense he kept falling back on was that he had a full-blooded Indian on his Interior Committee staff. He kept referring to him as 'my Indian'! He could not talk with sensitivity about issues." Because of his condescending attitude, the session proved "a disaster."

Jackson is a captive of the past. He is backward-looking on issues and tends to regard his experience as definitive. As one of his Seattle friends put it: "He thinks he's seen it all before." Because he has been so successful campaigning among the 3.5 million people in the 39 counties of Washington State, it was only natural that he would try to transfer his experience to a national race. "He's been a one-man show in his House and Senate races," says a former aide. "He knows every county chairman and previous chairman. . . . He thought he'd run for President the same way he runs for the Senate. He never appreciated the necessity of having people out ahead of him—advancing, organizing. Time and again, he'd fly out first class with his press secretary. That was all! He thought he'd actually keep people with a speech and a personal appearance. It was entirely the senator's lack of perception that was at fault." And, he emphasized, *"There was no one in a position to tell him otherwise."*

John Salter, who had long been Jackson's principal political operative and had had the benefit of working in JFK's 1960 campaign, apparently tried to get him interested in organizing a national effort but had no success. "Salter was wanting to get organized in the states," says the former aide, "but Jackson was involved in little details, like where to stay, how to travel. . . . Too bad, that uses up so much time and energy."

Gordon Culp, a Seattle attorney and former Jackson staffer, left his law practice to take charge of campaign scheduling. He agreed with the anonymous aide that Jackson "was more involved in campaign schedule details than he should have been. I had the job because everyone knew I was coming back here [Seattle] to practice law. You can't please everyone because there is no such thing as an optimum schedule. Scoop is automatically, intrinsically involved in details; it's part of his character. He's the same way with legislative efforts. That's creditable but impractical. He should have stayed out of details and fired whoever screwed up, but he doesn't do that either. I don't think he'll ever change."

Other aides have stories about Jackson's personally loading his own and his staff's luggage, and one recalls a campaign dinner in Florida. "It was in a side room in a restaurant, and afterwards Scoop comes up and asks who's paying. 'Is it all paid up?' he asked."

"Personal contact, that's Jackson's style," says a former political associate. "He'll leave D.C. on Thursday or Friday and make weekend appearances at a round of meetings and fairs and follow up with letters. Jackson's [state] organization is based on his meeting these people. Now, in 1972, how the hell do you apply that political style to the nation as a whole? National campaigning is totally alien to his style.... You can't campaign in 50 states like you do in 39 counties."

That last sentence could fittingly serve as the epitaph for Jackson's first presidential race. S. Sterling Munro, his administrative assistant, tried to run the Senate office as well as the campaign staff and wound up doing only half of each job. To make matters worse, there were "not enough people with finance and political experience to put together a national organization," says Culp. "And none ever was. . . . The primaries came rapid fire, and it was a traveling circus. I would agree with the criticism that there was no organization in place in the states."

Part of Jackson's problem was his inability to attract party workers and activists. "Scoop can't very well—happily—carve a way-out constituency which becomes a built-in campaign organization," says Culp. "He must do it out of the great bulk of voters. McGovern had a clear corner on the young, the only big pool of free campaign workers that exists. It comprises a valuable collection of bodies. . . . None of that sort of organization was available to Scoop or anyone else."

What that meant in practical terms, according to one campaign worker, was that Jackson's campaign in the largest state became " 'Mission Impossible.' We had trouble getting volunteers in California. We got 50 to 60 ex-Washington Staters who felt some loyalty to Scoop." To do well in California without an unlimited media budget, one needs tens of *thousands,* not tens, of volunteers. It was even worse elsewhere. Indeed, the number and fervor of political foot soldiers seemed to diminish with the distance from the Evergreen State.

Choosing which primaries to enter was a problem. Salter and a small contingent had scouted New Hampshire and recommended Jackson run there even though it looked as if Senator Edmund Muskie from the neighboring state of Maine would probably win. Jackson seemed to lean in that direction at first, and stories to that effect were leaked to the press. When he ultimately decided not to run in New Hampshire, the ostensible reason was that he could not afford to campaign both there and in Florida, whose primary was just one week later. But an equally important factor may have been his concern that William Loeb, the arch-conservative publisher of the Manchester *Union-Leader,* might endorse him. Loeb has the only statewide newspaper, and his endorsement would have carried considerable weight—but only in New Hampshire. Thereafter, Jackson would have had to bear the right-wing stigma. After he decided not to run in New Hampshire, Loeb endorsed Los Angeles Mayor Sam Yorty.

Tactics were another problem. Jackson has always been cautious about getting "out front" on an issue. He prefers to wait until he perceives it safe or the time propitious for belated leadership. (Israel is the best recent example.) On most matters he would rather "sit short in the straddle" and utter platitudes or simply duck the issue, as he did with health care in Wisconsin. That approach has paid off in Washington State, but he and his advisers knew he would have to seize some issues if they wanted to win votes in the primaries. And that is where Ben J. Wattenberg came in.

Wattenberg is easy to spot among the square-bodied, short-haired political heavies who form Jackson's flying squad. He's the lean fellow with shaggy gray hair, long sideburns and black, Viva Zapata mustache. But beneath that hirsute exterior ticks a cybernetic intellect which knows where the votes are and how they may be had. Co-author (with Richard Scammon) of

The Real Majority. Wattenberg taught the present generation of politicians that you need not be a Nixon to exploit "the social issue."

Many thought they saw a Svengali in Wattenberg, but he insists "the fact is the obverse of that. Jackson did not come to me, *tabula rasa,* and say, 'Find me a good strategy.' I believed in the stuff I wrote. I started listening to potential candidates and through good offices I got in touch with him. I went to the candidate because of what he was and what he has stood for for many years."

And what was that?

"Jackson has more coherent views than any other politician I have ever known. His strength is that he is not prepared to pick up any faddish rhetoric and policy. . . . He is prepared to speak his mind on things that are not popular."

In February of 1972 Jackson introduced "a Constitutional amendment to guarantee an equal public education without forced artificial busing." This amendment "will prohibit mandatory busing of children by declaring that every parent has the freedom of choice and the right to have his or her children attend their local neighborhood public school."

Many Jackson supporters and even some campaign aides were shocked and disgusted by what seemed to them a thinly disguised appeal to racism. All the familiar code words were there: "forced artificial busing," "freedom of choice," and "local neighborhood public school." Such phrases come easily to the lips of an unreconstructed segregationist like George Wallace, but what were they doing coming from the mouth of a senator who had supported every major civil rights bill? Where was the Scandinavian social conscience Jackson was so often said to have inherited from his forebears?

Wattenberg has a rationale: "Jackson explained his position on busing to me. There had been a court decision in favor of busing, and you could not overrule a court decision by simple legislation. . . . Eighty percent were against busing, and Jackson felt that he, too, was against it substantively. He decided the only way to change it is a Constitutional amendment.

"On top of all this he was running in Florida. He introduced it then in response to a given situation, but the intellectual processes that went into that view were sound and honest. I do not think it was a craven sellout. . . . And here's the payoff line: half the blacks are against busing."

One Jackson aide calls the anti-busing amendment "uncharacteristic and reprehensible. It was the part of the campaign I call 'Wattenberg Unchained.' . . . My biggest fear about Jackson becoming President is that Wattenberg would have substantial influence. Scoop is a very principled person, with a strong concept of right and wrong."

If Jackson thought he could "out-seg" Wallace, he had another think coming. In January of 1972 on a three-day swing through northern Florida, which had gone heavily for Wallace in 1968, Jackson made twenty-three stops and talked about defense, patriotism, his Presbyterian and Masonic memberships, and, of course, busing. "I repeat, I repeat," he said, "I am not a political hypocrite. I believe in human dignity for all people. The proof of that is that my daughter has a black teacher."

He convinced few people in that part of the state, and one good ole boy brought him up short when he asked Jackson why he had voted against ending the embargo on Rhodesian chrome. (This issue annually provides members of Congress an opportunity to give symbolic support to a white supremacist regime.) In a weak voice, Jackson explained that he had voted against ending the embargo to support "our British ally." Not surprisingly, Florida's diehard segregationists voted for the real Wallace, not the ersatz model from the Pacific Northwest.

"Jackson's big problem was recognition," contends Wattenberg. "Nobody knew who the hell he was. As we went into that campaign, the problem was how to get known. The way you get known is to win a primary. So you've got to pick one state. We put our whole stack in Florida, about $400,000. . . . I know of two or three polls that showed that had Wallace not been in the primary, Jackson would have won or been close to Humphrey. Humphrey got a lot of black and Jewish votes. . . . Primaries are high-risk poker."

"After the Florida campaign," one aide bitterly recalls, "Wattenberg took a poll and the election results and compared them. Then he tried to show us how the figures showed a shift to Jackson. I thought he had worked up charts a few nights before to handle *every* result the morning after the primary."

Wisconsin was next, but after Florida it was all downhill. "The Milwaukee paper the next day," Wattenberg recalls, "ran a headline: 'Wallace First in Florida, Humphrey Second, Muskie Fourth.' Jackson came in third but wasn't even mentioned.... Once you hit that—that you didn't get known—there was no way to bust out of it."

Gerald Hoeck, who has handled media for Jackson since 1948, agrees: "How do you become known and get people familiar with your positions? We needed to win a primary: we came in third. On election night, they covered everybody but Jackson. One did but the videotape equipment went awry. Another network taped it but didn't use it: they felt it was not a story. It's hard to become news unless you win one. There's no such thing as charisma. You win!"

If Jackson's militaristic rhetoric and Southern code words failed to cut substantially into the Wallace vote in Florida, they proved positively disastrous in progressive Wisconsin. When the ballots were counted there, Jackson was fifth with 8 percent of the vote.

After Wisconsin, his staff realized the campaign was in its death throes. The Ohio primary was four weeks away, Jackson had no organization in the state other than the "traveling circus" which moved with him from one primary to another, and money was getting short. "I ended up with $20,000 to spend on advertising in Ohio," recalls Hoeck incredulously. "Can you imagine that? Twenty thousand dollars for the entire state of Ohio!"

Jackson was fourth this time, but he still got only 8 percent of the vote. Before he went down to defeat, however, he launched a series of vitriolic attacks against Senator George McGovern which (in retrospect) provided the groundwork for the Nixon re-election committee's hatchet work that summer and fall.

By the time he got to Ohio, the neat, strategic plan laid out by Wattenberg had bombed. Jackson was no longer a serious candidate, but instead of acknowledging reality, he gave vent to his pent-up frustrations and began slinging mud at McGovern.

On April 25, in Youngstown, Ohio, Jackson called McGovern "the spokesman for some of the dangerous and destructive currents in American politics." Extremism of the left was gaining respectability, he warned, and "the main vehicle of this suicidal drift is the candidacy of Senator McGovern." Then, using that familiar Nixon tactic, guilt by association, he took a nasty swipe at the South Dakotan: "It comes as no surprise to me that Senator McGovern has just been endorsed by Yippie leaders Abbie Hoffman and Jerry Rubin. It would be unfair to conclude that because Hoffman and Rubin have endorsed McGovern, McGovern endorses Hoffman and Rubin. But it is perfectly fair to ask why these two hate-America leftist extremists, who have been in the forefront of violent demonstrations, should find Senator McGovern's candidacy congenial to their own problems.... Apparently the people who tried to wreck the Democratic convention from the outside in 1968 want to do it from the inside in 1972."

Three days later, in Cincinnati, Jackson criticized McGovern for supporting Henry A. Wallace for the presidency some 24 years before. "McGovern's 1948 candidate supported the Communist takeover of Czechoslovakia," charged Jackson. "McGovern's 1948 candidate wanted us to give away tens of billions of dollars in foreign aid to Joe Stalin's Russia." Wallace, in his view, was guilty of "appeasement" and, by implication, so were those who supported FDR's former Vice President and Agriculture secretary.

Jackson continued in this vein, much to his staff's dismay and to his own detriment as well. For example, the Cuyahoga County district attorney endorsed Jackson, and that should have been big news in vote-rich Cleveland. But Jackson once again teed off on McGovern's support for Henry Wallace in the 1948 presidential race. So, instead of the televised image of a bright young DA endorsing Jackson, viewers saw a bitter, irascible candidate who was headed for defeat and trying to drag an opponent with him.

Several weeks later McGovern was branded the "triple-A candidate" (acid, amnesty, and abortion). Many erroneously thought the author of that appellation was Jackson, when, in fact, it was Senator Hugh Scott, the Pennsylvania Republican. Their confusion was understandable because, after all, Jackson was the most visible and vitriolic of McGovern's attackers that spring.

At the convention in Miami, Jackson was the "ABM"

candidate (Anybody But McGovern), but the movement fizzled on the launching pad. After McGovern's nomination, Jackson half-heartedly endorsed him, but afterwards tried to avoid mentioning him by name. When asked point-blank by a reporter if he was supporting McGovern, Jackson replied: "I'm supporting the ticket."

No analysis of the 1972 campaign would be complete without some discussion of "the mother's milk of politics": money. (The phrase was coined by California's Jess Unruh.) A new campaign financing law went into effect on April 7, 1972, requiring that all contributions be made public. According to reports filed by Jackson's campaign committee at the General Accounting Office, the organization had about $100,000 on hand April 7 and raised an additional $200,000 before going out of business. This, however, was just the tip of the proverbial iceberg.

Only two of the Democratic candidates, Jackson and Wilbur Mills, refused to reveal who had contributed to their campaigns prior to April 7. Jackson clothed his reasons for not doing so in noble rhetoric. He had "promised" his contributors anonymity, and he would not go back on his "word." He indicated that some of the contributors were Republicans and government officials who might lose their jobs if their contributions were revealed. His staff also tried to blunt talk about Jackson's "secret list" by darkly hinting that other candidates had not been as forthright as they claimed to be. "McGovern's list was a phony list," said a Jackson military policy specialist. "I know of one man who gave McGovern $400,000, but you won't find his name on the list." (This false accusation was not fired in the heat of electoral battle; it was made fully a year after the 1972 election.)

Several magazine articles about Jackson in early 1974 made quite an issue of his secret list of campaign financiers, and it seemed certain to become a problem in the 1976 campaign. The solution Jackson hit upon was both simple and ingenious. His campaign treasurer, Stanley Golub, gave the list to Senator Sam Ervin's Watergate Committee. "Once the government requested it," says Golub, "we felt a responsibility [to turn over the list]. We called a number of contributors from here [Seattle] and Washington and told them we had given their names to the

Senate Watergate Committee. We also asked, again, if these were personal or corporate contributions. Claude Wild was the only one who demurred."

Wild subsequently admitted to the committee that he gave the Jackson campaign $10,000 in corporate funds from Gulf Oil Corporation. (Corporate contributions, of course, are illegal.) Another illegal contribution was made in Wisconsin when a Boeing employee spent $300 in traveler's checks supplied by his company to buy newspaper and radio ads for Jackson. These two illegal contributions were all that was known about Jackson's secret list until the list itself was made available to reporters by the Watergate Committee in August of 1974. (Curiously, the committee did not publish the list in its comprehensive, twenty-six-volume set of hearings and material related to the 1972 presidential campaign. One is thus led to speculate that Jackson may simply have engineered the committee's "request" for his secret list so the onus of releasing it would not be on him. In any event, that effectively defused its potential to damage his 1976 presidential campaign.)

Jackson's biggest backer was oil millionaire Leon Hess. He gave Jackson $225,000, much of it disguised as individual contributions from more than a dozen people. Other major contributors were Meshulam Riklis, the head of Rapid-American Corporation, who gave $100,000; Walter R. Davis, a Texas oil operator, who gave $50,000 in cash; and Dwayne Andreas, a Minneapolis soybean millionaire, who gave $25,000, also in cash. The total raised, before and after April 7, was $1.1 million, of which $166,000 was in cash. Even though these gifts were apparently legal, one now understands why Jackson was reluctant to make them public. Their size, the means by which they were disguised, and the heavy cash bundles were certain to be compared to the larger-scale Nixon operation; they hardly squared with the straight-shooter image Jackson tries to affect.

After the secret list was made public, the Northrop Corporation and Time Oil Company of Seattle each admitted making illegal corporate contributions of $1,000 to Jackson. Moreover, there are still unanswered questions about some of the publicly reported contributions.

Under the law which went into effect on April 7, 1972, it became illegal to give money to a political candidate in someone else's name. In reports filed by Jackson's committee at GAO are listed several late-1972 contributions from individuals associated with the Harvey Aluminum Corporation of Los Angeles. Two caught my eye: $1,000 from a bookkeeper and $3,000 from a secretary. When I called the secretary and asked if she had given her own money, she was evasive. "My contribution was returned before the 1972 election," she said. "I made out the check. . . . We can't get Mr. Harvey to explain it." Unless she gave her own money—and her evasiveness makes that seem unlikely—there may well have been a violation of the law.

To hear Jackson's people tell it, the problem in 1972 was money and recognition. Culp says there was "not that much money," but the secret list makes clear that Jackson raised $900,000 prior to April 7, 1972. Culp also calls "name familiarity a key difficulty" and suggests there was a cycle at work: money begets recognition, which in turn begets more money. Hoeck and Wattenberg appear to share that analysis.

There is some obvious truth to this point of view, but to ascribe Jackson's failure in 1972 to low recognition factor is to beg several important questions, the most important of which is: Why was he so unknown?

Since he had been in office for thirty-one years, lack of experience was plainly not a factor; nor was lack of prominence. Jackson has been one of the more visible congressional spokesmen on military affairs since the 1950s, and as chairman of the Interior Committee since 1963, he has been able to make a name for himself as a conservationist at a time when Ecology was becoming as sacrosanct as God, Flag, and Motherhood. He is a serious legislator, and the press has generally given his work the serious attention it merits. Thus, we can safely rule out lack of visibility as an important factor. The people who said, "No, I've never heard of him," when the pollster put Jackson's name before them did not recognize him for other, deeper reasons.

One stems from the nature of the man and his public work. Jackson is, no derogation intended, a backroom politician. He is most effective behind closed doors, one to one, or in committee. He is a superb tactician on the Senate floor, but a weak and ineffective orator whose speeches stir neither colleague nor constituent. Give him a secret Pentagon report, and he will tirelessly buttonhole one senator after another to collect (usually) a majority. The full Senate has held only a few secret sessions in recent years, usually to give Jackson an opportunity to sell his colleagues on Pentagon programs with classified Pentagon documents. Prior to 1975, he voted against measures to open committee meetings to the public unless a majority of the committee voted to close them. This, then, is a man who strongly believes that the public's work is best done beyond the public's eye.

Bills would not move through Congress without secretive, manipulative legislators: their talents and importance in the legislative process should not be underestimated. Such men, however, rarely become effective, inspirational leaders because, more often than not, they secretly hold the public in contempt.

There are few men on Capitol Hill who will work as hard as Jackson for a constituent in need, but should that same person or another suggest a position on, say, defense antithetical to his own, he will turn a deaf ear. (There are numerous examples of this, particularly in the early chapters of this book.) He serves the people of Washington State by steering government contracts and payrolls their way, and they reward him every six years with their votes. But, on matters of state, he hears only his own drummer. Such independence of mind would be a virtue if it were coupled with humility, but that trait is sadly lacking in Jackson. What often comes across in public forums, particularly under hard questioning, is his peculiar brand of closed-minded arrogance.

Jackson was disillusioned in 1972 because, after so many years on the national political stage, so few people knew who he was. The irony is that he was not *unseen*. His ubiquity in the electronic and print media put him before all but those few Americans in perpetual hibernation. The reason so few knew him, I suspect, is that he made either a negative impression or no more of an impression than the ordinary politician. Thus, the reason he failed so dismally in his first presidential race was not that he had such a statistically low recognition factor but that he made so little impact. The people saw just another run-of-the-mill politician when they looked at Scoop Jackson and promptly forgot him.

BASE

CHAPTER

2

The City of Smokestacks

JACK DOOTSON was waiting for me on the steps of the modest house on immodestly named Rockefeller Avenue. When I had called him from Seattle a few days before, he had sounded very interested—indeed, eager—to meet me and talk about his childhood friend and next-door neighbor, Henry Jackson.

It was late morning on a bright, warm day in mid-August. It would have been hot but for the westerly breeze which was moving the cool air of Puget Sound over the City of Everett. Dootson met me as I got out of the car, and we chatted in front of his house for several minutes. He then offered to show me the neighborhood and introduce me to some of the people who had known Jackson as a youth. I accepted, and we set off on a walking tour which took us the next four hours.

Henry Martin (for Martin Luther) Jackson was born on May 31, 1912, in the white frame house at 3602 Oakes Avenue. The address is something of an anomaly because the house actually faces north on 36th Street. There is no view in that direction, just other houses, but on a clear day—a rare event in this part of the Pacific Northwest except in summer—one can turn on the front step and see the volcanically formed Cascade Mountains to the east. Higher ground on the west blocks any view of the Sound, where floating logs are penned and herded into sawmills.

Life for the Jackson family centered on this house and neighborhood and, indeed, seldom went beyond the boundaries of Snohomish County. As Dootson and I walked along Oakes Avenue, he pointed to a towering stand of poplars about a mile south of the house. "Scoop's parents and sisters are buried there," he told me.

One departs this life but not his neighborhood in Everett.

The interstate highway has left its own concrete memorial along the eastern edge of Evergreen Cemetery, but the noise of the Seattle-bound traffic does not seem to intrude in the hilly, well-maintained graveyard. The most prominent Everett families have bought out the higher ground and erected monuments commensurate with their worldly goods, but to the children playing on a summer's afternoon, the large mausoleum bearing the name Rucker is less an object of awe than a local pyramid which must be scaled.

By contrast, the Jackson family gravesite is simple and unobtrusive. One would have a difficult time finding it without a knowledgeable guide. The plot is dominated by a large rhododendron, which, a month before, would have been in full and spectacular bloom, but now only a few mottled flowers remain. The roots of the shrub are in the upper-left corner of the plot, but the branches extend to the right across nearly all the matching headstones.

Marie Jackson
1907–1969

Gertrude Jackson
1898–1969

Jackson
Peter　　Marine
1868–1948　　1868–1957

Agnes Jackson
1900–1914

Peter Jackson was born Peter Gresseth on an island near the village of Aure in Western Norway and grew up on a farm. In 1885, he left Norway and followed the path of thousands of other Scandinavian immigrants to Minnesota. He then moved west in search of work, living for a while in Montana before settling in Washington in 1888, a year before it achieved statehood. The name "Jackson" was concocted out of the first name of his Uncle Jack and a Scandinavian "son." His American surname may have made his transition in the new land somewhat easier, but Norway never left his voice. Although he learned English, he always spoke it in the rising and falling tones of his native tongue.

Marine Anderson, the youngest of twelve children, was born in Alvenes, a Norwegian village north of the Arctic Circle. She too was reared on a farm and knew the harshness of rural life. When she was confirmed in the Lutheran faith, the family had to row across a fjord and walk seventeen miles to the Roerstad Church. Exposed to the North Sea, the route across the water became quite perilous in winter. With just four to five hours of daylight, trips to church had to begin the day before.

She left Norway for America when she was twenty-three and joined an older brother, Konrad, who had settled in Gig Harbor, a small village across Puget Sound from Tacoma. She eventually moved to Everett and became a charter member of the local Lutheran church in 1893. The church was a traditional meeting place for Scandinavian immigrants in search of marriageable partners, and it was in the new church that she met Peter Jackson, himself a charter member. In 1897 they were married there.

Henry was the youngest of five children and most likely his mother's favorite. In his early youth he was somewhat lazy: a situation which led to his sister Gertrude's giving him the nickname "Scoop," after a comic-strip character who appeared in the Everett *Daily Herald*. The cartoon Scoop worked in a newspaper office, where he cleverly manipulated others into doing his work. Gertrude saw the parallel, and the name stuck.

Having lost a teenage daughter to what was then called "inflammatory rheumatism"—Jackson speculates it was "infantile paralysis"—the family's indulgence of the baby was understandable. Lyle Waters, eighty-four, who lives across the street, remembers young Jackson as "a runt who didn't grow up or play hard until after he had his appendix removed." Next-door neighbor Dootson says that "Scoop would mow the lawn and sit down after a little bit." He did his chores all right—he feared his father's hand too much not to—but he did them without enthusiasm.

Gertrude taught at the Garfield School, and because she was fourteen years older than her brother, she was almost a second mother to him. Although teachers never considered him an exceptional student, he had no choice but to study hard if he wanted to live in peace with the disciplined and demanding Jackson women. Gertrude, in particular, was so familiar with the whines and excuses of schoolchildren that he never stood a chance of fooling her.

If he found it better to study than look for excuses not to, he was reinforced by the discovery that hard work can often make up for a lack of native ability. Moreover, when he brought home good grades, the stern Jackson women turned doting.

Somewhat undersized and a bit timid, Henry was not a good athlete as a boy. In fact, his friend John Salter suggests: "He was an awkward kid, the sort that bullies might have chased home from school." If that was the case, at least he did not have far to run because Longfellow School was just two blocks south on Oakes Avenue.

By the time he was a teenager, Henry was delivering the *Herald* in the afternoons. When Dootson, who is two years younger, took over route 22 in 1929, he was able to make as much as $75 in two months: a grand sum in those days. Henry spent very little of his earnings; he saved them. To this day he remains something of a miser when it comes to spending his own or campaign funds.

On page 1 of the *Herald* of July 2, 1927, the story in the seventh column carried the headline: "Herald Carrier Has Perfect Record for 2 Years; Wins Prize." It was the second year in a row Henry had won, and the paper duly noted the logistics of his feat: "Henry delivered 74,880 Heralds without a single complaint for non-delivery." What the story did not point out—and what the paper might not have known—was that he had passed out cards with his name and address on them and asked the people on his route to notify him, not the paper, if they had any complaints. It was a case of something for everyone: the subscribers got their papers; he got an award. It also provided him with an early "political" lesson he would not forget.

Marie was five years older than Henry and probably the most attractive member of the family. A bit of a rebel, she had long dark curls as a young woman but one day decided to have them cut and fashioned into one of the short styles popular in the 1920s. Her mother was almost sick when she saw the resulting "bob." Marie's rebelliousness may have been at the root of her failure to finish high school, but she never broke the family tie and, like Gertrude, never married. She later took commercial courses at Seattle Pacific College and earned some money "clerking," but most of the time she stayed at home and worked around the house to help her mother, who was often ill.

Marie and Gertrude remained together in the Oakes Avenue house the rest of their lives. In February 1969, after months of suffering, Gertrude died of cancer. That December, Marie was smoking in bed while she addressed Christmas cards. She apparently dozed off, dropped her cigarette and died in the resulting fire.

Arthur Jackson is ten years older than his brother Henry. He was at least as bright as his younger brother and much more athletic, neighbors recall. John Salter remembers Arthur as "a rough and tough guy as a kid—feisty." He definitely was not the sort a bully would have chased home from school.

Arthur never had a chance to develop his potential. The Jacksons were not poor, but, as in other immigrant families, the older children were expected to work to help with the family's finances. If the family prospered, then the younger children might be able to go to college. Gertrude's education at Bellingham Normal (now Western Washington State) may have been viewed as the sort of practical investment which could be recouped in her teacher's salary. Arthur, however, quit high school and got a job in a hardware store. Later on, he went to work with his father as a cement mason. Neighbors still remember the two men with wheelbarrows and the implements of their trade digging holes in which they would mix the cement. It was a slow and primitive method, but it had to do until they could afford a hand-cranked mixing machine. When they finally bought one, it was an object of considerable pride.

Some of their work was done in the neighborhood. The garage built into the hill on which the Jackson house sits is one example; the long retaining wall at 3610 Oakes Avenue is another. The facing on the garage is now broken in several places, exposing the rotted timbers beneath. But the wall on their neighbor's property, now nearly a half century old, has held up remarkably well. There is only one crack, on the far right end, and a good repair will guarantee that wall will still be standing long after there are no neighbors who remember the men who built it.

Crippling arthritis put an end to the athletic and hard laboring activities of Arthur Jackson before he was forty. Since then, he has been in and out of hospitals for operations and therapy. When he was a patient at the Mayo Clinic in Rochester, Minnesota, Jackson and his assistant, Salter, used to stop and visit him on their journeys to or from sessions of Congress. Arthur, who lost all movement in his hips and had to have artificial hip joints implaced, once complained to another visitor: "I'm nothing but a guinea pig here." Later on, he found work as a bookkeeper for Pacific Car and Foundry and stayed with that firm for some twenty years. He retired in the early 1960s after suffering a stroke that left him with a "very strong speech impediment," according to the senator.

Several of his friends told me that Henry Jackson and the rest of the family had helped pay for Arthur's many hospitalizations. Phil Sheridan, who was deputy prosecutor under Jackson and remains one of his close friends, told me that Jackson could not afford a car when he was prosecuting attorney or in his early years in the House of Representatives "because he was supporting his brother Arthur." Jackson confirms this: "I paid it all—several thousand dollars."

Yet, for some reason, there has long been a gulf between the two surviving children of Peter and Marine Jackson. In public and in private, the senator often mentions his parents (particularly his mother) and sisters and the strong, positive force they exerted on his life. Unaccountably, some of his friends of two and three decades were surprised when I asked them about Arthur. They had no idea Scoop Jackson even had a brother.

About the source of their estrangement I found only speculations. Salter thinks it may be a case of jealously: "Art resents Scoop and his success." That could be. An older brother could become bitter when surpassed by a younger one. But one would expect the more successful of the two to make extraordinary efforts to heal the breach. And, while I could not determine if such efforts have been made, the impression left with me by some of Jackson's friends is that he has simply put his older brother out of his mind. It is almost as if he did not exist.

One Seattle politician told me that Arthur had attempted to contact Carl Maxey, the liberal, anti-war activist who had opposed Jackson in the 1970 Democratic primary for his Senate seat. A Maxey campaign worker went out to visit him and returned to report that Arthur had complained about being "cheated out of his inheritance." Although the Jackson-Maxey race was bitterly fought—invectives flying from both sides—Maxey, I am told, decided against using Arthur's charge. "We felt it was essentially an internal family matter," this politician recalled. "It was a matter of our honor not to use it."

When I mentioned this incident to Jackson, he reacted sharply: "Well, that's just absurd. That's all I can say." However, he went on to add: "Sure, there was some dispute over property. . . . I purposely did not want to be included in the [his mother's] will, which I was not. There was a dispute over dividing of certain unimproved land and that was worked out so that there was an amicable settlement." About Arthur's alleged dissatisfaction, he said, "He never mentioned that to me, and I've been in touch with him regularly, continuously over the years." He also pointed out: "I talk to him, well, at least once a month."

Before I left Washington State, I located Arthur Jackson. He lives in Renton, a small town just out of Seattle, in a neat working-class neighborhood. ("He's cared for by two old ladies," Jackson later told me, "rather than being in a rest home.") The small, well-kept house had a large garden in the back and a "Brock Adams for Congress" sign was posted on the landing. (A liberal Democrat, Adams broke with Jackson on the Vietnam War and the two have remained at an "amicable distance" ever since.)

A small dog barked when I knocked, but it took several minutes before Arthur Jackson got to the door. He was holding himself up on heavy steel crutches, and the short trip to the door had obviously required a considerable effort. I introduced myself and asked if I could talk with him briefly about his brother and what it was like growing up in Everett in the 1920s and '30s. He said he no longer talked about "politics."

I asked if he still heard regularly from his brother. He said he did, but he remained adamant about not discussing even "nonpolitical" subjects. Although he seemed to understand my questions, he would not even respond with a yes or no. So, I left without learning from Arthur why such distance seems to exist between the two brothers. I had the feeling, however, that someone had prevailed upon him not to talk to the writer who had been poking about Seattle for the preceding two months interviewing the senator's friends and foes.

When I later related this incident to Senator Jackson and asked him about the apparent "resentment" of his brother, he replied: "Well, that's a supposition on the part of a lot of people. If there is, I have no way, really, of detecting it because if that were true I would know about it, I think. Naturally there's always differences within a family. But resentment, no. I don't think that would be a proper description. . . . You have to bear in mind now that we're talking about someone who's been seriously ill for thirty-five years. That's a long time."

When Jackson was a young boy, the Waters family across the street ran a small candy factory behind their house. Also nearby was a bakery. So, whichever way the wind blew, the neighborhood was bathed in delicious vapors. The air changed for the worse, Jack Dootson recalls, once "the Everett Pulp and Paper Company built its plant."

The odor left behind by the sulfate process fouled the air, and whenever the wind blew the wrong way, it inundated the city with the awful smell. Most accepted the situation as the price of "progress," but it nonetheless became a source of scatological humor. One joke of the time told of a woman who was changing her baby's diaper on the train. Having no place to put the dirty diaper, she threw it over her shoulder and hit the conductor, who had been dozing nearby. Awake now, and recognizing the smell, he jumped to his feet and called out: "EVERETT! EVERETT! Everybody off for EVERETT!"

"The City of Smokestacks" was what Everett once proudly

called itself: even the post office's canceling stamp carried the motto. Although most (but not all) of the pulp mills have since converted to the less malodorous sulfite process, several miles north of town smokestacks still turn the crystal air to gray, and the nose of the apocryphal conductor would still sense the train's approaching Everett.

There was hardly any middle class in the Everett of Henry Jackson's youth. The bankers and mill owners constituted a small elite, but the bulk of the city's thirty thousand population was working class. The broad backs of Scandinavian immigrants provided much of the heavy labor, and most bore their burdens stoically. They had little to gain and much to lose by opposing the mostly Eastern-born capitalists who controlled the local economy.

An object lesson was provided in 1916 when a contingent of International Workers of the World sailed from Seattle to lend moral support to striking millworkers in Everett. The unarmed Wobblies were met at the pier by the sheriff, company goons, and rifle-toting strikebreakers, who, minutes later, opened fire on the helpless men. At least thirty were wounded, and the reported death toll was five. But no one knows for certain how many died in the "Everett Massacre": as many as a dozen more deaths may have been covered up.

Everett eventually became a union town. Peter Jackson joined the local plasterers' union and served as its treasurer for twenty-six years. He was, in Salter's words, "one of the aristocrats of the labor movement." He was also, however, an independent contractor. This dual status later proved a boon to his politician son, who could talk to a union meeting one day about his father, the laboring man, and tell Jaycees the next about his father, the small entrepreneur.

Although they were working people, Jackson's parents, neighbors recall, were staunch Republicans. (Jackson suggests "independent conservative" is a more accurate description.) Lyle Waters told me that, when Jackson first ran for office, "Old Pete Jackson just stood there and shook his head and said, 'I can't understand why Henry wants to be a Democrat.' "

In fact, Jackson's politics as a young man apparently ran somewhat to the left of the Democratic party. His interest in government and history began in junior high when he participated in intramural debates. He won a place on his high school debating team for three years. One topic he argued was the four- versus six-year presidential term; another was "Resolved: That installment buying as a means of economic exchange is undesirable." So, when he entered the University of Washington as a freshman in 1930, he took a budding interest in politics with him.

Radicalism prevailed among the campus intellectuals of his day, and John Gavin, a law school classmate of Jackson, gives this tongue-in-cheek description of a typical metamorphosis: "When you entered as a freshman, you were a Communist; the next year a Socialist; your junior year a Democrat; your fourth year a Republican. And if you went to graduate school, you became a monarchist."

None of Jackson's friends recall his ever being a disciple of Marx and Lenin, but Salter says that Jackson's "political hero at that time was Norman Thomas. He was considerably to the left of the average college student of the time. He was aware there had to be changes and such, and he was actively working for them." He also "belonged to the Young Socialists' League."

Jackson's own recollection differs: "My interest in Norman Thomas . . . was that they wouldn't let him speak on the campus, and along with a lot of other kids, we thought this was an outrage. And we led the fight, unsuccessfully, to permit him to speak in the main auditorium. . . . We were successful, however, in getting him to speak at Eagleton Hall, which was the YMCA across the street from the campus. . . . I didn't belong to the Socialist Party or anything." He did, however, join "the League for Industrial Democracy," he said.

Salter suggests that Jackson's early economic and political thinking was "influenced by Scandinavians and their cooperative farmers' movement." He might also have brought some sense of class consciousness with him from Everett when he went to Seattle. Jackson himself indicates the Depression was a formative influence: "I saw women with good faces—obviously, by good faces, I mean you can tell their character: they were not just a bunch of hoboes or something—they were going from garbage can to garbage can to collect food to feed their families. And this left an everlasting impression in my mind, that a nation as rich and as strong and as powerful as the United States could be so disorganized, so crippled, to reach the point where people were literally starving: I thought [it] was outrageous. My feelings were for the kind of reforms and changes that we'd need to never allow that to happen again. And that's been the mainspring of my social and economic thinking all my life."

Whatever his earlier political leanings, Jackson had metamorphosed into a Democrat by the time he was in law school and actively campaigned for Governor Clarence D. Martin. Such a change actually required little movement in those days because Democratic politics in the state were so far to the left that James A. Farley, FDR's party chief and postmaster general, once cracked: "There are 47 states and the 'Soviet' of Washington."

Jackson "came to college a naïve hayseed," one classmate told me. Still a poor athlete and not the most brilliant student, he might not have been given a second look by the fraternities in more prosperous times. But, since there were only six thousand students—four thousand living off campus or commuting—the young man, an outsider most of his life, was invited to pledge Delta Chi. "He has remained a staunch supporter of Delta Chi over the years," his classmate said. Jackson was so proud of this affiliation that for several years his biographical entry in the *Congressional Directory* noted his membership in Delta Chi.

The adjectives fellow senators—allies as well as some adversaries—use to describe Jackson today are identical to those one hears from his law school classmates: honest, hard-working, loyal, serious. Though never an outstanding student, he may well have been the hardest working. High honors such as the Rhodes Scholarship competition, Phi Beta Kappa, and the law school's "Order of the Coif" eluded him; but he eagerly joined serious discussions about politics, philosophy, and economics. So serious was he that fraternity brothers despaired in their efforts to get him to go to dances and other social affairs. Although he did turn out for freshman track and became basketball manager, he gave up both to concentrate on his studies and make money in whatever "spare time" he could work into his schedule.

His natural inclination toward the serious aspects of college life was no doubt reinforced by a strong sense of obligation to his family. Although he had saved about $2,000 from his paper route and summer jobs, he might not have been able to go to college at all had his sister Gertrude not given him nearly $4,000 of her own savings; his parents gave him about $500. In addition, he washed dishes and waited on tables in the fraternity house to help pay for his room and board and ran a candy and cigarette concession out of his room, eventually becoming the distributor who supplied other fraternities and sororities. He also picked up and delivered laundry and dry cleaning at the various houses. By senior year he could afford to share an off-campus apartment with one of his friends.

Jackson never involved himself in campus politics, and his college friends could recall no remark or incident at the University which, in retrospect, seemed to foreshadow a career in electoral politics. Indeed, because he had such a knack for making money, most expected him to go into business law and make a pile of it by representing banks or timber companies. If such were his preferences, the Depression narrowly restricted his choices. Gavin recalls that, initially, "only three or four of our class were able to join private law firms." Another classmate, Jack Sylvester, found a firm which provided him an office but no salary. Those few who found jobs with salaries were fortunate if they started at $50 a month.

Jackson returned to Everett to look for a job while he waited for the results of the bar exam. He was hired by the local office of the Federal Emergency Relief Agency and wound up with a caseload of 175 families. Although people who wanted relief were supposed to come to the office, he knew many of the "old country people" were too proud to ask for it. So he took it upon himself to find out who did need relief by visiting the area he was responsible for and talking to local businessmen who knew who was needy as well as who was not. "I had a very strong feeling about the people who were suffering because of their pride," he told me.

Also working in the relief office was John Salter. The two men had first met when they were twelve-year-olds in the hospital about to lose their tonsils, but they had gone separate ways thereafter. Salter went to Catholic schools, except for his senior year at Everett High School, and then entered a seminary in California to study for the priesthood but quit one year before he was to be ordained. While it was simply happenstance which found the two men in the same office, they soon became close friends and developed a political relationship which has weathered forty years. Salter now jokes: "If I'd have finished, some say I'd have become the Cardinal Rasputin of Washington State politics." Given his considerable reputation for guile and craft—"Salter moves but leaves no footprints," says one beaten adversary—a more appropriate priestly parallel would have been Cardinal Richelieu.

Once back in Everett, Jackson began looking for openings in local law firms. He met Lloyd Black, who had developed a sizable practice, and the older man gave him a legal problem to research involving an unpatented mining claim. Black's clients were workmen who had a labor lien against the claim, and Black wanted Jackson to determine if there was a legal basis for sustaining the lien. "It just so happened," Jackson recalls, "that one of the cases we had in moot court involved the question of filing a property mortgage or a chattel mortgage on an unpatented mining claim. And the law of our state was . . . [that] an unpatented mining claim is personal property, and it's not real estate. So, if you filed a real estate mortgage it would be invalid against other creditors. Well, Lloyd Black . . . was amazed that I came up with a case and wrote out a brief with an answer—he didn't know it himself—and they won the case on that basis."

Jackson passed the tough technical test Black had given him, and after he received notice that he had passed the bar, he joined Black's firm. In his two years as an attorney in private practice, he handled the usual variety of legal problems: personal injury, divorce, estates, and real-estate transactions. Whenever Black had an important case go to trial, Jackson would interview the witnesses and assist him in court.

Black developed an interest in the younger man and encouraged him when he was considering trying to unseat Al Swanson, the incumbent Democrat who was then prosecuting attorney of Snohomish County. When he decided to enter the race, Salter became his campaign manager, and the two twenty-six-year-olds began preparing for their first major political battle.

The *Herald* of July 28, 1938, carried Jackson's declaration of candidacy on page 4. Steel-rimmed glasses, hair parted in the middle, sallow and thin-faced, lips tight in a perfectly horizontal line: the young man in the photo was the personification of earnestness. "My duty under the oath of office," he intoned, "is clear-cut and well defined, and I will do my best to comply with such oath of office and the duties pertaining to it." (He may have been earnest, but he was never—then or now—a phrasemaker.)

"We had no money, and we were going against the county [Democractic] organization. So, we had to use volunteer help. In fact, we were the first in the state to use house-to-house canvassing," recalls Salter. The few ads they could afford—or friends bought—invariably carried the visage of the tight-lipped, serious young man and a brief message: "Character. Integrity. Ability." The slogan at the bottom invited voters to: "Ask Those Who Know Him." With dozens of youthful volunteers knocking on the doors of the county's 100,000 residents—Jackson later reckoned that 200,000 of his campaign cards had been passed out—the message came across, and he beat Swanson in the primary by better than three to one. In November the county's largely Democratic electorate presented him with 72 percent of the vote.

In Snohomish County the police, bootleggers, gamblers, and madams had worked out a comfortable modus vivendi. Although a raid would occasionally be staged for public edification, the raided establishment would normally be back in business within days, if not hours. With loggers and millworkers from the county and points north and Seattleites thirty miles to the south in search of hard liquor and fast women, business was always brisk. That, however, was before Jackson became prosecutor.

The law at that time permitted the sale of beer and wine in public taverns, but hard liquor could only be served in homes or private clubs. "In a prosecutor's office, you get a lot of intelligence," notes Phil Sheridan, who was one of the three deputy prosecutors under Jackson. "There was a lot of crime in speakeasies and houses of prostitution. Wage earners would get rolled, and we'd get complaints from housewives. The liquor board had its own enforcement agency, and they would collect the evidence with respect to the sale of liquor using undercover methods like federal narcotics officers do today. They would bring the warrants to our office, and we'd check them for legality. If it was in the city, we'd line up the city and county police and the liquor board, and the raids would be timed so we'd hit a number of places at the same time. This way, one couldn't warn another."

The *Herald* of April 15,1939, carried a story about how Jackson, liquor board inspectors, deputy sheriffs, and city police (nineteen in all) simultaneously raided seven places which were illegally selling liquor. Ten days later, the paper reported three more raids. "If the law is wrong," Jackson told the reporter, "let the people change it. I can't and certainly it is the officers' job to close these places. It will be done if it takes a raid every week."

There were also "complaints," Sheridan recalls, "from housewives that their husbands were losing their paychecks to pinball machines, pull tabs, and punch boards. These were forms of gambling then prohibited by the [state] constitution." Although the city had been earning $900 a year in license fees from pinball operators, Jackson ruled that the machines were "gambling devices," hence unlawful, and issued an order which gave the operators two months to take their machines out of the county. He told the *Herald* that pinballs had become a "corruptive influence" because the syndicate handling them was "too powerful." He even acknowledged that he had been offered money to "keep still," but he refused to rescind his order.

Sitting in his comfortable Senate office, Jackson reflected on what had motivated him as a prosecutor: "I had a newspaper route that covered the area of the city where things were wide open. I would see police officers directly present in illegal operations: bootlegging, involved with bootleg joints and gambling joints. I was only thirteen or fourteen years of age, and it made a real impact on me. That was one of the factors which later led me to run for prosecutor. . . .

"Now, we had a notorious gambling joint called 'The Ranch,' which was one of the largest gambling joints on the Coast. And I had learned about a lot of unsavory characters that were involved . . . because I was working very closely with the FBI at that point. . . . I wanted to be sure in raiding 'The Ranch' that there was no tip-off and that the warrants were legally served. . . .

"After I threw them all out, I had operators of this sort of business [pinballs and gambling] call me or come to see me. They thought that I had had a fight over the amount of payoff that should be allowed. . . . Of course, I just unceremoniously tossed them out of my office."

If Jackson was ambitious when he was prosecuting attorney, he had yet to set his sights very high. Salter remembers Gertrude Jackson once saying that her brother "started running for President when he was two years old." When he was asked by his teacher, Mrs. Dootson, what he hoped to be when he grew up, he told her and the rest of the third grade of Longfellow School: "I want to be President." But, in his first year as prosecutor, Jackson's eye was not on the distant White House: it was focused on a goal much closer to home.

In 1939 a vacancy occurred on the Snohomish County Superior Court when President Roosevelt elevated Judge Lloyd Black, Jackson's legal mentor, to the federal bench. The county bar association, as was the practice, sent to the governor a list of three names in order of preference. Jackson's name was third on the list.

Although Salter opposed Jackson's becoming a judge, he nonetheless accompanied him to Olympia to see if Governor Martin could be persuaded to turn the list upside down. While they sat in his office, Martin put in a call to Jack Sylvester, who, a few years out of law school, had worked his way up to speaker of the state house of representatives. Unbeknownst to Sylvester, Martin had turned on the "squawk box" in his office so Jackson and Salter could hear Sylvester's comments about Jackson's qualifications for the bench. "I told the governor," Sylvester recalls, "that while Scoop had been a good prosecuting attorney, he had been on only a short time. He was too young."

Although he very much wanted the appointment, Jackson did not get it, and he was doubly peeved: at Martin, for whom he had campaigned, and at Sylvester, his classmate from law school. "For a number of months our close friendship was being tested," Sylvester remembers. "But in 1940 Jackson ran for Congress and was elected. We became good friends after that, but he was cool to me after that incident because he wanted that judgeship."

Jackson's trip to Olympia in 1939 revealed another characteristic that has marked—some would say plagued—his political career ever since: caution. Had he been appointed a judge of the Superior Court of Snohomish County, he might still be trying drunk drivers, wife beaters, and an occasional felon. He would have remained an important man in his home town, and I doubt he would ever have lost a night's sleep wondering what he might have become. That he ran for Congress the following year and was elected was largely a matter of luck: a four-term incumbent decided to run for the Senate. But there might also have been a pragmatic calculation as well. If you have to run every few years to keep your job, you might as well try for the more prestigious office and higher pay. Conditioned by the Depression, Jackson may well have chosen the "risks" of higher elected office because it was the best and, paradoxically, most secure job in sight.

CHAPTER

3

The Other Washington

JACKSON might have lived in comfortable obscurity in his native state and spent his productive years shuttling between local political office and private law practice, but two events beyond his control conspired to catapult him to the other Washington. One occurred when Representative Mon Wallgren unexpectedly decided to run for the Senate; he had already served four terms, and as Salter puts it, "it looked like he would be congressman forever." The other took place when Edward L. Bouchard robbed and brutally murdered two of his friends.

Jackson had already made quite a name for himself as a crime-fighting prosecutor, but raids on illegal bars and gambling houses are small potatoes compared to a sensational murder. So the Bouchard case presented Jackson with not only his greatest professional challenge but an unparalleled opportunity to win the highest laurels a small-town prosecuting attorney could hope for: the conviction of a brutal murderer.

The Everett *Daily Herald* followed the Bouchard proceeding closely. It was, says Phil Sheridan, who assisted in the prosecution, "a big murder trial. . . . It was a case that required a lot of preparation. We utilized the FBI laboratories and University of Oregon laboratories to collect data."

The case against Bouchard was overwhelming. When the police in Portland picked him up, Jackson recalls, "he had the dead man's billfold. They got a search warrant and went over the room and there they found a lot of the clothing which we were able to identify. . . . He was even wearing the dead man's underwear, if you can imagine that.

"When we got through collecting all of the evidence, we had before the jury all of the possessions of the two dead men. We were able to establish that he was in the area, that he had led them up into this area by his own admission. And when I confronted him with the fact that if he were innocent, I didn't want to proceed with this action; I wanted him to tell his version of this story as accurately as he could because his story wasn't credible: he just said he left them there and here he ended up with all this stuff. And I said that I felt that under the law, although I had no relish for it, that I would have to ask for the death penalty. And his reply to me was: 'Young man, I'm no good. I've been no good all my life. And if I were you, I'd do your duty.' And that was my last conversation with him."

The trial took two weeks, but the jury returned a verdict of first-degree murder after a brief deliberation. The judge then sent an interrogatory to the jury: "Do you find that the death penalty should be imposed?" The all-male jury took several hours this time but eventually reached unanimity and ordered the death penalty. "I found out afterwards," Jackson recalls, "that two of the men jurors broke down and cried. They said, 'It should be imposed, but we can't do it.' And that's what held up the verdict.

"The reason the death penalty was requested was that we had information from California that similar crimes had occurred in California where they had been garroted and hit over the head with an ax. And they were quite confident that this man probably was the one involved. I would not have asked for the death penalty had it not been for the overwhelming evidence and the fact that he himself . . . said, 'If I were you, I'd do your duty.' He had been convicted twice before of felonies: one involving the chloroforming of a madam in a house of ill repute and the other in a robbery. But it was a very trying experience. It's one that I didn't relish. It was one I couldn't escape from because I was a prosecutor, and I had a duty to perform. And I just did what I thought was my duty at the time."

On the day Bouchard was to be put to death at the state prison in Walla Walla, Jackson's office awaited news of the hanging. When a telephone call finally confirmed that Bouchard had indeed been executed, some of Jackson's staff, according to one person who was there, acted inordinately "happy with the news." Jackson himself was not in the office at the time, and Sheridan, who was, says he cannot "recall anything" of that nature. Jackson similarly recalls hearing nothing of such an incident but speculates: "That may have been the sheriff's office because they had been heavily involved in the investigative work on the case."

The Bouchard trial was concluded in the early summer of 1940, and on August 16 the *Herald* carried a story on page 2 headlined: "Congressional Seat Is Jackson's Aim." The hair parted in the middle and steel-rimmed glasses had not changed, but the new photo showed a somewhat less tense, nonetheless earnest, young man. The once perfectly straight line formed by his tight lips now had just the hint of a wrinkle. "He states that the immediate problem before the country is the preparation of a proper and adequate defense," the story said, "but that 'we should not lose sight of our continued desire to also better the standard of living of our people during these perilous times.' He has promised to work for an adequate and uniform federal old age pension law."

Jackson and Salter used the same sort of personal, door-to-door campaigning which had been so successful in the prosecuting attorney's race two years before. The ads in the *Herald* were also similar although the slogan on the bottom periodically changed. They started out using the original one, "Ask Those Who Know Him," but as the campaign wore on they changed it to reflect Jackson's considerable success in office. "He Has Served You Well as Prosecuting Attorney" read one. Another promised: "He Has Kept His Word as Prosecuting Attorney—He Will Keep His Word as Congressman." But the most interesting of all was the one which appeared during the closing week of the campaign: "A Man Who Has the Courage of His Convictions." (Was it merely a cliché or a hidden reference to the executed Bouchard?)

Although his Republican opponent, Payson Peterson, was able to buy a bigger ad in the *Herald* on election eve, Jackson took 57 percent of the vote the next day. The churchgoers rewarded him for closing local dens of inequity, and the bootleggers and gamblers wanted him out of Snohomish County. Although the Republicans had wisecracked about the two twenty-eight-year-olds who wanted to go to Congress, Jackson and Salter could not prepare for their journey to the other Washington: the latter as administrative assistant to the new congressman.

Jackson represented the northwest corner of the nation. His district was bounded by Canada on the north and the Pacific Ocean on the west; the southern boundary ran through the northern reaches of Seattle to the Cascade Mountains, which constituted the eastern boundary. The district was then largely rural in character, and even now the cities of Everett and Bellingham account for just 11 percent of the population of a geographically smaller Second Congressional District; most (54 percent) are suburbanites.

Isolationism was strong at the time even though the Nazi invasion of Denmark and Norway had disturbed many of the state's Scandinavian immigrants. Jackson navigated that current, pledging that he would "never vote to send boys overseas," says Salter. The month after he was sworn in, he voted against Roosevelt's Lend-Lease program of military aid for Great Britain, but in October 1941 he switched and voted for the aid. In another switch of sorts, he shelved his campaign pledge to "work for an adequate and uniform federal old age pension law."

Seeking to represent the interests of his constituents, Jackson sought and received appointment to the House Committee on Merchant Marine and Fisheries and remained there until he received a coveted seat on the Appropriations Committee in 1948.

Although a new legislator is supposed to be seen and not heard, each eventually gets an opportunity to speak on the floor of the House of Representatives. Like first love, a congressman's maiden speech is—to him, at least—an important and memorable affair. So, in the spring of 1941, while Hitler's armies were marching across Europe, Jackson grappled with his decision.

A friend from back home who was also in Washington at the time visited Jackson and Salter in the small Capitol Hill apartment they shared and came upon this scene: "Scoop and Johnny had barely gotten unpacked, and I can remember coming in and seeing five to seven people sitting around, looking through encyclopedias and old *Congressional Records* looking for a theme for his freshman address. This was the year of Lend-Lease and it was a very exciting time, but Scoop chose to talk about salmon, I think. That was my first glimpse of how closely he hews to the line, and I can remember thinking then that caution of that order will never prevail."

This recollection is somewhat in error. Jackson's maiden speech was not about salmon; the subject was herring. He had introduced an amendment to add $25,000 to an authorization bill for an "inquiry respecting food fishes," he told the House, "because the money necessary for scientific research into the supplies of herring available to commercial fishermen in Alaska had not been provided to the Fish and Wildlife Service." As a result, herring catches had dipped considerably.

Because fish oil was used by the tanning industry, he foresaw the shortage having a dangerous impact on nothing less than the nation's security: "The defense industries which rely upon herring oil will be seriously hampered unless something is done to push production back up to the average yield of approximately 5 million gallons of oil." He then ticked off statistics to back up his argument and pointed out that "the English Navy staged its sensational raid on the Lofoten Islands" of Norway to keep that nation's herring oil out of the hands of Nazi tanners. He concluded with this plea: "The $25,000 asked is very small. The industry's stake—$6 million—is large. Labor's stake—1200 jobs—is important. And the considerations of national defense demand that we take favorable action."

Although he sat down to applause, the House was not sufficiently moved and defeated Jackson's first amendment by voice vote. Fortunately, the United States and the Pacific Northwest's fishing industry survived, and American tanners received enough fish oil to keep the Marines from being called "Cotton-necks."

Jackson chose a mundane subject for his maiden speech, and both the choice and delivery set a pattern that would typify his approach to politics for the next two decades. He consciously decided to be, not a national politician, but a representative of provincial and constituent interests. Even in the late 1940s and early '50s, when he became involved in the development of atomic energy, his interest conveniently dovetailed with the growth in south central Washington of the vast Hanford Works, whose sole purpose was the production of fissionable material for nuclear weapons. (The government eventually poured some $2 billion into Hanford, but only one of the nine reactors is still in operation. The other eight have become surplus to the nation's needs.)

Jackson was also a vigorous proponent of public power at a time when conservatives called it "creeping socialism." He realized early on that the industrialization of his home state required cheap electric power which only the government could provide. The dream of liberals in the Pacific Northwest at that time was a system of publicly financed hydroelectric dams on the Columbia River run by a federal agency similar to the Tennessee Valley Authority. The legislator generally credited as prime mover of the plan for a Columbia Valley Authority was Representative Hugh B. Mitchell. When he later went to the Senate, Jackson took over as CVA's most vocal advocate in the lower body. Although he pushed the concept for years and ultimately got President Truman to support it, the ruling coalition of Southern Democrats and Republicans always blocked the bill.

Jackson quickly adapted to the Capitol's pork-barrel politics, and in addition to Merchant Marine and Fisheries, he sat on the following standing committees in his twelve years in the House: Appropriations, Civil Service, Flood Control, Indian Affairs, and Rivers and Harbors. He also sat on two select committees: Conservation of Wildlife Resources and Small Business.

For the provincial Jackson, these were ideal assignments. While others were concerning themselves with national or international affairs, he would be calculating how to get a larger civil service payroll for the Bremerton naval yard or how to finance a reservoir on one of his state's many Indian reservations. The newspaper boy who had won a prize for perfect service to his subscribers was now trying to do something similar for his constituents. Only this time, instead of handing out his homemade card and asking them to call if they had complaints, he was delivering millions of federal dollars and asking only that they pull the lever marked "Jackson" every even-numbered year. He soon became—and has remained—one of the most adept logrollers ever to have served in Congress.

If Jackson seemed more concerned with political pork than high national purpose when he served in the House, he correctly sensed that Congress is most likely to buy a legislative package when wrapped in bunting of red, white, and blue. Although his effort to equate herring oil with the nation's defense now seems ludicrous in the extreme, he hit upon a technique which he has successfully exploited hundreds of times since his maiden speech.

Reduced to its essence, the technique required one to believe that Jackson had found the horseshoe nail for want of which the battle would be lost. Such folk wisdom, like all analogies, must be closely scrutinized when lifted from the abstract and applied to such specific problems as herring oil or antiballistic missiles. Indeed, analogies are nearly always worthless if one's purpose is analysis. But advocacy is another matter.

It is as an advocate that Jackson has excelled since the time he sent Edward Bouchard to the gallows. He gathers facts, briefings and expert witnesses; studies the material until he has mastered the details; accentuates those details which support his case and downplays or ignores those which do not; and, finally, chooses the legislative vehicle most likely to succeed. His is no mean talent, as any senator who has crossed swords with him will attest.

Yet Jackson's considerable talent for advocacy has not been balanced by an equal capacity for disinterested analysis. The consequences of this serious imbalance become most evident when one compares the huge military force structures Jackson has advocated over the years to what, in retrospect, has proven necessary. Had the nation followed him in the 1950s and '60s, the Pentagon's budget, now approaching $100 billion, would probably long since have exceeded $150 billion—if it had not first caused the economy to collapse.

Jackson came to Congress somewhat of an isolationist: an accurate reflection of his district, which in 1940 was more interested in the price of cattle fodder than in international politics. The attack on Pearl Harbor had a strong effect on him, as it did on almost everyone. There was panic in many areas on the West Coast, and, Salter recalls, "they blacked out Paine Field [an air base just south of Everett], and we were almost shot by a sentry late at night when Jackson went out there to get a military plane back to D.C. to vote for a declaration of war." So, by the end of his first year in Congress, the erstwhile isolationist had become something of an internationalist.

If he had initially planned to use his committee seat primarily to look out for the good fisherfolk back home, Pearl Harbor compelled him to be concerned with the merchant marine. After the United States joined the conflict, he undertook a number of war-related assignments from the committee: investigating a tanker sinking one time, the structural defects of certain Liberty ships the next.

But the war had also reached him at a more personal level. Germany had overrun his parents' native land, and the agony of occupied Norway moved him emotionally. Although few have ever accused him of eloquence, his shortwave radio speech to the people of Norway in March of 1942 came from the heart. I have quoted it at some length here because it may well be the best speech he has ever made.

People of Norway and men of the Norwegian merchant marine, as United States Congressman from the State of Washington, I represent a district in which many of your friends and relatives now reside. I can tell you from my own knowledge that their hearts and thoughts have been with you every minute of your hardship and travail during the past months. Your indomitable courage and never-say-die spirit inspire them now when the Axis wolves are snarling at our very coasts.

I feel, too, that I have a special kinship with the Norwegian people. Although I was born in the State of Washington, my mother and father came here from Norway before the turn of the century. I am proud of my heritage. Never have I doubted for one moment that you hated and despised the treacherous Axis fiends who have pillaged and destroyed your homeland. Never have I doubted for a second that the people of Norway were united against their oppressors and would at the proper moment rise in wrathful justice to push them deep in the fjords through which they had sailed to make their treacherous attack.

Hitler has boasted that Norway has been knocked out of this battle. But can you say a nation has been knocked out whose government is still operating, albeit in another land, whose thousands of young men are fighting on land heroically side by side with their loyal allies, while hundreds are training to pilot destruction through the air to the Axis foes? Can you say that a nation is through when three-fourths of her merchant marine, over 750 ships manned by 25,000 officers and men, are daily threading their way through submarine and mine-infested waters to bring vital supplies to England and the United States and our other Allies? Can a nation be called "conquered" when 99 percent of its people are bravely resisting the Nazi overlords in spite of terror and persecution, firing squads, and concentration camps? Every day we in America hear of acts of courage which prove that Norwegians are fighting on the home front just as effectively as are their forces abroad. . . .

I would like to compare these Norwegian airmen and sailors to the intrepid vikings of old—these modern vikings on land and on sea and in the air. They have come out of the grim fastnesses of the North, not to conquer and discover new lands, but to seek new vistas of freedom and overcome oppression wherever and whenever it exists. Truly those persons of Norwegian ancestry in our country can be proud of the people in the land of their fathers.

If Jackson seemed a latter-day Pericles in his exhortation to the people of Norway, he appealed in his own land less to love of country than to that dark force which has periodically afflicted the Western American psyche: anti-Orientalism. For more than three years, he was one of the most vocal proponents of what was euphemistically called the wartime "relocation" of Japanese Americans. Although his innate caution at first restrained him from publicity seeking on any but noncontroversial federal projects for his region, his hostility toward persons of Japanese descent soon became evident in his dealings with constituents.

During my research in Seattle, I was shown an exchange of letters between Jackson and a constituent who advocated that the Nisei (second-generation Japanese Americans) be permitted an active role in the armed forces. What follows are excerpts from the letter this individual, a serviceman at the time, wrote to his congressman.

> I urge you to use your effort and influence to have the Nisei members of our Army sent to whatever fighting fronts there are or may be to the east of us. . . .
>
> The public knowledge that Nisei boys are risking and giving their lives, fighting for the same ends next to our Caucasian-American sons, husbands, etc. would be more effective than anything else in easing the friction here.
>
> In the minds of many of us there is a question as to the extent of their loyalty. Why not prove it conclusively by this means rather than making guesses with no factual basis?
>
> The Nisei soldiers, now stationed in the central part of the country, are doing nothing and becoming embittered and discouraged at being prevented from fighting for their own country and forbidden a chance to show their loyalty to it.
>
> Their performance in action may be expected to be courageous. They are aware of being in the spotlight and that they will stand or fall by their own behavior. . . .

This letter, written in February of 1942, proved amazingly prophetic because the Army eventually did organize an all-Nisei regiment which went on to become the most highly decorated in the European Theater. The author also wrote similar letters to other members of the state's congressional delegation, but their responses were little more than acknowledgments of having received the letter. Jackson, however, responded substantively.

> I appreciate very much your views regarding the removal of the Japanese and particularly the Japanese that are born in the United States. It is my personal opinion that it is more difficult to trust the

Japanese born in this country than the Japanese who are born in Japan and have immigrated to this country. Apparently there is more espionage perpetrated on the part of the second generation Jap than the first generation. In fact, one of my best Japanese friends who incidentally attended the University at the same time that I did and also graduated from law school at the same time turned out to be one of the leaders in the Japanese espionage in the City of Seattle. He always professed to me to be interested in better relations with Japan and gave every indication that he was loyal to this country. When shortly after the war broke out, I learned of his activities, I lost confidence not only in him but in the trustworthiness of the Japanese second generation. I realize this is an isolated instance, but have been informed by others that there have been numerous other cases of a similar nature.

Jackson had clearly succumbed to the anti-Japanese hysteria which afflicted many—but by no means, all—West Coast politicians. One exception was Harry P. Cain, who was then the liberal Democratic mayor of Tacoma. But Jackson would not listen to the dissident voices and soon dropped any pretense of objectivity.

That he also seemed to have lost his ability to think rationally is evident in his choice of language in the foregoing letter. Note, for instance, his characterizations. Instead of using accurate terms such as "Nisei" or "Japanese Americans," they become either "Japanese" or the pejorative "second generation Jap." It was as if the people of whom he was speaking were aliens, but in reality they were, like Jackson himself, native-born citizens of immigrant parents.

Next, take the crucial issue of loyalty. Although not one Nisei was convicted of an act of disloyalty against the United States, Jackson believed, with neither evidence nor finding of guilt, that "apparently there is more espionage perpetrated on the part of the second generation Jap than the first generation."

Finally, there is his disturbing personalization of the issue in the unsubstantiated accusation that a law school classmate had deceived him and "turned out to be one of the leaders in the Japanese espionage in the City of Seattle." Not only had he written off a friend without the due process of an evidentiary hearing, he stretched this admittedly "isolated instance" to shore up his prejudiced belief that "there have been numerous other cases of a similar nature."

If Jackson had confined his anti-Japanese feelings to a few letters to constituents and subsequently abandoned them when proof of Nisei loyalty had become manifest, it would merit only passing mention. Unfortunately, that was not the case. Although he cautiously kept his sentiments in check during the first year of the war, he then stepped forward to become one of the most vocally anti-Japanese members of Congress. His speech on the floor of the House on February 23, 1943, is illustrative.

We first heard much of Japanese infiltration tactics on Bataan and in the Philippines, but the Japanese had for many years practiced a different type of infiltration—infiltration into the vitals of our economic, political, and domestic structure. The disciples of Bushido, by insidious and indirect means, inserted themselves in a great many organizations in much the same fashion as the Nazis have utilized their front organizations. In our great Pacific coast cities they controlled much of the hotel and restaurant business although always there was a white manager who would front for them with the general public. They lowered prices to their own countrymen in the fresh produce and vegetable field, forcing out their white competition, only to raise prices as soon as they had monopolized this sphere of business. Always they had prominent civic leaders as their attorneys, paying them on a retainer basis. Whenever a situation came up in which they were interested, they had only to contact these individuals with their specious reasons to have them immediately come forward in their interest. Investigation will show that Japanese consuls in our large cities lavished expensive and sumptuous gifts on a great number of prominent citizens at Christmas and other appropriate occasions. . . .

After my study of this question, I wish to assure the Members of this House that there is not the slightest doubt in my mind but that the Japanese consul, taking his orders directly from Tokyo, ruled the Japanese colonies in our country with an iron and dictatorial hand; thus there was a society within a society and a race within a race. Every 2 years the Japanese consul in the large Pacific coast cities was changed and a new consul came in, bearing direct orders from the "Son of Heaven" in Tokyo. He directed the establishment of

Japanese language schools; he managed the complicated Japanese financial system through the Japanese banks, owned and controlled in the land of the Samurai. The consulate office was the fountainhead from which flowed all directives to Japanese residents, both alien and native to this country, and was also the center of espionage and propaganda activity to which came all the data which the Japanese were able to gather regarding our Pacific coast line and the isles and inlets of the Alaskan Peninsula. . . .

The War Relocation Authority and the Federal Reserve Bank Board now have all the information regarding the financial assets and economic enterprises of the Japanese in this country. Now that we are at war with Japan, we need not be concerned with diplomatic niceties. Is there any reason why this information should not be made available to the American people? Do not the American people, and particularly the residents of the Pacific coast, have the right to know the extent of the economic stranglehold possessed by Japanese residents on the domestic economy of our country? I for one must insist that the American people have a right to be fully informed on this subject.

Fantasy had distorted Jackson's perception beyond the rational and, again, affected his language. Note, for instance, two locutions: "Japanese colonies" and "Japanese residents." The proper term in the first case is "Japanese American communities"; in the second it is "Japanese Americans" or simply "citizens." But Jackson, who by his own reasoning could have been called a "Norwegian resident," could not bring himself to refer to the Nisei as either Americans or citizens. After all, such "niceties" as the Bill of Rights apply to citizens. Alien residents, however, are another matter.

The overt purpose of Jackson's speech was to introduce a resolution "asking that a special committee of the House be set up to investigate Japanese activities in the United States and its possessions." Had the resolution become law, its author most likely would have become chairman of the committee. So, as an advocate, he had a tremendous incentive to prosecute his case on the reverse of the proposition that one is innocent until proven guilty: he would have treated all Japanese Americans as suspects until they had been cleared by a form of loyalty board.

Following the speech, a colleague, John Z. Anderson of

California, engaged Jackson in a colloquy to determine if he would be willing to let Nisei prove their loyalty through military service. His opposition to the idea came through in their exchange on the House floor.

Anderson: . . . Will the gentleman give the House his attitude on the present War Department project of developing a Japanese unit within our own armed forces?
Jackson: . . . From what we have been able to gather up to date I think it is pretty clear that the Japanese we trusted most are those who often proved to be the most treacherous. . . .
Anderson: Does not the gentleman believe that the utmost care must be taken in separating the wheat from the chaff, so to speak, before any Japanese in this country are permitted to join our armed forces?
Jackson: That is right. I do not see how it is possible for the War Relocation Authority or any other branch of the Government to determine the loyalty of the individual Japanese on the basis of the information we now have on hand.
Anderson: The gentleman comes from the Pacific coast and knows the reaction of the people out there just as I do.
Jackson: That is right.

(Instead of going along with Jackson's guilty-until-proven-innocent proposal, the Army established the 442nd Infantry Regimental Combat Team, an all-Nisei unit. The month after Jackson's speech, a skinny eighteen-year-old named Daniel Ken Inouye enlisted in that unit as a private. The son of Japanese immigrants to Hawaii, Inouye rose through the ranks and won a battlefield commission in November of 1944. He lost his right arm in combat and was later awarded the Distinguished Service Cross, the nation's second-highest military decoration. He is now the junior senator from Hawaii.)

Jackson continued to call attention to what he called "the Japanese problem in the United States." On April 15, 1943, he quoted approvingly the remarks of the commanding general of the Western Defense Command which appeared in a newspaper article.

"A Jap's a Jap," and "it makes no difference whether he is an American citizen or not," Lt. Gen. John L. DeWitt said yesterday in opposing "the sentiment developing to bring back some of the Japanese to the west coast. . . .

"I don't want any of them. We got them out. They were a dangerous element. The west coast is too vital and too vulnerable to take any chances."

Jackson then added his own assessment:

> I think there is a tendency on the part of the American people to minimize the importance of the Japanese situation in the United States, particularly because the events in the far Pacific have been favorable to us during the past few months, although the situation is serious at the present time.
>
> I have a resolution pending before the Committee on Rules calling for an investigation of the entire Japanese problem in the United States. There are conflicting rumors, charges, and counter charges continually concerning the Japanese problem. The greatest confusion exists in the minds of the American public regarding this question. I submit, gentlemen, Congress has the responsibility to investigate all the facts in this situation. I believe it can best be handled by Congress delving into the whole question and solving it in a realistic matter of fact and humane fashion.

Jackson continued his efforts, and in a Seattle *Post-Intelligencer* story on May 17, 1944, headlined "Jackson Urges Watching Japs," he was reported to have "announced progress in his efforts to obtain the enactment of a resolution setting up a special permanent congressional committee to keep watch on all Japanese affairs affecting the United States." Congress, however, still took no action on the resolution.

Japan formally signed the document of unconditional surrender on September 2, 1945, on board the battleship *Missouri* in Tokyo Bay. That realistically killed whatever small chance had existed for Jackson's resolution, but reality had yet to have its impact on him. So he persisted, adding new "facts" to his advocacy.

On October 17, fully one and a half months after Japan's surrender, the *Post-Intelligencer* carried a page 5 story with the headline "Army Bestiality True Jap Nature—Jackson." It began: "The United States should be brought to the understanding that the utter bestiality of the Japanese army in war is more nearly representative of Japan's true nature than is the present ingratiating conduct of the conquered population, Rep. Henry M. Jackson, Washington Democrat, asserted today."

He renewed his request, the story continued, for a permanent committee to maintain watch "on all things Japanese affecting the security of the United States." He referred to reports of atrocities committed against American prisoners of war and criticized " 'do-gooder' efforts now under way in this country to save from deportation 5,500 American-born Japanese who formally declared loyalty to the Japanese emperor, and thus voluntarily gave up their citizenship when they believed Japan had a chance to win the war." He called General MacArthur's occupation program "immensely satisfying to the West Coast, where the Japanese and their true instincts are understood as nowhere else in the country."

By war's end, 112,000 persons of Japanese ancestry had been forcibly "relocated" away from the area within 40 miles of the Pacific Ocean; about 70,000 of them were Nisei and, thus, citizens. Three Supreme Court decisions upheld the relocation; so, as a practical matter, their chances of getting restitution for lost houses and businesses through the courts were nonexistent. Consequently, they turned to Congress, but those who finally did receive favorable action on their claims were fortunate if they got ten cents for each lost dollar. Jackson now admits he was wrong about the Nisei during World War II, and he supported postwar congressional appropriations for partial restitution. On the House floor on March 12, 1952, for instance, he spoke briefly in favor of one such measure and inserted a letter from the legislative director of the Japanese American Citizens League setting out that organization's position.

On May 31, 1952, the day he turned forty, Henry M. Jackson declared his candidacy for the United States Senate seat held by Harry P. Cain, the one-time Democratic mayor of Tacoma, who had since become a conservative Republican. By this time, Jackson had closed his breach with the Nisei, and he could now present himself as the candidate of all the people. In announcing his intentions, however, he said little about his Republican opponent but alluded to a foreign one: "I know from first-hand reports the danger posed by the Soviet Union. . . . I know America must be strong, and I know that America cannot go it alone. We need allies. The rearming of those allies is the cheapest way to avoid world war III."

And so the Yellow Peril gave way to the Red Threat.

CHAPTER

4

Grass Roots: The Thirty-nine Counties of Washington State

"FIND 'EM AND VOTE 'EM."

Abraham Lincoln distilled into those five words the essence of successful campaigning. Computers, electronic communications, and mass-marketing techniques may do it faster; but they simply do the very thing stump speakers, handbills, and courthouse cronies alone once did. They locate potential supporters, give them the candidate's pitch, and see that they get to the polls on election day.

The thirty-nine counties of Washington State have elected Henry M. Jackson to the United States Senate every six years since 1952. Each time he has gotten a larger plurality than the time before: 56, 68, 72, and 82 percent respectively. Such lopsided margins may be commonplace in the one-party politics of the deep South, but they are rare in the Pacific Northwest. Jackson is the exception, and the way in which he has applied Lincoln's maxim could provide an object lesson to anyone who seeks to win and hold public office.

Although he can easily command hundreds of thousands of dollars when he runs for reelection, his approach to campaigning has changed very little since he ran for prosecuting attorney of Snohomish County in 1938. More money has permitted him to streamline his operations—hiring a private plane instead of riding in a friend's car, for example—but the approach is the same.

Here is how he now describes his first campaign: "I had these little cards. . . . We had about 100,000 people in the county, and before the election was over we'd used 200,000.

"To every fair, to every gathering of more than two people—I'd be there and shake hands. It was a highly personalized effort on my part, plus a whole army of young people who went door to door. This is the old doorbell ringing, and it was really novel because it hadn't been done on any large scale, such as we had undertaken. We covered every town—Everett was the largest town of course—and we blocked out the whole town, and we had groups that went out and covered it door to door.

"For the Congress [in 1940] we blocked it out the same way in the other counties. I was not endorsed by our county chairman. I ran against the organization, so to speak. . . . We simply wore out the other side, just sheer effort. And we had to do it all in just a short time.

"There were six on the ticket. Mr. Bargreen had run before so he was known all over the district. And the advantage that I had was that I'd defeated the incumbent [prosecuting attorney] three to one or four to one in the primary and then won about three to one in the general election; so I had a strong base. But one thing I learned out of that election is that [just because] a person votes for you for one office it doesn't follow that they're going to vote for you for another office.

"We just had to work around the clock because we had about four to five weeks between the closing day for the primary and the primary election, and it was just a prodigious effort to get around all those areas. Now, I had contacts because I was president of Young Democrats in the county, and I'd campaigned for [Representative] Wallgren after I got out of college in '36 and for Roosevelt. . . . But the tactic was basically the one of extending the same approach that I'd followed in my county to all the other counties."

As this rambling reminiscence indicates, Jackson's approach to campaigning was both personal and methodical. Residential areas would be broken down by precincts and neighborhoods, and volunteers would knock on doors and hand out campaign literature. He would know what times the shifts changed at each mill and would get to as many of them as often as he could. No place of business was too small, no location too inconvenient when votes were at stake.

Phil Sheridan told me of an incident which illustrates the point: "I recall attending a Jefferson-Jackson Day dinner in Anacortes. They had the normal political dinner and speeches, and there may have been a hospitality hour before. Anyway, it was close to midnight by the time we left. On the way back to Everett, we passed a Cooperative Plywood Plant, and Jackson said, 'Let's go in here. I think they'll be changing shifts.'

"So we got out of the car, and he said, 'Let's go see the boom men first.' They were the ones who steered the logs in. So we walked out along this narrow catwalk which was not very well illuminated and not wide enough for two people to pass each other. It was about a block and a half long—it seemed that long. It was a wet, damp night, and I was concerned about our safety, falling into the Sound.

"We got to the boom shack, and he was soliciting their votes as they ate lunch at midnight. They shared coffee out of their thermos with us, and he answered questions and took the names of some of them and mailed them information. He was one of the pioneers of that type of campaigning."

Another time, Jackson thought it would be a good publicity stunt to visit the Coast Guardsmen in the lighthouse on Tatoosh Island a few miles off Cape Flattery in the Pacific Ocean. It is the far northwestern tip of what was then the nation's most northwestern congressional district. Accompanying him were a reporter and Gerald Hoeck, who has handled his campaign publicity since 1948. The three men went out to the island in an amphibian. Hoeck describes the scene: "When we got out there, they dropped this large bucket, and the three of us went up spinning. Scoop spent about an hour and a half talking politics, and as he was leaving he said, 'I hope you fellows will vote for me.' There was silence for a second and then one of them spoke up: 'Congressman, I'm afraid none of us are registered to vote in Washington.' "

Jackson got a newspaper story out of the trip; so it was not a wasted effort. But, even without the reporter, Jackson might still have gone, and he probably would not have bothered to call in advance to make sure there were registered voters at the lighthouse. Detailed planning is not that important to his approach because there is no way you can completely plan fourteen- to eighteen-hour work days on the campaign trail. While he naturally has a general plan which schedules him for particular events and places, such as county fairs and political dinners, from there on it is a matter of shoe leather and handshakes.

Jackson is a singleminded man, and he pursues politics at a frenetic pace. One time, when his plane arrived late, he went directly to a fund-raising reception without first stopping to clean up. The young woman who was responsible for his arrangements caught up with him while he was pumping hands and talking to small groups of people all over the room. Their conversation, as reconstructed by an observer, went something like this:

JACKSON (turning briefly away from his listeners): I need a room where I can shave and wash my face and hands.

WOMAN: Senator, the room is ready.

JACKSON (again, in a quick aside): I need a room where I can shave and wash my face and hands.

WOMAN: Senator, the room is ready.

JACKSON (in still another aside): I need a room where I can shave and wash my face and hands.

WOMAN (trying to contain her exasperation): Senator, would you like me to bring you your razor?

JACKSON: Yes. (Short pause.) But where will I wash my face and hands?

Jackson's seriousness, unfortunately, is not lightened by a sense of humor. Neale Chaney, the state party chairman and a longtime ally of the senator, remembers what happened when he tried to inject a light note into a speech before the State House Democratic Caucus in Olympia. "Vic Myers, the ex-lieutenant governor and band leader, was the M. C., and Scoop was the main speaker. Vic got up and kept the audience laughing for about 45 minutes. Then Scoop got up and started his speech with seven one-line jokes that fell like lead weights. The funniest thing he said all night was: 'So much for levity.' "

Jackson has few hobbies or interests other than politics. Although he occasionally goes fishing, he gets restless without newspapers, radios, and telephones. Judge William Beeks, a friend of long standing, told me that Jackson's fishing companions would sometimes disconnect the radio and "just let him think it didn't work." The ruse apparently worked because Jackson has absolutely no aptitude for gadgets. (Chaney tells of the time Jackson was driving him around Washington with the radiator pouring out steam. When Chaney asked if he had put water in the radiator, Jackson looked at him quizzically. "We had a lot of water put in at a service station," says Chaney. The great reciter of nuclear statistics seemed unaware that car radiators require water.)

If Jackson is serious to the point of humorlessness, he is not ineffective. His memory for names and faces is legendary in Washington State. "He can recall a lunch we had twelve years ago, who was there, and what we talked about," says Beeks. He is also unfailingly polite. Several people who entertain him socially told me that he always stops by the kitchen to thank the help for the meal they prepared and served before he leaves. His common touch is genuine, and the election results reflect it.

He also gives the appearance of consulting widely with state politicians. Although he was certain enough that he would run for the Senate in 1952 to have John Salter move to Seattle two years before the race, he nonetheless traveled the state to ask the advice of every county chairman and local pol he could find. It was not "advice" he wanted so much as personal contact, and he was effective at it. As one Seattle attorney puts it: "You could probably talk to five hundred people who to this day think they convinced Scoop to run for the Senate."

Although Jackson has never lost in the eleven times he has submitted his political future to the voters of Washington State, he nonetheless runs scared. Gordon Culp, a Seattle attorney and former member of Jackson's staff, says, only half in jest: "If the vote in a little town is 212 to 4, he wonders what went wrong with the 4."

After he was elected to the House in 1940, Jackson was so proud of having won 57 percent of the vote that his biographical entry in the January 1941 edition of the *Congressional Directory* noted that he had won "by a large plurality." Because there is a separate statistical section in the book, such a comment is unnecessary; moreover, it is considered poor taste to crow over the size of one's electoral margin in what should be a straightforward listing of biographical data. Someone apparently squared the new congressman away because the next edition appeared in May without the boastful phrase.

Jackson's concern with how well he is doing, or has done, at the polls borders on obsession. Irvin Hoff, a former aide to Senator Warren Magnuson, recalls a time in 1958 when he and Salter were talking in Jackson's Seattle office about the coming election. "Jackson was in the bathroom shaving with the door open. Salter winked at me and started talking out loud about how we were weak in Kitsap County and how we'd only won it last time by 1,500 votes. Jackson then pops his head out the door and says, 'It was 1,559.' "

If Jackson began his political career concerned with his margin of victory, the Republican near-sweep in 1946 could only have convinced him that building a big vote "cushion" was not only prudent but necessary. The red-baiting tactics which launched the political career of Richard M. Nixon in California that year were not unknown in the Pacific Northwest, and Jackson's liberal voting record and leftist inclinations in college were potential soft spots. He moved smartly to counteract that liability, Salter says, "by bringing the International Labor Organization's maritime conference to Seattle in 1946. The ILO was strongly anti-communist, and he was on the radio forty-six times in that period." It proved to be a wise move because when the smoke cleared only Jackson was left of the four Democratic congressmen and the senator who were up for election.

Henry Seidel met Jackson in 1947 when he was a soil conservationist working in the sparsely populated San Juan islands in northern Puget Sound. San Juan County was the smallest in the state, with about three thousand people, and it accounted for about one percent of the vote in Jackson's congressional district. Although he has since become one of Jackson's more vocal liberal critics, Seidel was favorably impressed when he first met the young congressman and occasionally traveled with him when he visited the San Juans.

"Scoop worked hard at leg work," Seidel recalls. "He'd go out on Lopez Island and meet people, and they got to know him as a person. He lived very modestly. I was making $2,000 a year as an agronomist, and I felt I was better off than he was. He never paid a lot of attention to his clothes or appearance.

"We went to Lopez Island once in 1948. It was mostly a farming community, and Scoop was speaking that night at a meeting hall. He came across as earnest, forceful, and serious and went over well. I remember we stayed at Mrs. Tralnes' house. She was a Norwegian woman, and he had a very strong following among the Norwegian farmers. They never asked him for anything. They were just proud of him."

Although Jackson was compiling one of the most liberal records in the House, he would mute his liberalism in these appearances. "He told me," says Seidel, "that if you wanted to get elected in Washington, you had to talk conservative and vote liberal because no one looks at the way you vote." Sixteen years later, Jackson said much the same thing to a reporter for *Seattle* magazine: "People don't support you because of the way you vote in the Senate. They vote for you out of respect. If they think you're a damn fool, your vote isn't going to change their minds."

Although he downplayed the importance of his voting record when he campaigned, he was well aware that certain issues can galvanize the public's attention. Having been one of the few congressmen who voted against establishing the House Un-American Activities Committee in 1945, he was still somewhat vulnerable to charges of being "soft" on communism even though he supported the ILO and became a vigorous cold warrior the following year. So, when the McCarran Act, which established the Subversive Activities Control Board and required communists to register with the attorney general, came to a vote on September 20, 1950, Jackson sat through both calls of the roll until he was certain his vote would not affect the outcome and then voted for it. This greatly upset his staff, but two days later, after President Truman had vetoed it, he regained his conscience and voted to sustain the veto. His opponent later tried to make an issue of this second vote, but it did not stick. So many people in the Second

Congressional District had met or heard Jackson that they could not possibly have been convinced that their stolid, homespun representative was a "fellow traveler."

Another key to Jackson's success is that he never stops campaigning. In the two years before his 1970 reelection, he reportedly returned home all but six weekends. His presence is felt in other ways as well. Press releases several times a week turn into news stories in the media and create an impression that he is hard at work in behalf of local interests, which he usually is. Even more important, he takes seriously his role as ombudsman (a Scandinavian concept) in presenting his constituents' complaints and requests to an often lethargic bureaucracy. More often than not he succeeds, and word-of-mouth advertising spreads news of his effectiveness to friends and neighbors.

One does not have to scratch very hard to find individual stories of his effectiveness. One young journalist in Seattle, who has been a harsh Jackson critic, sought and received help from his office in getting Selective Service to reconsider its denial of his request for conscientious-objector status. The board reversed its initial determination and found him a CO.

Phil Sheridan told me that a University of Washington professor once called Jackson on the weekend to see if he could help a Peace Corpsman who had returned home with an exotic tropical disease which threatened to take his arm. Jackson called the military and had them arrange for a medical specialist to be flown from London to Michigan to consult with the young man's physician. His arm was saved as a result, and one day he came to Jackson's office to shake his hand and thank him. Even that reward was unsolicited.

Jackson has also used his power to help communities in the state. When the Army decided to move out of Fort Lawton, a choice piece of Seattle real estate on Puget Sound went up for grabs to other federal agencies, and the Coast Guard seemed to be eyeing a large chunk of it. Ed Devine, who was then the deputy mayor of Seattle, recalls Jackson turning to a staffer and saying: " 'See what you can do about it.' " As a result, the Coast Guard apparently decided to look elsewhere. Jackson then drafted a bill, guided it through the legislative process, and the City of Seattle now has Fort Lawton for a park.

When eight of the nine nuclear reactors at the Hanford Works became surplus to the nation's needs, Jackson put his influence behind the Tri-City Nuclear Industrial Council and other groups in the Richland area which were seeking to diversify their industrial base. He engineered a breakthrough when the Atomic Energy Commission agreed to "segment" its contracts so that large corporations, such as General Electric, would be forced to take the long-term interests of an area into account when they got major contracts. In the past, companies would train their people on government money only to relocate them (to the detriment of the local economy) when the contracts ran out. By using the contractual process to compel these corporations to invest in a few long-term projects in the Tri-Cities, that area's economic downswing was successfully reversed.

Jackson has served his state and constituents as if in fulfillment of a unwritten social contract. In exchange for their votes, he has been their advocate and ombudsman before the impersonal machinery of government. But this contract is not without catch.

Always willing to listen to people with problems, Jackson seems to close his ears to those with ideas. When he believes he is right, he is not only unshakable; he can be downright hostile to opposing points of view. This criticism does not come just from his political adversaries; allies and friends have experienced his closed-mindedness as well.

Irving M. Clark, Jr., a Seattle attorney who is an ardent conservationist, calls Jackson "the most important figure in the history of Congress on conservation." Clark was active in his 1970 reelection effort on the 'Conservationists for Jackson' Committee. Yet, Clark says, "I found him unreachable on the Vietnam War. I wrote him a four thousand word memorandum on the war, and I got no response. Not even an acknowledgment."

James Whittaker, who gained considerable fame in 1963 when he climbed Mount Everest, is another conservationist who has supported Jackson in his Senate races. In 1964, for instance, he was active on Jackson's finance committee. Concerned about the war, he asked Senator Robert Kennedy to join him in a 1966 lunch meeting with Jackson to discuss the

Johnson administration's policy in Vietnam. "I thought it would be constructive for Senator Jackson," Whittaker recalls, "although Bobby advised me it would do little good." Jackson simply "reacted and justified his position . . . and I found the lunch interesting but nonproductive with respect to Vietnam."

In a two-hour interview, Gordon Culp had mostly laudatory things to say about his former employer. But, when I asked him if Jackson could admit a mistake, Culp replied: "I think he has a problem there. . . . To disagree with him as a constituent is to risk personal animosity. That's the view of many, but I don't think it's an exercise in arrogance." He also acknowledged that Jackson "can't bring himself to say: 'I don't know.' "

I put the question more bluntly to John Salter, his friend and political associate for nearly forty years. "Suppose someone on Jackson's staff thinks he is way off base on an issue. Is there anyone who can look him squarely in the eye and say, 'Bullshit'?"

Salter paused for a few seconds pondering his reply and then answered simply: "No."

An important key to Jackson's electoral success has been the breadth of his constituency. Conservatives find him an ally in his votes for heavy military spending and aid to troubled corporations (*e.g.*, Boeing's supersonic transport). Law-and-order advocates like his no-nonsense speeches and espousal of the death penalty for certain crimes. Moderates will never catch him voting against an increase in social security payments or aid to education. He can point to his votes on civil rights legislation before minority groups, and nearly every year he scores 100 percent on AFL-CIO issues. So his natural political allies are many.

By contrast, his natural adversaries are few. There may still be a small contingent of right-wingers who never forgave him for his vote against HUAC in 1945, but they are insignificant at the polls. The one group which does present a serious challenge—or, more accurately, a nuisance—to Jackson are liberal Democrats. Although the 1970 primary results suggest they represent only13 percent of the population of Washington State, they may well account for a majority of the party's activists. (His relationship with liberal Democrats in Washington State is the subject of the next chapter.)

Before he was appointed to the federal bench, William Beeks practiced law in Seattle and served as finance chairman in Jackson's 1948 and 1952 races. When I asked him the types of people who contributed, he was candid: "Mostly from people who had dealings with government, but Jackson was always so careful never to receive corporate funds and never to take money from anyone who was seeking something at a particular time. I suppose that anyone who gives money probably does so in the hope that it may one day open a door or be of benefit to them sometime."

Jackson's Senate campaigns are now heavily financed by Republican money—a situation which led his 1970 primary opponent, Carl Maxey, to characterize him as "a short, fat, white Republican masquerading as a Democrat." But in 1952 he had to scramble hard for money as well as votes. Fortunately for him, the incumbent senator, Harry P. Cain, was a rube straight out of central casting. "Bitter, irascible and loose-lipped" was the way Richard Neuberger, a reporter (later senator) from Oregon, described him in *The New Republic*. But even rock-ribbed Republican *Time* numbered him among the eight Senate "Expendables."

Cain had a knack for putting his foot in his mouth: "I have been said by many to be the number-one real estate lobbyist in America. I have never resented this title." But the self-inflicted wound which probably destroyed him was his long, bitter, and *public* squabble with his wife, which ended in divorce.

Jackson, on the other hand, was described by Neuberger as "having few enemies because of a placid disposition." He, of course, worked exceptionally hard campaigning around the state, but his victory may well have been more the result of Cain's default.

Once in the Senate, Jackson became determined to stay there, and he continued his pattern of emphasizing regional and constituent interests rather than national affairs. A 1958 campaign pamphlet, "Jackson Is Doing a *Great* Job," told the story of his first term the way he wanted voters to see it.

On the second page was a picture of Jackson surrounded by

six young people and the caption: "Idol of thousands of young teen-agers, Senator Jackson typifies the clean-cut young Senator who meets national problems head on. Here, after the network 'Youth Wants to Know' program, Jackson chats with panelists." But, in the two-page center spread, the angles were strictly local. Under "Atomic Energy," he was credited with leading the fight for a $15 million plutonium recycle reactor for Hanford. His contributions to "Defense" were also calculated in locally spent federal dollars: "Jackson helped keep the B-52's and jet tankers rolling from Boeing plants by impressing the Defense Department with continuing need for long-range jet aircraft. His efforts also resulted in authorization and appropriation for the multi-million dollar Forrestal-class drydock for Bremerton." Such were the ways of "the clean-cut young Senator who meets national problems head on."

Jackson was so accustomed to thinking of politics in local terms that he could even relate the specter of nuclear war to votes back home. "I say to my colleagues frankly," he said on the House floor in 1951, "that if the horror of atomic war should be loosed upon us, I could not face my own constituents—I could not face my own conscience—unless I had today protested against the magnitude and the severity of the cut in the civil defense appropriation requested of us."

The image boggles the mind: Jackson campaigning amid the atomic rubble of Everett, walking from fallout shelter to fallout shelter, reminding the survivors of his vote for civil defense.

Jackson's legwork in the Senate on behalf of the state's economic interests seemed calculated to win him the support of traditionally Republican big business. Although he is now sometimes derided as "the Senator from Boeing," he was once anathema to the president of that company, William Allen, who, I am told, used to refer to the freshman senator as "that goddamned socialist." But Allen and William Reed, whose family owns the Simpson Timber Company, later became convinced that Jackson was good for business and proposed him for membership in Seattle's exclusive University Club. Several members objected at first because he was a Democrat, but a subsequent effort succeeded.

The member who provided me with the foregoing information told me that the club's 250 members are "the cream of the crop." Although it is supposedly a social organization in that members simply do not bring business associates to lunch there, for a politician, membership is clearly an imprimatur which can be turned into big business support for reelection. A glance at Jackson's more recent lists of campaign contributors seems to indicate he has obtained just that.

Women are excluded from the club except for a New Year's Day reception, when they are allowed inside the sanctum sanctorum with their husbands. I asked this member if the club had any other "exclusionary policies." He laughed. "We discriminate on the basis of race, color, and creed," he told me. Translation: Jews and blacks need not apply.

Jackson has been a member of the University Club for nearly twenty years, but he pays the cheaper, out-of-state dues. Added to his membership in the Elks, Masons, Shriners, and the exclusive Chevy Chase Club in the capital's Maryland suburb, this brings to five the number of "social" or "fraternal" organizations of which he is a member that have a history of discrimination on racial or religious grounds.

Washington State has two of the weakest political parties in the nation. One source of their weakness is a measure reformers of the 1930s enacted which ended party registration for voters; another is the "blanket" primary. Unlike "open" primaries, in which the voter in the privacy of the booth can choose either—but only one—party's line from which to select candidates, in Washington State he can pull levers on any line. This freewheeling crossover gives Republicans a powerful voice in choosing which Democrats will stand in the general election and, of course, vice versa. So the importance of political parties in developing and recruiting candidates for office has effectively been nullified.

A brief look at one potential gubernatorial candidate shows just how chaotic the situation can become. Robert Anderson, the bright and personable mayor of Everett, came from the business world into politics. Because voters do not register by party and the mayoralty election is nonpartisan, he has never had to declare in public a political affiliation. Yet he is widely thought to be a potentially strong candidate for governor. Being a good politician, he is "considering the options" rather than making a hasty choice. Indeed, each party has wooed him because they need him more than he needs them. If the time comes for him to make a decision, he will be able to choose the party whose nomination he is more likely to win and then fly its banner as a flag of convenience.

State politics are based on the "star system," and rising politicians are normally a part of the firmament which surrounds one of the two senators or governor. A party label accrues, but loyalty to one's patron is the more recognizable badge. One can be reasonably independent in campaigns for local office, but congressional and statewide office seekers invariably gravitate toward one of the stars. Indeed, unless one is independently wealthy—and campaign reform laws have been eating away at that advantage—it is practially impossible to finance a major campaign without access to a star's moneymen. The financial resources of the state Democratic party, for instance, seem barely adequate to cover the rent for its headquarters: a collection of windowless cubbyholes in one of Seattle's seedier office buildings.

John Hempelmann, who came within an eyelash of being elected to the House in the First Congressional District in 1972, provides a good example of how Jackson can use his star status to help a young politician. Hempelmann went on the payroll in Jackson's Senate office in 1963 and eventually got bitten by the political bug himself. "Scoop worked on me to go to law school at the University of Washington. The idea was for me to go home and get ready to go into politics," he says.

Hempelmann was graduated from law school in 1969, and although Jackson wanted him to run for Congress the following year, he demurred. Instead, he became cochairman of "Young Lawyers for Jackson" in the senator's reelection effort. In May of 1972, Jackson and a labor official were in Oregon, where Hempelmann was working on Jackson's abortive presidential race. The three were talking about the congressional contest in Washington State, and when they got to the party's nonexistent prospects for the First District, "Jackson pointed at me," Hempelmann recalls, "and said, 'There's your candidate. I've been trying to get him to run for three years.' "

Jackson's help was crucial. "I raised $83,000 and spent $84,000," says Hempelmann. "Scoop was directly responsible for $25,000 to $30,000. I got money from unions and Jackson presidential contributors who wanted to give money to Jackson when he was no longer campaigning; he channeled it to me and other candidates. I got money from New York, D.C., and California. . . . He did radio and TV ads for me and arranged for Ted Kennedy to do radio and TV ads for me. Kennedy came off the Senate floor to do films with me on the Capitol grounds.

"Jackson came out four times. Kennedy came out once for a group of Democratic candidates—me included. Every time he [Jackson] came out we got great television coverage, and free television is valuable. Scoop even rode a bicycle with me twenty-two miles across the district from Fort Lawton to Sand Point on a Saturday. Both papers on Sunday carried big picture stories."

Hempelmann was ahead on election night but lost by 2,600 votes when the absentee ballots were subsequently counted. "I would never even have come close without him. I still meet people who say, 'I voted for you because if you're good enough for Jackson, you're good enough for me.' "

Although he concedes that some liberals may have voted against him because of Jackson, that defection may have been more than offset by Hempelmann's dovish stand on Vietnam. Although Jackson was a militant hawk, he did not regard his protégé's position as anything other than a difference in policy; it was not Jackson's political acid test.

So Jackson does not expect or require that a politician under his sponsorship be a miniature version of himself. What he does demand is loyalty, and his herculean effort for Hempelmann is indicative of how he can repay it. The younger man is clearly intent on reciprocating: "I really love the guy. I'm going to be with him in '76 or any other time he wants. And I may disagree with the way he runs the country or on foreign policy, but no one will ever convince me he's not honest."

A wise politician always remains in with the "outs," and Jackson has generally been quite decent toward defeated opponents. Harry Cain, who lost his Senate seat to Jackson in 1952, stumped Florida for him in his first presidential primary twenty years later. "Big Bill" Bantz, who went down to defeat with just 32 percent of the vote in the 1958 Senate race, later received, according to Salter, Jackson's help in seeking a federal judgeship. (He did not get it, however.) In 1970, Jackson and his Republican opponent, Charles Elicker, were at the same reception in Chelan County. When it became clear that few of the people there knew who the other man was, Jackson graciously introduced him around the room.

If "rehabilitation" has characterized his dealings with fallen opponents, "retribution" has been the theme in his relationship with liberal Democrats. The most pointed example was what one of his staffers calls the "rip-off" of eight McGovern delegates to the 1972 Democratic Convention from Washington State. (This is treated in detail in the following chapter.) But it extends also to more petty incidents.

Vern Koenig was an early leader in McGovern's delegate search in Washington State; he now runs a political advertising agency in Seattle. "The say he [Jackson] never forgets," Koenig says. "And I'm told he's asked people what I do for a living.... The implication was to see I would not do business."

Paul Pedersen, the chairman of McGovern's effort in the state, was told that Jackson had encountered an executive of the corporation which employs him. " 'How can someone so radical [Pedersen] work for so conservative a company?' " Jackson reportedly asked. (On another occasion, however, he was reported to have asked plaintively: " 'Why doesn't Paul Pedersen like me?' ")

When McGovern became the presidential nominee of the Democratic party, Senator Magnuson agreed to become the titular chairman of the state effort, and Pedersen was to become cochairman. Jackson and other state political figures were to be listed in a column in the left margin on the McGovern-Shriver stationery. When Jackson saw the proposed letterhead, he exploded. " 'I'm not going on if Paul Pedersen's cochairman. No way,' " he reportedly said. To assuage him, Pedersen agreed to have his name "lowered" into the margin so it would not appear above Jackson's.

Henry Seidel was Representative Brock Adams's administrative assistant until he retired in 1970. Jackson once arranged a lunch meeting with Adams and some labor officials, and Seidel was pointedly excluded. He later learned why. The topic at lunch was why Seidel ought to be fired. His opposition to the Vietnam War was what had apparently set Jackson off. (He may have felt Seidel had led Adams to break with him on the war.)

Henry Jackson began his political career cautiously, seeking to build the widest possible electoral base. He talked conservative and voted liberal and managed to convince the great middle he was one of them. He voted for civil rights while maintaining membership in whites-only fraternal organizations and became the champion of Soviet Jewry while reaping benefits from the gentiles-only Chevy Chase and University clubs. A most agile politician, he has avoided tough issues most of his career while he has carried on this amazingly successful balancing act.

Once in office, he strengthened his base by using the full weight of his position to serve the special interests and citizens of his state. They, in turn, have fulfilled their part of an unwritten social contract by returning him to the Senate with ever-increasing margins of victory. Although he has ignored the institutional needs of his state party, he can deliver money and votes to those of his party's candidates he deems worthy. This has reinforced his personal power.

Jackson was trained to be a lawyer, but since he was elected to office at age twenty-six, politics has been his only profession. He is among its master practitioners, and one simply cannot imagine him out of office. Who is Scoop Jackson? If there is a "private man," he has become so totally absorbed by politics as to be indistinguishable from the public figure.

CHAPTER

5

The Klickitat Shuffle: Screwing the "Radiclibs" Back Home

POLITICS in the Democratic party in Washington State have polarized around the figure of Henry Jackson. The liberal-progressive wing from which he sprang more than three decades ago now finds him anathema—a feeling he reciprocates. His political strength comes from moderate to conservative Democrats and Republicans, with the latter providing much of his campaign financing. Four of every five voters support him on election day, but rather then ignore his liberal opponents, or seek rapprochement, he seems to have deliberately sought to alienate them. His efforts in that regard culminated in 1972 when the Jackson juggernaut "stole" (an opponent's word) or "ripped off" (his own staffer's phrase) eight McGovern delegates to the Democratic National Convention.

The break between Jackson and the Democratic liberals in his state began slowly in the 1950s. Jackson has always been exceptionally thin-skinned, and he tends to react harshly to what more balanced politicians would brush off as minor irritants. Once such irritant presented itself in the form of Alice Franklin Bryant, venerable Seattle peacenik, writer of letters to editors and unsuccessful candidate for high office.

The trident-in-a-circle is now a common piece of costume jewelry, but in the 1950s the so-called peace symbol usually appeared hand-drawn on a placard which said, "Ban the Bomb." The specter of nuclear holocaust served as a motive force in the politics of that time but mostly to justify heavy military outlays, and the label "liberal cold warrior" did not then seem a contradiction in terms. On the other hand, the "peace wing" of the Democratic party had few spokesmen and almost no following. So when Bryant decided to challenge Jackson's renomination in the 1958 primary, most took it for the quixotic gesture it was. Not Jackson, however.

The place is Lake Sammamish; the occasion a Democratic picnic in the summer of 1958. An observer describes the scene: "It was getting kind of late in the afternoon. People had been eating and drinking beer all day. There was a ball diamond there, and they put a dais at home plate for the speeches. Alice Franklin Bryant was opposing Jackson for the nomination, and she was at the lectern giving him hell, banging on it. The only people sitting on the field were those who had had too much beer and didn't feel like moving or had fallen asleep. But Jackson was sitting behind a tree nearby, out of sight but taking it all in, when Al Rochester [a former Seattle city councilman] walks by. Jackson grabbed him by the leg and said, 'Al. Do you hear that? We've got to do something. She's gaining on us!' "

Some time later the liberal Metropolitan Democratic Club listened to a speech by Nobel prize-winner Linus Pauling about the dangers of atomic fallout. At the end of his remarks, the scientist surprised his audience by making an impromptu endorsement: "If I were a voter in this state, I would vote for Alice Franklin Bryant."

Henry Seidel, who was then president of MDC, thought nothing of the remark, but the word was flashed to Jackson in Washington, and he reacted to it as a declaration of war. Two hours later, Seidel got a transcontinental phone call from a very irate senator, demanding to know why Pauling had been invited in the first place. Although he asked for and received an apology from MDC, it took two years, according to Seidel, before Jackson could be coaxed into appearing before the two-hundred member group again.

Jackson was also upset by liberal delegates to the 1960

Democratic Convention who would not switch from Stevenson to Kennedy when Jackson was being considered for the vice-presidential nomination under JFK. Liberals, in turn, were disturbed by his seemingly gratuitous slap at the United Nations in several 1962 speeches and his threatened obstruction of Kennedy's partial nuclear test-ban treaty the following year. They perceived their fortyish freshman liberal turning into a fiftyish mossback.

Jackson's enthusiastic support for the Johnson administration's policy in Vietnam eventually turned what had been a crack into a chasm. By 1968, his liberal opposition had become more than just vocal; it was organized.

While liberals were preparing for local caucuses to try to elect delegates for Senators Robert Kennedy and Eugene McCarthy, Jackson was coordinating the effort for Vice President Hubert Humphrey through his neighbor Everett attorney John F. Wilson, who later became chairman of the delegation to Chicago.

Liberals succeeded in getting 14½ delegate votes while Humphrey picked up 32½, but a question arose concerning the balloting in populous Pierce County, which includes Tacoma. Maralyn Chase, who was state secretary for the McCarthy campaign, claims: "There was one more vote cast than was eligible, and Jackson's people came out ahead by one vote."

So Humphrey won that district's four delegates. But, when the ballots were destroyed in an incinerator a few days later, smoldering suspicions burst into flame, and the burning of the ballots became a *cause célèbre* among McCarthy supporters. Although Wilson maintains a recount would not have affected the outcome, he acknowledges that "the cosmetic aspect—burned ballots—was not good. They even had a ballad to sing about it in Chicago."

The events in and around Chicago, the Vietnam War, and the Pierce County "pyre" served to solidify the McCarthy and Kennedy forces after they returned, and they subsequently joined together to oppose their common adversary, Henry Jackson.

Jackson's renomination in 1970 was a foregone conclusion, but liberals wanted to confront him on the war and other issues.

Carl Maxey, an attorney from Spokane, undertook the challenge even though, as a practical matter, he had no chance of success. Not only was he from a less populous part of the state, he was black (in a state where only 2 percent of the population is) and had a white wife. Nonetheless, Maxey and his supporters knew their quarry well, and if they did not exactly put a scare into him, they soon found—and began hitting—his exposed nerves.

One Jackson campaign commercial showed him walking with one of his children in a park his legislation had created. Maxey looked but saw something else: "Every time I see Jackson in that television commercial, walking in the woods with his child, I see the trees, and I'm reminded of the coffins they are sending our children home in from Vietnam."

Such remarks outraged Jackson, who spoke of Southeast Asia in geopolitical terms and avoided—or simply never saw—the larger moral questions. He was a man of the Senate, where even his fiercest adversaries were civil enough to call him "the gentleman from Washington." No such courtesies were forthcoming from Maxey and hundreds of young people, some of whose placards accused him of murder. When he spoke on campus, he would sometimes be pelted by marshmallows, and several observers have told me that his hands and body would often be shaking as he spoke. Having come to office in an era when politics were supposed to end at the water's edge, he just could not understand how a dispute over foreign policy could create such hostility.

The King County (Seattle and suburbs) Democratic Convention handed Jackson a stinging rebuke in May when it endorsed Maxey, 508 to 485. At the state convention in Spokane two months later, a liberal platform was adopted over Jackson's opposition. But the primary election in September was no contest: Jackson got 84 percent of the vote. Though he won overwhelmingly when it mattered, he could not forget—nor, apparently, forgive—those he deemed responsible for his humiliation.

Mike Ryherd was then the Democratic party chairman of King County. A liberal, Ryherd tried to maintain a semblance of neutrality in the senatorial primary. After Maxey received the King County endorsement, for instance, he told the Seattle *Times*: "The activists in the party have become more liberal. . . . If they want to work for a candidate, that's fine. But they shouldn't try to shove it down everybody else's throat."

When Ryherd later decided to run for county assessor in 1971 and won the primary, he had high hopes of uniting all factions of the party behind his candidacy. When he learned that he might not get the endorsement of the AFL-CIO's joint labor council, a meeting was arranged at John Salter's house.

Having been Jackson's principal operative for nearly forty years, Salter's political standing in the state rests entirely on the supposition that he is speaking and acting for the senator. Several people attended the meeting, but it ultimately boiled down to the following exchange between Salter and Ryherd which I have reconstructed from the accounts of observers.

SALTER: A lot of people are going to say you're not objective as party chairman because your wife is a paid McGovern worker, and your campaign manager is her partner.

RYHERD: Look, one thing you have to understand: my wife's politics are her own. I don't tell her what to do.

SALTER: I find that kind of hard to believe. Don't you two ever confer in bed? . . . Face it, there's no way labor's going to feel comfortable with you as long as your wife is working for McGovern. It makes it appear that you're also for him.

RYHERD: I thought I'd been clear about that. I'm not going to endorse any presidential candidate as long as I'm party chairman.

SALTER: Maybe you ought to consider resigning as chairman.

RYHERD: I've already said that I would resign *after* I've been elected.

SALTER: Well, I still think there's going to be a problem.

RYHERD: Why? My labor record has been impeccable, and it would be a real shame to blow this seat because it's really crucial to low-income and labor people because the assessor can raise or lower their property taxes.

The meeting ended inconclusively, but Ryherd was soon to learn that his stand had cost him dearly. Of the meeting his campaign manager, Vern Koenig, recalls: "They were like surgeons: they have a polite, gentlemanly chat and then get down to business. They know exactly what part they want to cut out."

Within a few days things began to happen. "The *P-I* [Seattle *Post-Intelligencer*], which had endorsed Mike in the primary, withdrew its endorsement in the general. Attorneys who could give $25 didn't. And, needless to say, we didn't get the labor endorsement," recalls Koenig.

When the votes were counted election night, Ryherd recalls, "I lost, 101,000 to 99,000, before the absentee ballots were counted." How much of a hand Jackson had in the loss is in dispute, but liberals across the state, who were waiting to see if Jackson was going to make a peace gesture, thought they got his message. He would use his political clout to continue his vendetta against them even if it meant electing Republicans to office. They would see no olive branch, just the mailed fist.

In spite of the large sums of money he can raise and the overwhelming vote he receives, Jackson has a serious problem which has plagued his state—and, clearly, national—campaigns: he attracts relatively few volunteer workers. The young people who rang doorbells for him in the early days are now middle-aged and inclined to limit their political activities to voting and, perhaps, writing a check. The Democratic activists in his state, as elsewhere, tend to be young, issue-oriented, and liberal. Jackson not only has little to offer them, he seems to have gone out of his way to repulse them. So, when he decided to run for President, he knew his liberal opponents at home would attempt to defeat him in the caucuses. Because they had taken nearly a third of the delegates to Chicago in 1968 and embarrassed him two years later in King County, he took them seriously and had his staff launch a statewide effort to capture the entire delegation: fifty-two votes.

State delegates to the Democratic National Convention were selected in four stages. Precinct caucuses in March chose delegates to attend either the legislative district's caucus (in the large counties) or the county convention (in the smaller ones) in April. They, in turn, went to the congressional district's caucus in May, where most of the delegates to Miami were selected. The remaining delegates were chosen at large by the state convention in June.

Because the average precinct caucus, according to John Wilson, attracts just eight people, liberal activists stood a good chance of winning some of the delegates if they could get out the vote. They did just that and won six delegates from the Third Congressional District and two from the Fifth. They might have won four more in the Fourth but for a curious maneuver engineered by Jackson's Seattle staff.

A nose count before the congressional district caucuses showed that McGovern would handily win the Third and had a good chance of winning the Fourth unless a way could be found to send more Jackson people to the latter caucus. Eventually they saw a way to do it with the delegates from Klickitat County.

Situated on the Columbia River in south central Washington, Klickitat County is sparsely populated and largely agricultural in character. It is the sort of area where Jackson runs well, and to no one's surprise he won all five of the county's delegates to the state convention. What set this county apart from similar ones was that the line which separated the Third and Fourth Congressional Districts ran through it.

The state rules quite clearly stipulated that delegates to the congressional district caucuses could vote only "in the Congressional District in which they reside." With two of the county's delegates in the Third and three in the Fourth District, there would have been no question about where each should vote had all the delegates attended their respective caucuses. They did not, however.

Tom Dickson, a young attorney who was on Jackson's staff at the time, describes what happened: "It was very close in the Fourth Congressional District. We had read the rules for choosing delegates, and we saw an opportunity to use the rules to turn a losing proposition into a winning one. The rules said delegates would attend the caucus in their congressional district. Two of the people in the Third could not go. One had an employee die and had to go to the funeral. The other had a meeting in the county. We found that out when we called to see if we could wheel this deal. Whether it was by design or a stroke of luck is argumentative, irrelevant. We referred to it as 'the Klickitat shuffle.' "

In place of the absent delegates from the Third Congressional District, two alternates from the Fourth were chosen. Thus the county sent no delegates to the Third's caucus and five to the Fourth's. This meant that two more Jackson delegates went to the Fourth's caucus than would have had the original delegates all attended, and it turned out that those two extra votes were Jackson's margin of victory.

What Jackson's staff had engineered was not contrary to the rules of the party; indeed, it was a most clever exploitation of a loophole in a rule which did not take into account the possible consequences of a county's being divided between two congressional districts. Moreover, having taken all but eight of the delegates, Jackson was certain of controlling the credentials committee and state convention should McGovern's people challenge the fruits of "the Klickitat shuffle." Nonetheless, the defeated McGovern delegates felt strongly that they had been victimized; so they retained Thomas McCarthy, a liberal attorney from Bellevue, to represent them.

McCarthy and Paul Pedersen, who was chairman of the McGovern campaign in the state, met John Salter for lunch at the College Club to discuss a "deal." McCarthy recalls: "We discussed the challenges, and he said they would challenge us in the Third and Fifth unless we dropped our challenge in the Fourth. Paul and I told him that we could only make recommendations to my clients. I remember that he just could not believe that these people would not do what we told them to."

McCarthy presented Salter's suggestion to his clients, but they refused to drop the challenge. "I passed the word to Jackson's people," he says. "No deal."

Jackson's staff sought a second, larger meeting, and one was arranged at Seattle's Sherwood Inn. Jack Tanner, an attorney from Tacoma, represented the Jackson camp. "He did most of the talking," McCarthy recalls. " 'We are going to have the votes at the state convention,' he said, 'and unless you drop your challenge in the Fourth, we're going to vote down your challenge and knock out your delegates from the Third and Fifth.' "

Dickson remembers Tanner putting it even more bluntly: " 'Take it our way or no way.' "

Dickson avers the compromise offer was sincere, but others in Jackson's retinue may have regarded it simply as a necessary prelude to stripping McGovern of his eight delegates. (In this latter construction the McGovernites would only have themselves to blame for having refused to compromise.) When I asked Dickson why they did not just defeat the challenge to the Fourth District and unilaterally put their proffered deal into effect, he resorted to a legalism, "preservation of interest," for their challenges to McGovern's delegates in the Third and Fifth.

Whatever the motive, the stage was set for a confrontation when the credentials committee met in the Bowl Room of Seattle's Olympic Hotel on June 23, 1972.

The agenda item when the committee convened at 1:30 P.M. was the Jackson challenge to the six McGovern delegates from the Third Congressional District. The basis of the challenge was that 38 more votes than were mathematically possible had been tabulated in the election of Thurston County's delegates to the Third District's caucus. (There were 152 valid ballots and 29 choices per ballot: a total of 4,408 votes. The tabulation, however, was 4,446 votes.) The five members of the tallying committee consisted of three Jackson supporters, one Muskie and one McGovern supporter. The count took three hours, and when the McGovern supporter requested that the count be verified for accuracy, he was voted down, four to one. One of the counters, Mrs. Vern Petit, later submitted a deposition which concluded: " 'I feel we made an honest attempt to count the ballots correctly at the convention, and although I, as a Jackson supporter, am sorry to see him lose his delegates, I feel the convention result was fair and should be accepted as part of the democratic process.' " (All quoted material from the hearings of the credentials committee has been extracted from a verbatim transcript made by a legal stenographer hired by McCarthy.)

The arguments apparently swayed no one. Jackson's people had the votes, and the committee voted to unseat the six McGovern delegates, 31 to 9.

Next on the agenda was the McGovern challenge to "the Klickitat shuffle," but after the first vote, there was no doubt about how the committee would go. The arguments were laid out for the record, but both sides realized that debate was perfunctory. The McGovern challenge was easily defeated, 26 to 11.

Next came Jackson's challenge to the two McGovern delegates from the Fifth District. It was based on alleged errors in two legislative districts in Spokane County; however, the meeting in one district was run by a Jackson supporter who may have intentionally created an error so the loss could later be challenged. Moreover, if in fact there were errors, there was no evidence—only assertions—presented to show how the outcome would have changed. Although the case was flimsy, Jackson had the votes.

But, before the vote was taken, a young McGovern supporter, Pat Stiley, rose and made an emotional plea to the committee: "I might point out to the chairman himself and to the thirty-five members of the body that you have done more than defeat us in battle, and not just me but thousands of people in Spokane and thousands of people throughout the state. You have humiliated us and humiliated us unnecessarily and without reasonable cause for it, and you are driving us from your party. If that is what you have wanted to accomplish, you have done it. If that is not what you wanted to accomplish, you have a lot of housecleaning to do."

Carl Maxey also stood up and made this caustic observation: "Tomorrow, the readers of the *P-I* and *Times* and *Review* and all of the rest of the papers throughout the state will look up and say of Henry Jackson: 'My God, he ate the whole thing.' And it will be a testimonial to the avarice of this man and to the ridiculous conduct of those people who are supporting him."

When the votes were counted, Jackson's challenge had been sustained, 28 to 10. It had taken a few hours to go through the motions of parliamentary democracy, but in the end the Jackson-dominated credentials committee had done what it had been expected to do: stripped McGovern of the eight delegates to Miami he had "won" in the caucuses.

The matter of who would and who would not go to Miami having been resolved, the committee turned to lesser issues. One of them was whether McGovern's delegates from Thurston County to the *state* convention would be seated.

Tanner moved to sustain the Jackson challenge, but to the surprise of everyone the committee split, 16 to 16.

Neale Chaney, the state party chairman, was then chairing the committee, but he refused to break the tie. According to parliamentary procedure, he should have ruled that the motion failed for lack of a majority, but he did not. "Obviously Jackson's people had a hard time swallowing that one," says McCarthy. "But the glares that were going around the room had an effect." Chaney called for a new vote, counted the hands and announced: "The challenge is sustained, 22 to 14."

Chaney has been a Jackson loyalist since he rang doorbells for him in the prosecuting attorney's race in Snohomish County in 1938, but Chaney's conscience must have been disturbed by the credentials committee's arbitrary exercise of power. Just before he adjourned the meeting, he expressed that concern: "I think that you should reflect very, very carefully on what has been done here today because I think that we can have a blood bath tomorrow, or we can sit and hold a convention. Now, I have been a party to negotiations, spent the most of two weeks between the McGovern and Jackson leadership. As state chairman, I am going to recommend to the convention tomorrow that they reject all challenges, and I am going to ask the leaders and the Jackson and McGovern forces to sit down and withdraw their challenges. . . . Now, my little speech here may cost me my election as a national delegate but be that as it may. I thank you for your time."

Chaney's proposal was doubly sensible. By voting down all the challenges, the convention would restore the eight McGovern delegates, thereby healing some of the day's wounds, but it would also permit the state to send an unchallenged delegation to Miami. After all, the same sort of might-makes-right approach at the national level could result in Jackson's being stripped of some of his delegates. (In fact, McCarthy carried the McGovern challenges all the way to Miami, only to have McGovern's political director, Frank Mankiewicz, get him to drop them as a "unity gesture" toward Jackson.)

Chaney never put his proposal to the convention. That night he met briefly with Jackson behind the platform before the senator's dinner speech. "Jackson was overheard that night dressing Chaney down," says McCarthy. Chaney disagrees: "As state party chairman, he [Jackson] would not try to tell me what to do." But, he adds: "There was no doubt in my mind he wanted all the delegates because as a candidate for President you'd want to go in with your whole delegation intact."

When Jackson stood up to begin his speech, he knew he had the entire state delegation in his pocket. All that remained was for the convention to put its rubber stamp on the actions of the credentials committee. Although his national campaign had collapsed in disaster the month before, he now stood victorious on his home ground. It was a time for magnanimity, but Jackson was in a different frame of mind.

Instead of extending a hand to the defeated liberals of his party, he tried to tie them to straw men he called "extremists": "The American people are fed up with those who advocate amnesty, legalized prostitution, and legalized homosexuality. Some states are putting it into their platforms. . . .

"Now, they're fed up with tax schemes that will place the load on those who work for a living, especially those earning from $9,000 a year on up, while some propose handouts of a thousand dollars for every American. Isn't it high time, isn't it high time to make it possible for every able-bodied American to work and to stop this nonsense of handouts for people when we ought to be talking about putting them to work?"

The speech continued in that strident vein. One King County party official still recalls it as "the most horrible episode in my entire life. It was a very vitriolic attack on 'interlopers,' that the party must get rid of these kooks and return to 'the real majority.' "

Even some of the senator's supporters took a dim view of his speech. Randy Revelle, a Jackson delegate to Miami who later became a Seattle city councilman, says: "I had hoped Jackson would give a conciliatory speech, but instead it was a fighting, sleeves-rolled-up speech. I just left shaking my head. Some of us had called for moderation, reasoning that eight delegates were not that important. There was a meeting of Jackson delegates after the banquet, and the tone of that meeting was set to some extent, unfortunately, by his hard-line speech. I felt it was a speech he didn't need to make. It just made no sense to antagonize the opposition and engender bitterness."

Another Jackson supporter puts it more bluntly: "That [speech] was what the Jackson mob did *not* need."

On Saturday, the state convention moved quickly to ratify "the Klickitat shuffle" and the work of the credentials committee which had given the eight McGovern delegates to their favorite son. Jackson reveled in the moment. At last he had gotten from his state what he felt was his due: 100 percent.

AMBITION

CHAPTER

6

The Early Senate Years

WHEN JACKSON campaigned for the Senate seat held by Harry Cain in 1952, he compared what he had done for the state against his opponent's meager record. In a statewide radio broadcast a month before the election, he boasted: "There hasn't been a single project developed in Washington State during the past twelve years that I haven't taken an active hand in promoting. I challenge anyone to point out one major project in this state that my opponent has led the fight for in Congress."

He was particularly critical of Cain's vote against greater appropriations for more power at Grand Coulee Dam. "Imagine, with our state facing a brownout in its defense operations—at Hanford, at Boeing, at aluminum plants in Spokane and Vancouver, and at the Bremerton Navy Yard—with thousands of fertile acres thirsting, with $10 billion worth of new enterprise at stake, this man, Harry Cain, turned his back on his constituents and voted against his own state, against national security, and against the prosperity of this region."

Perhaps because he really had no regional accomplishments to point to, Cain resorted to the same sort of tactics which propelled Richard Nixon to office in California: red baiting. "My own opponent has ducked any chance to discuss his sorry record of playing ball with the left wing. He seeks to sound like a statesman when in fact he has in the past closed his eyes to the threat of communism and participated in the muddle-headed policies which have led us to Korea. Such men as Jackson and [Representative Hugh B.] Mitchell of Washington are conditioned in the school that gave away a large part of the world to Russia after World War II."

Although Jackson generally ignored charges of this sort, he was not above a little retaliatory mud-slinging. "My opponent can talk from now until doomsday, but he cannot escape the fact that he and left-wing Glenn Taylor were the only two senators who voted against the 70-group Air Force. He cannot escape the fact that he voted against arms aid to Korea and Europe prior to the communist attack."

Jackson carried his anti-communism into the Senate, but he was primarily concerned with the threat overseas. Although he no doubt would have preferred to devote his energies to regional issues to solidify his political base—as he had done so successfully in the House—he soon became embroiled in the premier issue of the day: the internal "communist menace."

The Eisenhower landslide in 1952 gave the Republicans a bare majority in the Senate, and one consequence was that Senator Joseph McCarthy became chairman of the Permanent Subcommittee on Investigations. Jackson did not relish being assigned to that panel, but he could not escape it. And before long he found himself in the floodlit Caucus Room—scene of investigations from Teapot Dome to Watergate—for McCarthy's inquisition into the alleged infiltration of the government by communists.

Having voted against HUAC and the Internal Security Act of 1950 and for Alger Hiss's pension—he correctly believed that denying it amounted to an unconstitutional bill of attainder—Jackson was understandably reluctant to tangle publicly with McCarthy. Indeed, the Wisconsin Republican had made a special trip to Washington State to campaign for Harry Cain and had poked at such soft spots. Several friends say Jackson was "frightened" of McCarthy, and their assessment seems accurate. Although McCarthy's counsel Roy Cohn denied it happened, John Salter claims that Cohn privately threatened Jackson after one particularly heated subcommittee session, saying: " 'You sponsored and wrote to the White House on behalf of two known communists, and I'm going to get you.' "

"We spent the next forty-eight hours," Salter recalls, "going through ten years of files and did find one who was a communist, but it was just a standard letter for a constituent." Although Cohn never mentioned the matter again, Jackson's panicked weekend going through drawer after drawer of the most ordinary correspondence indicates how very vulnerable he must have felt to insinuations he was a "fellow traveler."

Characteristically, he assumed a low profile in his first year on the subcommittee but joined the other Democrats, John McClellan of Arkansas and Stuart Symington of Missouri, in a highly publicized walkout in protest against the chairman's dictatorial power in the hiring and firing of staff members. (Ironically, two decades later when Jackson became chairman, he arrogated similar power to himself.) The Democrats rejoined the panel in February 1954 and attended the star-chamber proceedings, but if Jackson was outraged by McCarthy's performance during the televised hearings, he kept it from surfacing. Symington, who was also a freshman, had no such reluctance and frequently engaged the chairman in verbal duels. "Sometimes Scoop put his hand on Symington's knee to keep him from getting too excited during the hearings," recalls Salter. No such restraint was necessary for the ever-cautious Jackson. Although the hearings made him familiar to people on the street, the books about that era and the film *Point of Order* accord him only passing mention. It is no oversight.

The dramatic confrontation between McCarthy and Boston attorney Joseph Welch marked the beginning of the decline of the Wisconsin demagogue. On June 9, when Welch posed his famous question—"Have you no sense of decency left?"—McCarthy could not adequately respond because his conduct had long since supplied the answer. Then and only then did Jackson, who senses weakness in others as surely as a shark smells blood, join in the kill.

On June 11, with minority counsel Robert F. Kennedy passing him hastily scribbled questions, Jackson once again became a prosecuting attorney as he cross-examined McCarthy about the qualifications of his investigator, G. David Schine—zeroing in on a paper Schine had written which grandly planned the destruction of world communism.

"The broad battlefield is the globe," wrote Schine, and he

went on to describe how everything from the clergy to pinups and overseas Elks' clubs might be drafted into democracy's holy war against communism. It was a ludicrous document, and Jackson skillfully exploited it in his questioning of McCarthy. Schine, for instance, had suggested a "Deminform" to spread information about democracy abroad. This prompted Jackson to ask mockingly: "Isn't that word 'Deminform' pretty close to 'Cominform'? Aren't some of the people going to get mixed up?"

On down the list he went, his questions barbed with ridicule. "Is he [Schine] going to infiltrate the clergy?" And: "I don't know whether they have an Elks lodge in Pakistan. I belong to the Elks."

The audience in the closely packed Caucus Room laughed at each thrust and so did millions at home as McCarthy, whom Welch had exposed two days before as a demagogue, was transmogrified further into a buffoon. He would never again be taken seriously, and in December the Senate, by a vote of 67 to 22, administered the *coup de grâce* in the form of a motion to censure.

With the McCarthy era behind him, Jackson reverted to his accustomed role of provincial politician. A seat on the Interior Committee gave him a voice in the disposition of the federal government's vast Western land holdings while membership on the Armed Services Committee allowed him a vote on military contracts and bases for the folks back home.

It is not surprising, then, that the public record of his first two terms in the Senate contains relatively few references to national or international affairs. He seems to have been preoccupied with such matters as keeping the cheap electrical power and water of his region from being diverted south to fuel California's population boom. Because of the symbiotic economic relationship between Washington and Alaska, he naturally worked hard to help create the forty-ninth state. But, except for an occasional speech about the Soviet Union, he seemed entirely content playing ombudsman for his constituents and steering ever larger federal payrolls to his state. His interest in atomic energy, however, was somewhat—though not much—broader.

Jackson first became involved in nuclear affairs in the House when he was appointed to the Joint Committee on Atomic Energy. With the economy of the Tri-Cities in south central Washington so dependent on the Hanford Works, he had a strong incentive to win a Senate seat on the committee and did. Thereafter he immersed himself in the technology of the atom so he might be recognized a Senate "expert."

Unsuited by temperament to an analytical role, he soon became an unabashed advocate of nuclear power as a panacea for the ills of mankind. In 1955, for example, he proposed that the United States dot the deserts of the Middle East with nuclear reactors: "These atomic furnaces will produce overnight energy to pump water over arid fields, turn the wheels of new industry and lay the groundwork for increased productivity in areas where dire want is a round-the-clock reality." (Ironically, when President Nixon traveled to the Middle East in June of 1974 and advocated the very thing, Jackson rushed to the Senate Press Gallery to denounce the scheme as an "absurdity": "I never thought he would go so far as to peddle nuclear power plants to the Middle East. . . . We should spend the money on the eye disease that hits half the kids there.")

No region on earth would have been deprived of the blessings of atomic energy in Jackson's scheme of things. After a 1960 visit to Antarctica, for instance, he suggested that the United States build nuclear power plants on that pristine continent. And, of course, he found imaginative uses for the atom at home. One Seattle journalist recalls a Jackson trip to eastern Washington in the late 1950s when he turned every question he was asked into a discussion of nuclear power. "Farmers would ask him about falling potato prices, and he'd talk about how atomic energy could be used to process potatoes and stabilize prices. He has this knack of falling back on his past experience—or his last briefing."

After he was reelected in 1958 by a comfortable, 68 percent margin, he began to devote some serious attention to matters which had national significance. Although he had written articles and given speeches about national security during his first term, those efforts required relatively little time. With his political base more secure, he now felt he had room to branch out.

Almost every politician was a cold warrior in those days; so defense was a politically safe issue, and being identified as a hard-liner was political ammunition Jackson could use against any right-wing opponent. Thus his appointment to chair a specially created Government Operations' Subcommittee on National Policy Machinery in May of 1959 gave him an opportunity to investigate an important, if narrow, area at no political risk to himself. It was, characteristically, a cautious first step on the periphery of the larger arena, but he now had a national issue to look into, and he approached it with his usual thoroughness.

The subcommittee's focus was clearly on procedure, as distinct from content, and Jackson himself noted that his investigation was "concerned with the administration of national security—with getting good people into key foreign and defense posts and enabling them to do a job. It is not inquiring into the substance of policy." With his task thus circumscribed, Jackson delved into the workings of the National Security Council, Strategic Air Command, Pentagon planning, Science Advisory Board, State Department, and Foreign Service.

Three years later Jackson continued his investigation into the machinery of government with his Subcommittee on National Security Staffing and Operations. Although the staff reports issued by both panels seemed to have little influence on the Kennedy and Johnson administrations, they provided Jackson with an understanding of the inner workings of the Pentagon and State Department no other legislator has yet equaled. Most importantly, it gave him insight into which people and which subagencies can initiate, revise, or obstruct national policy and a realization that if you can control the players you can greatly influence the game.

CHAPTER

7

Scoop and Maggie

WASHINGTON STATE has long been represented in the Senate by Warren Magnuson and Henry Jackson, and it would be hard to imagine two Democrats more unalike. Although both are of Scandinavian descent in a state which was heavily settled by Nordic immigrants, and they cooperate with one another to serve their constituents and local economic interests, the similarities end there.

To the political observer it is clear that each has his own electoral constituency. Although both are supported by centrist Democrats, many of the party's liberal leaders who actively oppose Jackson appear on the letterhead of Magnuson-for-Senate committees and help raise money for the senior senator's campaigns. Jackson has cultivated Republican businessmen, and they have responded by heavily underwriting his campaigns. While they are not so impractical as to burn their bridges to Magnuson, they are not nearly so comfortable with the Senate's foremost consumer advocate as they are with the more business-oriented Jackson. Hence, the campaign contributor lists of one do not greatly overlap the other's. They cooperate in each other's campaigns—one usually serving as honorary chairman for the other—and they have even loaned staff members for such races. Neither, however, does very much to strengthen the state party. Both are products of the "star system," and each plays to his own audience.

A poll of senatorial assistants taken in the fall of 1973 by

Ralph Nader's Capitol Hill News Service ranked Jackson first in "effectiveness" and Magnuson second. Shortly thereafter, the Seattle *Post-Intelligencer* ran a cartoon of the two senators in boxing trunks, calling them Washington State's one-two punch. It symbolized, says one Seattle journalist, "the smugness people feel in this state about having two strong senators. Other Far West states are not strongly represented."

In fact, no state outside the deep South enjoys similar clout in the Senate. With Jackson chairman of the Interior Committee, Magnuson heading Commerce, and both on the Defense Appropriations Subcommittee (Jackson ex officio), the Evergreen State usually gets more than its share of federal greenbacks. Although they could not prevent the 15 to 18 percent unemployment wave from engulfing Seattle and Puget Sound in the early 1970s, their chairmanships and seniority helped turn the situation around. A glance at the state's federal tax burden compared to federal outlays in the state indicates their effort was of considerable magnitude.

In 1970 the people and businesses of Washington State paid $3,434,470,000 in taxes to the federal government and received slightly less ($3,415,188,946) in federal spending in the form of contracts to state businesses, payrolls, individual benefits, and the like. Two years later the situation changed markedly. Although the state's federal tax burden rose slightly to $3,574,210,000, federal outlays skyrocketed to $5,100,948,611. To put it in more meaningful terms, between 1970 and 1972 the federal government increased its spending in the state from $1,002 per person to $1,496.

Not only did federal spending per capita jump 50 percent, but every federal agency increased its budget, and the state's relative standing in comparison to other states in spending by each agency also went up. In some instances it was a modest increase: from 5th to 4th among the states in spending by the Atomic Energy Commission. But the jump in most cases was large: 18th in Defense Department spending in 1970 to 12th in 1972, 26th to 19th in spending by NASA, and 6th to 2nd in Department of Interior funds.

No doubt there were other factors at work in this massive influx of federal dollars. Unemployment was more than just a local problem; it was an economic disaster which might have had serious political repercussions in President Nixon's campaign for reelection. Nixon's need for good public relations in economic matters, however, seems less significant in comparison to the power of Jackson and Magnuson to block or delay defense, trade, and other important legislation. In short, Nixon may have wanted to "purchase" Washington State's nine electoral votes with federal money, but it stretches credulity to assume he would have spent an extra $1.7 billion if that was all he expected in return.

One reason the senators work so well for their state is that their areas of expertise are so different they seldom come in contact with one another as legislators. Businessmen with military, oil, or timber interests naturally turn to Jackson, while those concerned with aviation, automobile insurance, or foreign trade seek an audience with Magnuson. At the more mundane level of constituent service there is also some degree of specialization. So Magnuson's staff is likely to steer people with immigration and naturalization problems to Jackson's office, and the reverse process may occur if an individual is having trouble dealing with, say, the civil service bureaucracy. Their professional relationship, then, is a textbook model of how two well-placed senators can logroll with one another to their state's maximum advantage.

Although Jackson and Magnuson work well together, they have never been close on a personal level. "Tense" is the adjective friends of each often use to characterize the relationship. That may or may not be, but no one ever suggests their relationship is "warm."

In style and temperament they are in no way alike. Although both were bachelors until quite late in life, the fun-loving "Maggie" made no secret of his interest in the opposite sex and, indeed, flaunted it so openly that his opponent in 1956 tried to make it a campaign issue. "Yes, I'm not afraid to admit it: I like girls," was his televised reply, recalls a former aide, "but mother always warned me to beware of men who like boys."

Contrast Magnuson's humor and openness about his social life with the junior senator's apparent feeling that everyone must be watching him. In 1958, for instance, a friend saw him wearing sunglasses on the Fauntleroy (West Seattle) to Harper ferry (now defunct) and thought it strange because he had never seen him hide behind a pair of shades. When he asked about "the disguise," Jackson replied that he did not want to be recognized on his way to see the woman he was dating in Port Orchard. She, like Jackson, was single so it was not a matter of averting a scandal. He must simply have felt that he was living under a microscope.

Magnuson is gregarious and mixes easily with people. Friends who have entertained Jackson, however, say he tries too hard to be the center of attention. At one dinner party, for example, a famous scientist had been holding the attention of the table until Jackson insinuated himself into the conversation and then monopolized it by ticking off in great detail the legislation he had sponsored to advance the cause of science. No matter what the subject, they say, he will try to steer the conversation to politics or one of the few other topics with which he is familiar.

In the course of my interviews with individuals who have dealt personally with Jackson, no one could remember his ever taking a second drink. When he would go to Magnuson's apartment in the Olympic Hotel after a political function, he would sip his drink, converse briefly, and then take his leave. "He always had a speech to give the next day in the San Juan Islands," cracks one Seattle politician. Magnuson, on the other hand, would no more decline a drink than a dowager would a dividend.

Jackson's mother was "obese" (his word), and he inherited her tendency to put on weight. To keep from completely filling out his genetic code, he carefully restricts his diet, takes large doses of vitamins, and exercises. Magnuson, however, has long since surrendered to the desires of the flesh and in profile resembles nothing so much as the Capitol dome. He has a sense of humor to match his size and enjoys pulling an occasional prank, whereas Jackson's utter humorlessness has led to his becoming a "victim" on more than one occasion.

One time when Jackson was chiding Magnuson about his weight, he decided to play along with the game. An observer reconstructs the scene:

JACKSON: You know, if you exercised regularly, you wouldn't be so darn heavy.

MAGNUSON (playing along): What kind of exercises do you mean?

JACKSON (sensing an opening, takes off his jacket): Here, I'll show you what I do.

(While Jackson was demonstrating push-ups and sit-ups, Magnuson hit the button under his desk, which summoned his secretary.)

MAGNUSON (to secretary): Tell Bill Allen [the president of Boeing] I can see him now.

At that point Jackson jumped to his feet and rushed to put on his jacket. Bill Allen was not there, of course, and Jackson, I am told, gave up trying to get his more rotund colleague interested in his physical-fitness program.

Magnuson can be effective at the podium when he is giving hell to the Republicans. The more straitlaced Jackson comes off as a cross between a fundamentalist preacher and a teacher droning before an amphitheater filled with freshman. He reels off facts and figures as if he were embellishing a computer print-out, and his efforts at humor or imagery are often counterproductive. In a Seattle speech in 1969, for instance, he got carried away talking about China's growing military might and the need for the United Sates to keep its defenses strong against a future attack from the Far East. Reaching for a metaphor to emphasize his point, he raised his voice and loudly declaimed: "We can't afford to have any *chinks* in our armor!"

Some of the party dignitaries at the head table doubled over to keep from laughing but with little success. Unable to connect their reaction to what he had said, Jackson peered over his glasses like a schoolmaster who had just been hit by a spitball, glowered at his naughty class, rustled his notes, and continued to lecture.

Images are always deceiving in some measure, and that is very much the case with Washington State's two senators. Magnuson appears to be a real-life version of the beer-bellied, backroom pol one sees in the films of a generation ago, while Jackson seems to be the straight shooter of *Mr. Smith Goes to Washington.* Although it demands too much of the imagination to envision Magnuson in actor Jimmy Stewart's role, the opposite of their images is closer to reality nowadays.

Magnuson's image as a wheeler-dealer and purveyor of political pork nearly cost him his Senate seat in 1962, when a Republican nonentity came within four percentage points of unseating him. The warning was heeded, and out went the shirt-garters-and-galluses crowd and in came the bright young lawyers. His active interest in consumer issues dates from that wholesale turnover in his staff. Moreover, to make sure he gets a continuous stream of new blood, he initiated a talent search at the University of Washington's law school, where a panel of professors annually chooses an outstanding graduate to join his staff. In terms of the general caliber of the two offices, every knowledgeable observer I encountered in Washington State agreed that Magnuson's was far superior in brainpower to Jackson's.

By contrast, one Seattle journalist talks about "the orderly young men who work for Jackson . . . He gets the obedient and hard-working. Maggie gets the smart ones." The difference in quality becomes most evident, he claims, after they have left the staff. "Former Magnuson lawyers have made it on their own while Jackson's people have to be 'parachuted' with his help into good positions."

Loyalty is very important to Jackson, who, unlike Nixon, repays it in kind. With his extensive knowledge of the defense and foreign policy bureaucracies, he can easily move his people into and out of government jobs and go to bat for them with other federal agencies and private concerns as well. As one Seattle attorney puts it: "He places his people in all the different agencies. If you had a convention of all of Jackson's people, you'd need a big room."

His contention is borne out by several former aides who freely acknowledge that Jackson had gone out of his way to help them after they left his staff. "Maggie is not that way as much," says one of his former aides. "Maggie would be embarrassed to fight for a subordinate's job. . . . I think he runs the cleanest operation in the Senate. If he didn't, it would be a big campaign issue. But Scoop gets away with it and seems to see nothing wrong with it."

When loyalty is the primary attribute required of a staffer, the boss runs the risk of surrounding himself with sycophants. Although it would be inaccurate to characterize Jackson's entire staff as "yes men," they are a far cry from the more detached analysts Magnuson actively seeks. Their scope and functions are also different. Every afternoon Magnuson holds a staff meeting he calls his "children's hour." The size and membership of this group of staffers change frequently, but their collective role does not. It is to inform, jar, and argue with their boss about any and all matters of professional concern.

While members of Jackson's staff claim he is generally accessible, he tends to rely more heavily on written memoranda and briefings by officials of the executive branch. Verbal input from his staff is likely to be limited to discussions about tactics: who may introduce which amendments and how Jackson may wish to respond. It is not likely to affect the substance of his views, which have been formed through long hours of study and hardened by even longer years of advocacy. The free-wheeling exchange, salty language, and confrontation of the boss that go on during Magnuson's "children's hour" would be as out of place in Jackson's office as a ham sandwich at a kosher banquet. What Jackson wants of his staff is work rather than ideas, deference not challenge.

"Winning isn't the only thing: it's everything" summed up Vince Lombardi's approach to football, and it also characterizes Jackson's attitude toward legislative politics. When he has his mind set on moving a bill or amendment through the Senate, he has no qualms whatever about putting the screws to his opponents. With his iron grip on the Interior Committee, he can stop and start projects at will in practically every state, and he is not above threatening to use that power to get votes on unrelated issues. Even his allies have come under strong pressure when they wavered. His treatment of former Senator Clinton Anderson of New Mexico provides perhaps the most poignant example.

Jackson became chairman of the Interior Committee in 1963 after Anderson stepped down to take the chairmanship of the Aeronautical and Space Sciences Committee. Seventeen years his senior and elected to the Senate in 1948, Anderson was in many respects Jackson's mentor; he had even introduced the younger man to the woman he would marry. In the debate over the Safeguard antiballistic missile system in 1969, Jackson was the leader of the Nixon administration's effort, and he expected his old friend to be voting with him. But even though Anderson had voted the year before for the Johnson administration's Sentinel ABM, scientists from Los Alamos had raised such serious questions about the wisdom of Safeguard that he did not declare a position, pro or con, until the night before the vote.

After days of intensive lobbying by both sides, Anderson decided to vote against Safeguard and had his press secretary draft and release a statement to the press. Jackson, of course, found out about it that evening and arranged to have breakfast with Anderson the next morning. When Anderson returned to his office after that meeting, one staffer recalls, "He was nervous in dealing with me. I told him it would be a problem to change his mind now, that a switch might make him look foolish."

On the Senate floor just before the vote, this staffer sought out Anderson, who "came to the back of the chamber to talk to me. Scoop did too. He said the Brooke amendment had changed the issue so thoroughly that the vote before the Senate had changed radically." It was not true, but truth at that moment apparently meant less to Jackson than winning. When it came time for Anderson to cast his vote on Senator Margaret Chase Smith's amendment to limit Safeguard, Jackson, according to several reporters who were in the gallery above the floor of the Senate, practically shouted in his ear: "No, Clint. Vote no."

The Smith amendment failed to carry on a vote of 50 to 50, with Vice President Agnew adding an unnecessary tie-breaker. So Anderson's vote was the key to victory, and Jackson was jubilant. But the price of victory had been the older man's humiliation.

"When Anderson left the chamber," his staffer recalls, "he was surrounded by reporters who wanted to know: why had he switched? He had no good answer. It was an embarrassing scene." After word of what had transpired on the floor reached Anderson's office, "his staff was in tears," says a reporter who was there.

"Anderson's pride was hurt substantially. He felt he had

been bulldozed," says the staffer. So in 1971, when Jackson pulled all the stops to lobby for Boeing's supersonic transport, he voted against it. Jackson was reportedly so enraged that he told his erstwhile mentor: "This is the parting of the ways, Clint." Their once-close relationship cooled after that incident, but the breach may since have been repaired.

In contrast to Jackson, who behaves as if he had a proprietary interest in the votes of his Senate colleagues, stands Magnuson, the master of the soft sell. One political associate remembers being particularly agitated over an issue in a conversation with Magnuson, who said nothing but listened patiently. When the man had finished, Magnuson simply asked: "What were you mad about last summer?" The man thought for a few moments but could not recall, which of course was Magnuson's point. Individual legislative triumphs, as important as they may seem at the time, may turn into Pyrrhic victories if you alienate too many allies in the process of winning.

In the case of the Safeguard ABM, Jackson's victory in 1969 won approval for a four-site system, but three years later it was restricted to two sites by the U.S.-Soviet ABM treaty and ultimately reduced to one in 1974. Similarly, the killing of the SST, according to informed Seattleites, was the best thing that could have happened to Boeing, which later found itself with so many unsold jumbo jets that "you could have walked across Paine Field from wing tip to wing tip for all the 747s they couldn't find buyers for." Yet Jackson alienated a number of senators on these and other issues to obtain short-term advantages which have not only evaporated but also cost him dearly on subsequent issues.

Magnuson takes an entirely different approach, according to a former staffer. "He never goes up and says, 'I hope you'll be with me on this issue.' Instead, he'll ask: 'How's your wife?' Or he'll talk about football and then leave without saying a word about his amendment. His theory is simple: 'He knows what I was really talking to him about, and I want to make it easier for him to vote for me if he can. If he can't, I don't want him angry.' "

Another staffer has a slightly different impression of the way Magnuson operates. "He loves to get a bill through

Congress, and he likes to win, but it's the soft sell. He tries to see things from their [other senators'] perspective, and he doesn't ask too often. Sometimes he tries to intimidate the younger guys, but he whispers in the ears of what he calls 'the old bulls.' He has a reputation for getting things done.... He always pulls votes on issues."

Says a third former aide: "Maggie operates on instinct. He doesn't want long-winded briefings. He absorbs things fast and makes a decision. Jackson is more cautious. He wants to plow through the facts; he's more studious; he wants more background. Maggie leapfrogs to a decision. He is more effective around a legislative body because he recognizes and accepts the give and take. He senses how he can get an objective without scars. Scoop drives toward it and is less inclined to consider others' feelings."

Magnuson has long been considered a Senate "whale," but Jackson was thought by many to be a "minnow" until President Nixon decided the junior senator was his idea of an "ideal" (John Ehrlichman's word) Democrat. Magnuson has the self-confidence of a man who has found his station in life and is content with it. Jackson, on the other hand, has had presidential ambitions burning in his gut since at least 1960. While Magnuson tries equally hard to succeed in his legislative endeavors, he does not take defeat so personally as Jackson. If the issue is important, he might simply write new language for an amendment or devise a different parliamentary stratagem and try again until he does succeed. Jackson has no such detachment and considerably less self-confidence; so legislative battles are for him a test of "manhood" (a characterization several close observers have used).

Jackson claims that the human suffering he saw during the Depression influenced his social and economic philosophy, but one finds little objective evidence of its effect in his thirty-five year career in Congress. Although he has a generally progressive voting record on issues such as civil rights, medical care, and aid to the needy, he has never taken—indeed, he seems to have carefully avoided—any leadership role in such matters. While Magnuson has been out front on no-fault automobile insurance and truth-in-packaging and in other areas which directly affect a person's well-being, Jackson has been preoccupied with "things." The number of new ballistic-missile submarines or the number of acres in a new national park certainly have an impact on jobs and the quality of life, but they are at least one remove from the more basic human concerns Magnuson is identified with. It is not that Jackson does not care: his many good deeds for constituents and friends argue otherwise. I suspect it is simply because he is more comfortable dealing with abstractions, such as nuclear deterrence and land-use policy, than with the more ordinary problems of human beings.

Jackson made his committee choices a decade before Magnuson found consumerism; so his lack of leadership on flesh-and-blood issues did not arise simply to avoid overlapping his senior colleague. They were conscious expressions of preference. Having made them, however, he deferred to Magnuson and others, judgment on human issues and expected similar deference in return, particularly on defense matters. This arrangement worked quite well until the late 1960s, when the Vietnam War and military spending became issues of conscience no legislator could safely "horse-trade." When Magnuson broke with Jackson on them—voting, for example, against ABM and against funds for defoliants in Vietnam—their relationship became extremely brittle: a situation their staffs exacerbated further.

In 1969, Magnuson was one of the last senators to decide how he would vote on the ABM. So Richard Perle, then quite new to Jackson's operation, decided, unsolicited, to brief Magnuson's office on Safeguard in hopes that the word would filter upward. "We were kidding Perle about things," an aide recalls. "Someone said, 'Shit, Richard, the only reason you want the damn thing is to make fat cats rich. . . . By the time they're fired, you'll be dead.' It was a pretty low level of discussion, and it drove him up the wall because he was so serious. Finally, he got so incensed he said, 'I have no choice but to go directly to Senator Magnuson and tell him about what a poor input he's been getting from his staff.' And with that he picked up his books and charts and stormed out."

Although Perle's naïve zeal might be ascribed to his inexperience, the true-believer attitude afflicts some of

Jackson's most experienced staff members. Dorothy Fosdick, who has been his principal foreign-policy aide for more than two decades, is perhaps the greatest zealot. In an incident remarkably similar to young Perle's, she once told a Magnuson aide that "she'd have trouble supporting Maggie ever again if he didn't vote against troop reductions in Europe." The intolerance of a Perle and Fosdick seems to mirror the closed-mindedness of their boss.

"Getting the wagons in a circle" characterizes the attitude which pervades Jackson's staff, and their acute defensiveness has led more than one observer to conclude they are "paranoid." For instance, in the summer of 1974 Washington State's Republican attorney general, Slade Gorton, announced he would not run for the Senate against Magnuson; in fact, he showered praise on the senior senator. He had nothing but harsh words for Jackson, however, and hinted he might run against him in 1976. Magnuson was naturally relieved when the popular Gorton dropped out of the race and courteously returned his complimentary remarks, ignoring of course what Gorton had said about the junior senator. Jackson, I am told, was enraged, and a few of his staff went so far as to speculate to reporters that someone on Magnuson's staff had actually written Gorton's remarks. It was an absurd notion but not so surprising considering the superloyalists Jackson seems to favor on his staff.

Everything is black or white: you're either with us or against us. It is the mentality which spawns enemies' lists. The attitude on Jackson's staff may differ in degree, but it does not differ in kind from that of Richard Nixon's White House.

CHAPTER

8

Chance Missed: JFK and the Vice-Presidency

THE MOST difficult office to campaign for is the vice-presidency. First there is the matter of constituency. Presidential and congressional candidates can present their case to an electorate; the would-be vice-president must appeal to a constituency of one: his party's presidential nominee. Because the convention chooses that person one day and his running mate the next, predicting who that constituency of one will be well in advance of the event may require as much clairvoyance as political savvy.

Then there is the problem of timing. If the would-be vice-president declares his support of a particular presidential aspirant months before the convention and works to advance that person's candidacy, he has probably foreclosed his chances of getting the number-two spot if he guessed wrong. Even if his candidate is nominated, he might still be bypassed in favor of a more calculating politician who, when the outcome was in the balance, helped clinch the nomination.

Finally there is the matter of "image." What sort of man would openly campaign for an office which, former Vice-President John Nance Garner said, was not worth "a pitcher of warm spit"? An upcoming politician might *want* the post as a stepping stone to the Presidency but so might a second-rater whose career is approaching dead end. Wanting the vice-presidency, then, is all right, but appearing to want it is a posture to be avoided. A presidential nominee may not want his running mate to outshine him, but he also does not want a "loser." After all, his choice will provide the public with their first measure of his ability to make executive decisions. That certainly proved true of Nixon's choice of Agnew.

Jackson has twice run unsuccessfully for the vice-presidency. His election to the Senate in 1952 against the Eisenhower tide and his visibility on the televised Army-McCarthy hearings brought him to the attention of the public and, more importantly, his party's leaders. That plus his liberal voting record made him of interest to Adlai Stevenson, and when Jackson visited Chicago, he often met privately over dinner with the former Illinois governor. Those meetings seem, in retrospect, to have been of a piece with Jackson's quiet campaign for the office.

Supporters in Washington State and congressional allies such as Mike Mansfield enthusiastically boosted Jackson for the vice-presidency, and on the eve of the party's 1956 convention, *Congressional Quarterly* profiled him as the leading Western hope for the number-two spot. *CQ* suggested his principal asset was the geographical balance he might bring to the ticket but thought his bachelorhood would be a major liability if he were paired with the divorced Stevenson. The case for the freshman senator was hardly compelling, and when Stevenson let the convention choose his running mate, it soon became clear that the party did not take Jackson's candidacy seriously.

Had he lost in the balloting for the vice-presidential nomination it would have been a blow, but Jackson's pride must have been deeply wounded when he was not even *nominated* in an open convention. Friends suggest this experience made him determined to prove himself as a vote getter in his 1958 reelection race. To his good fortune, the Republican party selected William "Big Bill" Bantz to run against him. It was hardly a contest, and Jackson won 68 percent of the vote. Yet, even though he had only token opposition in the primary and an inept opponent in the general election, Jackson filed campaign expenses which were second highest for incumbent senators. (He missed being first by $34.) Winning reelection to the Senate was not enough: he wanted to win big so his party would be favorably impressed with his "electability."

Jackson played the game more cleverly in 1960. He did not openly declare his support for John Kennedy until the week of the Los Angeles convention, but he cooperated with Kennedy's campaign organization from the start. He "loaned" his administrative assistant, John Salter, to JFK's "Irish Mafia," and Salter was heavily involved in its early strategy sessions. Although Kennedy also wanted to borrow Irvin Hoff, Magnuson's AA, he chose to work for Lyndon Johnson's candidacy in December of 1959. Salter says, "Irv Hoff and I worked out an understanding that he'd go for LBJ and we'd go for JFK." Although Hoff recalls no such "deal," the State of Washington (as usual) wound up with its bets neatly covered.

A Jackson for Vice-President committee was formed by state party leaders in Seattle in June. One of its flyers was a map which painted the states west of the Rockies bright green and pointedly noted that the region's population exceeded 30 million. The increasing importance of the West and Jackson's proven vote-getting ability were strong points in his favor, and once again *CQ* profiled him on the eve of the convention. This time he was billed as "a favorite in his own and several other Western states for the Democratic vice-presidential nomination."

Kennedy arrived in Los Angeles about 150 votes shy of the nomination. If there was a deadlock between him and Johnson, Senator Stuart Symington of Missouri, who seemed to be everyone's second choice, stood a chance of becoming the party's compromise candidate. Kennedy had to pick up additional delegates, but the obstacles were formidable. Governor Robert B. Meyner of New Jersey, for example, controlled his state's delegation and planned to have its 41 votes cast for his favorite-son candidacy. If he calculated correctly that there would be no victor on the first ballot, his delegation might decide the outcome and win for him the vice-presidential nomination. (He miscalculated, and the 41 votes cast in his name won for him nothing more than a footnote in the convention record.) Unwilling to give away the second spot to Meyner or another favorite son before an actual deadlock,

Kennedy and his lieutenants went fishing among wavering or uncommitted delegates. Their bait was the vice-presidency.

Robert Kennedy had been close to Jackson since his days as minority counsel on the Permanent Investigations Subcommittee, and he said, both privately and publicly, that Scoop was his candidate for the vice-presidency. John Kennedy, naturally, was noncommittal. Although he said he would choose a Protestant who was not from the East for a running mate if he won the nomination, he refused to be more explicit—and understandably so. Winning the presidential nomination was the first order of business, and if Jackson wanted to be Kennedy's vice-president, he would have to help him secure that nomination and prove in the process that his appeal went beyond Washington State and his own election.

The Saturday before the convention RFK called Jackson and implied that his brother personally preferred him for the number-two spot but made no promises. He did, however, hint that the choice might hinge on how well Jackson did convincing additional delegates and party leaders to back Kennedy. It was unmistakably a test, and Jackson jumped eagerly, though somewhat unsurely, into the battle.

On Sunday he made the rounds talking to party leaders such as Chicago Mayor Richard Daley, and on Monday he publicly announced what everyone had known all along: that he was supporting Kennedy. He visited several state delegations on Kennedy's behalf and also tried to convince his own delegation to back Kennedy, but with little success. Magnuson switched from LBJ to JFK because he wanted to help Jackson get the second spot on the ticket, and so did the governor, Albert Rosellini, but no other member of the delegation would budge. (He was particularly upset with the liberals, who would not abandon their emotional and *impractical* support for Adlai Stevenson.) When the roll was called, Kennedy got 14½ of the state's 27 votes; Stevenson was second with 6½. Jackson had failed to translate his personal vote-getting power into political influence within his own state's delegation, and he did no better in other states. JFK and his hard-nosed crew no doubt reduced their estimate of Jackson's value to the ticket accordingly.

The twenty-four hours following Kennedy's nomination were long ones for Jackson. "I was out to 5 A.M. celebrating

JFK's nomination," recalls Salter, "and at 7 A.M. Bobby called and said to come over. Jack and I met in the bedroom with some others and talked. . . . He told me to come back at 11:30, but it was clear from the start that the ballgame was over." Salter's instinctive judgment proved correct although he guessed wrong about who Kennedy would choose. "I thought it would be Symington," he says.

Jackson, Salter, and a few other aides sat around their hotel suite waiting for the phone to ring. At noon Kennedy called Jackson and asked him to come to his room. When he got there, Jackson learned that the Veepstakes now had a third entrant: Lyndon Johnson. No decision had been made, but Kennedy promised Jackson that he would be the first to know once a decision had been reached. So he went back to his room and waited several more hours for the phone to ring. When it finally did at 3:20, Kennedy told him that Johnson had agreed to be his running mate. Kennedy then asked Jackson to be chairman of the Democratic National Committee. "He began declining," recalls Salter. "I was tugging at him and finally got him to say he'd consider it and call back. . . . [Lawrence] O'Brien leaked it to the press, and the next day we met Jack." The result was that a very reluctant Scoop Jackson, a product of the star system in the loose, almost nonparty politics of Washington State, agreed to become chairman of the national Democratic party.

Sometime after Jackson accepted the DNC post, he told reporters he had "a complete understanding" with Kennedy that he (Jackson) would "handle the entire campaign," but he soon found he was "chairman" in name only. Robert Kennedy ran the campaign, and he and other insiders rarely sought Jackson's advice. Nonetheless, he campaigned hard, particularly in "the Bible Belt." When Nixon disparaged Kennedy, it was Jackson who often rose in defense, charging the Republican candidate with "demagoguery." When the Rev. Norman Vincent Peale took a jibe at Kennedy's Catholicism, it was Jackson, a Lutheran turned Presbyterian, who immediately called a press conference to denounce Peale for "bigotry." Although he did not design grand strategy for the campaign, he could take pride in the effective, workmanlike job he did.

On election night he was disappointed that Nixon won his

home state by 30,000 votes, but Kennedy's failure in the West was more than offset by pluralities in the East and South. Johnson's regional strength had provided Kennedy his margin of victory and confirmed the wisdom of his choice. Had Jackson been on the ticket instead, Kennedy would probably have lost.

Jackson did not enjoy being party chairman, and he set what was then a record for brevity of tenure when he submitted his resignation before Kennedy's inauguration. Jackson and Salter had had more than a few collisions with the "Irish Mafia" during the campaign, and those tensions did not dissipate when Kennedy entered the White House. The most obvious symptom was the new administration's slowness in finding a suitable post for Salter. He was subsequently made congressional liaison for the International Cooperation Administration, but it was dull, unchallenging work compared to Larry O'Brien's job as White House liaison, the post Salter (unrealistically) coveted. Two years later Salter rejoined Jackson's Senate staff.

Jackson also suffered some disappointments. His careful work as chairman of the Government Operations Subcommittee on National Security Staffing and Operations had made him the leading congressional expert on the nation's defense-policy mechanisms, but he was seldom consulted by the new administration in such matters. With Robert McNamara and his "Whiz Kids" ensconced in the Pentagon and the aloof Massachusetts crowd in the White House, Jackson was odd man out. The final indignity may have been the failure of the Kennedy family to be represented in December of 1961 when Jackson surrendered his bachelorhood on the altar of matrimony.

In 1961 Jackson sided with congressional conservatives who came close to killing the bill which subsequently created the Arms Control and Disarmament Agency (ACDA). That was the first outward indication of a political breach with Kennedy. Then, in March of 1962, Jackson gave a widely publicized speech before the National Press Club entitled "The US in the UN." He spoke about "an undue influence of UN considerations in our national decision making" and questioned "whether the involvement of the UN in our policy making has not at times hampered the wise definition of our national interests and the development of sound policies for their advancement." He downplayed the importance of the world organization in keeping the peace, preferring instead a system based largely on American military power: "The truth is, though we have not often spoken it in recent years, that the best hope for peace with justice does not lie in the United Nations. Indeed, the truth is almost the reverse. The best hope for the United Nations lies in the maintenance of peace. In our deeply divided world, peace depends on the power and unity of the Atlantic Community and on the skill of our direct diplomacy."

At that time, billboards exhorting the United States to "Get Out of the UN" were second only to "Impeach Earl Warren" in the more reactionary hinterlands. So liberals were aghast that one of their own was mouthing such heresies, albeit in more muted tones. Delivered several weeks before Congress would act on UN appropriations, Jackson's speech damning the world organization with faint praise was viewed, probably correctly, as giving aid and comfort to the right-wing, anti-UN bloc in Congress.

The partial nuclear test-ban treaty was signed in Moscow on August 5, 1963. Jackson's initial reaction was to question the credibility of any test ban the Soviet Union would sign, and he withheld support for the treaty until the middle of September. When he finally spoke in favor of it, he actually seemed to be laying the groundwork for its eventual abrogation.

> The essence of my view on this treaty, which has been referred to as a limited treaty, is that it is indeed limited. Actually it is not a treaty, but a loose commitment, a statement of present intentions of the parties not to engage in nuclear weapon test explosions in the atmosphere, in outer space or underwater. This nation's commitment will rest on the assumption that certain conditions are met—including the condition that the surpreme interests of this nation are not jeopardized. Should those interests be jeopardized we shall be released from our commitment.

To say the least, it was a rather novel interpretation of a treaty which, when ratified, would become "the supreme law of the land." The *New York Times,* which had often favored

Jackson by publishing his speeches and articles on defense, compared him in an editorial to the hawkish, ex-bomber pilot who was then Air Force Chief of Staff:

> The endorsement given to the nuclear test-ban treaty by Senator Jackson, one of our more influential legislators on military affairs, was the most equivocal bit of support it has had since General [Curtis] LeMay told the Foreign Relations Committee that he was for the treaty but probably would have been against it if it had not already been signed. The spirit of Senator Jackson's remarks is that the only true security for the United States lies in continued mistrust of the Soviet Union and in the maximum pile-up of nuclear weapons.

Life sometimes becomes more trying for a senator when his party gains control of the White House, and Jackson was not prepared for the loss of prestige and influence he suffered when his friend John Kennedy became President. Democrats who had once looked to Capitol Hill for answers to questions and policy decisions now turned to the White House. McNamara and the bright Ivy Leaguers throughout the executive branch captured the media's, and hence the public's, imagination and probably heightened Jackson's latent inferiority complex. The press seemed only mildly interested in his subcommittee's careful study of national security operations, and the only way he could get anyone to take him seriously was by threatening such liberal sacred cows as ACDA, the UN and partial test-ban treaty. Out of frustration he had become an obstructionist.

In the early 1950s Jackson used to play softball at a Georgetown park with the Kennedy brothers. He befriended Robert Kennedy in the McCarthy era and supported John Kennedy much earlier than the cold logic of his vice-presidential ambition required. Perhaps he felt both men had turned on him by denying him the prize he thought within grasp and humiliated him by making him a figurehead in the subsequent campaign, or he may simply have resented his exclusion from "Camelot." Whatever the reason, Kennedy and Jackson had a falling-out.

Although Jackson would now have history remember him as a close Kennedy ally, his actions during and since the Kennedy years indicate that his break with the *family* was complete and, no doubt, bitter. In 1967, for instance, when Robert Kennedy made a major Senate speech breaking with President Johnson's policy in Vietnam, Jackson delivered Johnson's rebuttal on the Senate floor while his staff swept through the press galleries with copies of his remarks and a presidential letter which rebutted Kennedy's speech point by point. When RFK ran for President in 1968, Jackson actively opposed his candidacy. In 1971, when Edward Kennedy was seeking reelection as Senate whip, Jackson voted for his opponent, Robert Byrd, who won by a single vote.

Coincidence or vengeance? Without getting into Jackson's brain one cannot be certain, but when he was campaigning in the Florida primary in 1972, one of his campaign aides recalls that Jackson seemed to make quite a point—indeed, too much of one—about changing the name of Cape Kennedy back to Cape Canaveral.

CHAPTER 9

Oh! Henry! An Innocent Among Women

HENRY JACKSON was a half year shy of his fiftieth birthday when he married the former Helen Eugenia Hardin in 1961. A number of his friends recall being very surprised when they heard the news. As one of them puts it: "He was already married—to his work."

Some cynics thought they saw an element of calculation in his marriage. They assumed his brush with destiny at the 1960 Democratic Convention had given him presidential ambitions, and he had simply decided that a wife and family were necessary should he run for the White House. "There's nothing accidental about Scoop Jackson," says one Seattle journalist who has known him since the 1940s. "He goes to church for a purpose and to the exercise machine for a purpose."

Women dominated the household of Jackson's youth. His mother and sister Gertrude were authoritarian figures who were quite capable of putting him in his place when he was a boy and saw no reason to stop when he became a senator. Usually it would come in the form of good-natured balloon popping, such as the time his mother reacted to a television appearance by wisecracking "You should have been an actor."

Even after he had begun his climb in the competitive world of politics, he relied on the Jackson women for little things. Gertrude, for example, would help him shop for clothes when he came home during a congressional recess, and his sister

Marie would do his laundry. During one such visit, his next-door neighbor, Jack Dootson, dropped in and found Gertrude and Marie standing behind their brother in front of a mirror. One by one, they took his ties, draped them around his neck and knotted them. He then carefully loosened each one and took it off so that when he returned to Washington he would not have to tie them himself.

When he first went to Congress, he spent so much time carrying water for his constituents that he did little socializing. Although his assistant, John Salter, developed a bit of a reputation as a ladies' man, "Scoop was a plodder," says a woman who knew him then. "I can't imagine a greater innocent with women."

"He was absolutely naïve about women," agrees Salter, who recalls how Jackson reacted once when a woman he had asked out turned him down. "It was Saturday afternoon, and he had called to see if she wanted to go to the movies that night, and he couldn't understand why she said no. So I asked him if he had taken her out before, and he said he had.

" 'Did the two of you get along?'

" 'We seemed to.'

" 'Well, when was the last time you took her out?'

" 'Oh about two months ago.'

" 'Have you called her since then?'

" 'No.' "

"His whole life was the Congress," says a former congressional aide who knew him in the House. Even his meager social life had a way of turning into business. "I remember running into a couple of guys from his office late one night. They had caught him in the office with a woman he had been dating, and they were laughing.

" 'What were they up to?' I asked.

" 'Well,' they said, 'we walked in and saw Mary Lee's mink stole draped over the chair.'

" 'Yeah,' I said, 'but what were they doing?'

" 'Well, she was sitting in the chair—typing.' "

Jackson lived austerely in Washington. The cluttered bachelor apartment he shared with Salter was just a few blocks from the Capitol. He was helpless in the kitchen so he rarely ate dinner at home. Most nights he would stop at the United Methodist Building, which he passed on the walk to his apartment, and eat an inexpensive meal. His was a spartan and regimented existence.

If the female employees of the House and Senate can be accepted as honest witnesses, when Congress is in session, the Capitol contains the greatest concentration of married middle-aged lechers in the United States. Young bachelor legislators, however, are a rare commodity; so Jackson soon found himself being paired with single women at dinner parties. But most of the women he dated he met (literally) at the office. Capitol Hill has always had more than its share of bright, attractive women; moreover, they were likely to be knowledgeable in Jackson's one and only area of interest: politics.

One woman who worked on his Senate staff in the 1950s says that "he went out with almost every single woman who worked on the staff who was not engaged or seriously attached to someone." She accompanied him once on a trip to New York and recalls spending "a day in Central Park, riding on the merry-go-round. He does have a relaxing, nonsensical side, but he didn't let it develop very far.

"Another time we went dancing at the Mayflower Hotel. I took off my shoes, and someone came up and told me that ladies had to wear shoes. I remember him answering: 'There are other ways to tell a lady.' "

Jackson is paternalistic toward his staff, particularly its female members. "He always wanted to feel responsible for employees, and one reason he would not hire pages was because they were so young," recalls another woman who was on his staff. "He always made a point of making sure that people working late had a ride home. . . . There were orders to his staff not to let women go home at night without safe transit."

With one exception (Dorothy Fosdick on foreign policy), the women on Jackson's staff did not hold substantive positions. "We were not paid well compared to other staffs nor were we given much responsibility," says one. Adds another: "He was able to listen to women as long as they were not in a position of power. . . . He respected the brains of women, but he also had traditional ideas about women and their need to be taken care of." "He put them on a pedestal," says the first ex-staffer.

Jackson has long held "traditional ideas" about a woman's place. Once, when he was campaigning for reelection to the

House, the question of whether married women should be permitted to work if their husbands held jobs was a hot issue because jobs were still scarce. Jackson was opposed, he recalls, because he believed "priorities should be given on a family basis. . . . The husband or head of the family should have a preference."

He seems to realize that such notions are a political liability nowadays because after he made the foregoing remark, he added: "Women's lib was not even thought of [then]." Nonetheless, he voted against the Equal Rights Amendment in 1970, and when the matter came to the Senate floor again in 1972, he decided to remain in Wisconsin campaigning for the Presidency rather than return to Washington along with his senatorial opponents Humphrey, McGovern, and Muskie. He clearly feared the consequences of a second negative vote because he did not "pair" his vote with another senator's to put himself on the record one way or the other. He simply ducked.

Jackson is generous with his friends in matters of the spirit. If one of them is sick, he will call, write, or visit; he has even been known to call their doctors. But, when it comes to matters of the wallet, friends say, he is a "tightwad." So, when Jackson decided to give a stag party for Salter before his marriage, he tried to honor his highest aide for the lowest price.

"The party was going to be on a Sunday night," recalls a friend. "And Scoop called me three times over the weekend to make sure I was coming because he had to tell the caterer how many. Then he chose the cheapest thing on the menu, chicken à la king, as the main course, but because he had cut it so fine with the caterer, there wasn't enough to go around. I remember Scoop kept trying to rush us through the chicken and get everyone to eat dessert. Well, Mike Mansfield caught on to his game and started hustling people to ask for seconds on the chicken. Mike had this marvelous glint in his eye as he went around telling people: 'Scoop's pushing the chicken. Let's have some more.' "

His frugality was also evident to the women he took out to dinner. "He was always conscious of how much something costs," recalls one. "We used to have dinner sometimes at the Rainbow Inn or Grill. They had mostly casserole dishes, and it was serve yourself. If you didn't take everything you were supposed to get on the plate, they'd refund part of the price."

The women who most interested the freshman senator were invariably young, attractive, and from families (as the euphemism goes) "of means." He dated Marilyn Atwood, the daughter of an Anchorage, Alaska, newspaper publisher, for about two years. She recalls him joking "that he'd been working hard all his life and wanted to marry someone with money so he could retire."

Atwood, who was in her late teens when she started dating the fortyish Jackson, recalls him being "very sensitive and concerned about what people think. If we were having dinner in a booth of the Olympic Hotel and the people in the next booth were talking politics, he'd listen and have me listen on the other side to see what they were talking about.

" 'I have only average intelligence,' he used to tell me, 'and I have to work hard.' So he would read about nine papers a day, and I'd usually wind up with the real estate section. . . . I'd be watching "I Love Lucy," and he'd read. He said he had to do his homework because he felt he had an exam every morning.

"His career was all-important. He was not romantic enough, but he was very respectful of my desires and feelings. He liked to go out with girls, but he didn't want people to think he was getting married.

"He gave me a Christmas present once, and I can remember him holding it behind his back and being very shy. He was very cute and very humble about what he bought and said something like: 'You probably already have something like this.'

"He was always taking vitamins. He'd laugh and say he needed twice as many when he took me out. He was always dieting, and one drink was the most he'd have in an evening. More often than not, he'd just have a glass of ginger ale.

"If we couldn't get [airline] reservations, he wouldn't pull rank as a senator. He'd approach the desk humbly—not like the big shot—carrying his hang-up bag. He's still a warm, humble person, and I can't conceive of a man who came from his humble beginnings changing overnight."

Helen Langer first met the freshman senator when she was a journalism student at the University of Washington. The niece of Senator William Langer of North Dakota, she was visiting her uncle and sitting in the Senate gallery when Jackson happened by with friends. "He asked me to come by for tea that afternoon," she recalls, "but I didn't because I thought it would be an imposition. So he called me at my uncle's apartment to find out why.

"He has an ego, but so do all politicians. He could not have been nicer to me. But I knew what the life was like from my uncle. There's a lot of falsity and superficiality to political life, and my values were not in that vein. . . . The Washington whirl did not impress me all that much. It was nice to go, but it was certainly not the beginning and end of life.

"Our values matched in that I didn't have to go to expensive restaurants. Scoop would talk of his Norwegian thriftiness—Salter would call it stinginess—but that's not an objectionable trait. He's a poor boy from a small town, and I don't know if he'll ever get over it. . . . Owning the house he does now [in Everett] is a big symbol for him, a symbol that he's arrived.

"One reason we got along was that I could tell him off. He respects people who'll stand up to him. . . . But he's a perennial boss. He'd try to tell my mother how to run the business. [She owned a bank.] Cab drivers the same thing. He always wants to take charge. It's an idiosyncrasy of his that can be tiring. He's like that all the time, and he doesn't like to admit he ever gets tired.

"He doesn't have the greatest sense of humor. He was not very good at letting loose or playing charades. I had a feeling he was never a little kid, that he never had the fun and games which would loosen him up. . . . There was no cultivation of the arts and that was a disadvantage socially. . . . He lacked good taste in dress, but I think I did turn him around on that.

"He's like an elephant: he never forgets. He's also stubborn. If he believed something, he'd stick with it. He has the character to stick with it and a lot of pride and stubbornness. . . . He bends over backwards to help people. The phone would always be ringing at home in Everett. He would be living in a fishbowl. He was a good listener—that's a wonderful quality—a good country boy and a super politician.

"Scoop and I went out for nine years. I dated him when he came here [Washington State], but it was not a steady relationship for either of us. . . . The difference in age was too great for me. No one could have done a better selling job in trying to get me to marry him. . . . I guess I was not in love with him. I did not want to hurt him because I think he's such a good person. I certainly wish him every success."

Nineteen sixty seems to have marked a turning point for Jackson, the time he began to take seriously his chances of fulfilling the secret dream of every young politician: the Presidency. His near-miss in the Los Angeles convention's Veepstakes and his campaign role as chairman of the Democratic National Committee lifted him from provincial obscurity to some national prominence. One consequence was that he was now numbered among the rich and near-famous middle-aged geezers on the most-eligible bachelor's list.

A woman he occasionally dated at that time recalls sensing "a feeling he felt inadequate. He was a first-generation American, not smooth and stylish like JFK, and it bothered him that he did not have more savoir faire. . . . One time he said to me: 'They say I'm one of the most eligible bachelors. If that's so, why can't I find a wife?' "

If his lament became a prayer, it was soon answered. On January 3, 1961, the day the 87th Congress convened, he ran into Senator Clinton Anderson of New Mexico in the elevator on their way to the floor of the Senate for the swearing-in ceremony. Accompanying Anderson was his new receptionist, Helen Hardin, and Jackson could not help but be attracted to the tall, lithe strawberry blonde.

Tea dates in the Senate Dining Room and at the Carroll Arms Hotel across the street from the Senate Office Building were soon followed by bicycle outings in Rock Creek Park. In early September, the press heard rumors of their impending marriage and confronted Jackson, who coyly replied: "I have never been against marriage despite the evidence of forty-nine years, but even bachelors must leave the door open." Thus he confirmed the rumors while diplomatically leaving the announcement to the bride's family. On December 16, they were married in Albuquerque's Central Methodist Church, where the bride's late grandfather, Clyde Campbell, had once been pastor.

It was the second marriage for Mrs. Jackson. In 1955 she had married a New York physician, Frederick W. Fuller, but the marriage ended in divorce. While living in New York, she earned a master of arts at Columbia University and moved to Washington following the divorce to work for Anderson, a friend of her father, who was the president of American Gypsum.

Twenty-one years younger than Jackson, she is thoroughly a politician's wife. Gracious, soft-spoken, almost shy on political speech-making tours, she is a perfect foil to her publicly gregarious, arm-pumping husband. She dresses tastefully but does not affect the sort of stylishness which might make other women envious. Her hair—more blonde these days than strawberry, thanks to a color specialist—is a simple bouffant held in place by heavy doses of hair spray. (I have seen her face a stiff breeze with not a strand out of place.)

By all accounts she is one of Jackson's greatest assets. Bernice Stern, a King County councilwoman, says, "I think he's got a great wife, who's a heck of a lot smarter than she lets on. She's also got that capacity to look at him adoringly when he's told that same story a hundred times."

A few, however, find her impenetrable. One Seattle society matron, who has known Jackson for decades, comments: "Helen seems to me a paper doll he could call his own. She's so candy box, two dimensional. To know Helen is not to: she's so totally even. . . . She looks as polished for the role as Pat [Nixon] herself—somewhere between Pat and Tricia. She's a very good performer for what she does. I have nothing against her. She's more seen than heard. . . . It's impossible to be unkind to Helen."

Like most political wives, Mrs. Jackson avoids speaking publicly about contentious issues. Friends suggest, however, that her attitudes are somewhat more conservative than her husband's. One recalls having lunch with her in the Senate Dining Room when all she seemed to talk about was "what those hippies might do to her car." Parked on the Capitol grounds, where a special police force takes extraordinary pains to look out for members of Congress and their property, the specially tagged Jackson car was in no danger.

Mrs. Jackson has proven to be quite adept at dealing with

the press. After she returned with her husband from a 1974 trip to the People's Republic of China, women's page reporters naturally wanted to interview her. Instead of holding one meeting for all of them, she was sophisticated enough to do the interviews one at a time. The result was several stories prominently displayed on the women's pages, each an "exclusive."

After fourteen years of marriage and two children, Jackson has the home and family he wanted. At Christmas, the four Jacksons join some of their Everett neighbors and go caroling. So important is this family event that he even called his neighbor John Wilson one year to see if it could be delayed until Congress adjourned. "It's amazing to see the look of neighbors when they see the potential President singing away with his children," says Wilson, "but he's just naturally homespun."

Jackson's office is on the first floor of the old Senate Office Building, and Senate employees on that floor tell me they sometimes see him with his children, often carrying them on his shoulders down the somber corridors. One wonders: does he ever think about how such a scene would photograph in the Oval Office?

ISSUES

CHAPTER

10

The Land

IT MUST have been a slow news day because the media rarely devote serious attention to the American Indian. But the television cameras were there in force on the morning of July 21, 1971, for the Interior Committee's hearing concerning a "new national American Indian and Alaska Natives policy," and Jackson was in the chair. That it would be more a media happening than a substantive inquiry became apparent soon after he introduced the first witness: Robert B. Jim, chairman of the Yakima Tribal Council.

JIM: "Senator and gentlemen of the committee, it gives us a great honor to be able to take a little of your time. As we have discussed previously, we are honored that you . . . [are] one of the chiefs of the Yakima Tribe, honorary member, Chief Why-Ya-Ma-EE-Nuck-Nu-Wi-Sha-Tee-Ehum, the name we honored you with in February 1970 when we adopted you as a member of our tribe."

(At this point Jackson ordered the discussion to go "off the record" so reporters could write down his honorary title. Then, once the TV cameras were ready to roll, he resumed.)

JACKSON: "You might explain what that title means."

JIM: "It means 'the Eagle Who Watches Over the Land and the People,' and that is the name bestowed upon you after consultation with the elders and the great honor that they had for you as a senator and for having the consideration to come to our tribe."

Jackson flashed a huge, telegenic grin. He had just brought off a brilliant *coup de théâtre,* the sort that network anchormen cannot resist running at the end of the evening news to leave their viewers smiling. That the exchange had been calculated strictly as a publicity gimmick seems an inescapable conclusion because a few minutes later he turned over the gavel to Senator Clinton Anderson, left the hearing, and did not return.

When he served in the House, Jackson was chairman of the Indian Affairs Committee for several years, and as chairman of the Interior Committee he is the most powerful senator in such matters. Nonetheless, he did not accord them very high priority for most of his career. In 1964, for instance, on a campaign tour in Okanogan County, Jackson and his aides were driving through a reservation when he wondered aloud about the number of Indians who lived there. A magazine reporter recorded what followed: "An aide put the number at 4000. Jackson peered thoughtfully out the window, then muttered, 'Hell, they don't vote,' and his car sped on."

Although he did not dispute the accuracy of the quote, Jackson complained "bitterly, resentfully" to an executive of the corporation which published *Seattle* magazine because he felt the quote had been used in a context which—unfairly, in his view—made him appear unconcerned with Indians. He claimed he had meant the remark only in jest.

Such image consciousness in an election year is understandable, but criticism of Jackson's attitude toward Indians arose for more concrete reasons. In a 1971 Law Day address to students at the University of Washington, Vine Deloria, author of *Custer Died for Your Sins,* asserted that Jackson had been "more detrimental to Indian causes than any other senator in the past hundred years." Deloria's criticism centered on the policy of "termination" which Congress had begun in 1953 to force Indians off their reservations and into the "American mainstream." Jackson had unreservedly supported that policy and had repeatedly tried to terminate the huge Colville reservation in his own state. Although some Indians favored termination because each would get a few thousand dollars in compensation, the long-term implication of that policy entailed nothing less than the destruction of entire tribal cultures.

Jackson sought to mute his critics by replacing the Caucasian who was the committee staff member responsible for Indian legislation with a Blackfoot Indian who had been reared on a reservation in Montana. It was a wise move that led to Jackson's sponsoring such substantive measures as the Indian Education and Alaska Native Claims acts. Moreover, two weeks after Deloria's speech, Jackson made a complete reversal and introduced a concurrent resolution expressly repudiating termination and acknowledging "the Federal responsibility to protect Indian lands, resources and rights."

There are still critics who maintain he does not do enough for Indians, but for the most part he has shown considerable flexibility in dealing with this and other issues which have come before his Interior Committee. Unlike his anachronistic waging of the cold war, he has not been a rigid ideologue where the land and its native peoples are concerned. Although he may not possess the aesthetic sensibilities of a Thoreau, he has to his credit some of the most important environmental legislation enacted by Congress. Ecologists who are critical of his support for the trans-Alaska pipeline and off-shore oil exploration turn positively effusive with praise for his efforts on the Wilderness, National Trails, Redlands and Canyonlands, and other laws.

Because it is the *art*, not science, of the possible, politics necessarily involves the balancing of interests. "Ambition must be made to counteract ambition," said James Madison, and this concept seems to be the operating principle in the Interior Committee. No one familiar with his work would ever mistake Jackson for a legislative visionary in search of that holy grail called "the public interest." Rather, he has established his committee as a forum where competing private interests may contend and compromise in determining what the law will be.

Although others on the committee might prefer a more disinterested approach to determining the public interest, they have little to say about the way it is run. Interior is a one-man show and likely to stay that way as long as Jackson is in the chair. His control is so complete that subcommittee chairmen have no say at all in the choice of their staffs. Although he allows them some latitude in drafting legislation, he has been known to "steal" the credit for what they have done. A case in point occurred in 1972 with strip-mining legislation.

Senator Frank Moss of Utah had begun work on a strip-mining bill early in the year and eventually reported it to the full committee. Because he needed the support of committee Republicans, he did not include the strong environmental safeguards he preferred but expected the full committee to correct that deficiency by amendment. Although the bill was on the committee's agenda from mid-July to early September, Jackson did not get to it until September 13, after which it was reported to the Senate. About two weeks later, the Senate passed a resolution calling for a moratorium on federal coal leases, and Jackson sensed the timing was right for a more comprehensive measure. But, instead of perfecting the one Moss had introduced (and his committee had approved) by amending it on the floor, he set his staff to work writing an entirely new measure for which he claimed sole authorship and all the credit. As one Senate observer sarcastically put it: "He came in riding on a white charger."

It was another in the string of publicity gimmicks which had alienated so many former allies. Indeed, not one Democrat on the committee supported Jackson in his abortive presidential bid in 1972, and when the 93rd Congress convened in 1973, four of them chose not to be reassigned to the panel. Such defections are indicative of the disdain committee members have for the chairman's autocratic ways.

Jackson's bills are seldom architectural masterpieces; no one familiar with what the Senate can do would ever call him a legislative craftsman. He is, on the other hand, a superb parliamentary tactician. Not only is his sense of timing acute, he usually can assess the protagonists in a legislative battle and almost instinctively determine the minimum each side will accept. Although he sometimes runs roughshod over his colleagues, he gets results which, if not perfect in a technical sense, are acceptable to the parties in pursuit of a "Madisonian compromise." His is no small talent.

How Jackson operates may best be seen by looking at specific pieces of legislation he has shepherded through Congress. I have chosen two: the North Cascades Act of 1968 and the National Environmental Policy Act of 1969. The former shows how he skillfully plays off competing interests in his home state: in this instance, the timber and mining interests which help finance his political campaigns versus Washington State conservationists. The latter is a case par excellence of a legislative navigator negotiating the shoals of competing congressional interests. (Because of its national importance, I will deal with NEPA at greater length.)

Patrick Goldsworthy, a biochemist at the University of Washington, moved to Seattle from Berkeley in 1956. At that time the timber companies could do pretty much as they pleased in the national forests, and he was appalled by the "logging roads going into beautiful wilderness areas. It seemed cutting the trees was the wrong thing to do. How could one do something about it?

"In 1957 we formed the North Cascades Conservation Council. [Goldsworthy has been its president since 1958.] We were very small then, but we've now got about 2000 members, mostly in the state. . . . We felt the need for a single-purpose organization. We were initially concerned with Glacier Peak but eventually expanded to cover the Cascades from the Columbia River to the Canadian border."

It was not simply the council versus the timber and mining companies; the Agriculture Department's Forest Service was also involved because the chief of that agency had considerable control over national forests and was naturally reluctant to lose that power. Jackson came down early on the side of the conservationists by spearheading the drive in Congress which culminated in the Wilderness Act of 1964, but the price of passage was going along with the House Interior Chairman, Representative Wayne Aspinall of Colorado, who insisted on permitting mining companies to continue prospecting in wilderness areas.

The chief of the Forest Service designated a Glacier Peak Wilderness area in 1960, but, Goldsworthy says, the council was "not satisfied because we felt it should have been larger—about twice as large. . . . So we started talking to Jackson in 1960, and he expressed interest but asked us to 'come back when you can demonstrate public support.'

"So the North Cascades Conservation Council started a long publicity campaign. The Sierra Club did a film. We wrote articles and learned how to get into the press. There was little press interest at first, but Glacier Peak made it a bit more news. The North Cascades battle was very newsworthy, and we generated enough public support so that the Forest Service got nervous. In 1963 President Kennedy appointed a North Cascades study team of Agriculture and Interior officials and other government officials. At the same time, we published a book setting out a North Cascades Park prospectus. In 1965 the study team report laid out who opposed and who supported the park . . . [and] it gave Jackson a feeling that this was a big issue in the state. We also got petitions with about 30,000 signatures and lots of letters."

Jackson responded by holding two days of hearings in Seattle in February of 1966, and the testimony ran heavily in favor of creating a park. In fact, the list of witnesses who testified and persons who wrote letters filled thirty-four pages in the hearing record: an impressive display of citizen support. "We packed the place," says Goldsworthy, "so Jackson would feel secure putting his name to the thing."

The study team had recommended a park of about 700,000 contiguous acres, which naturally delighted the council, but a rather powerful coalition of special interests opposed so large a park. Seattle City Light, the city's essentially autonomous power agency, had a large hydroelectric generating facility at Ross Dam on the Skagit River; individuals and corporations held some five thousand mining claims in the area; truckers were interested in the North Cascades Highway which would provide a northern road link between the eastern and western parts of the state; and the timber companies naturally hated to see so many billions of beautiful board feet of timber being wasted on trees. So Jackson temporized.

In the bill he introduced in 1967, he separated the study team's proposed park into northern and southern portions by a sort of "Polish Corridor" which contained the dams, lakes, and highway. This was designated the Ross Lake National Recreation Area, a classification which potentially opens it to activities ranging from boating to clear-cutting the timber. He subsequently chopped off the lower tip of the southern portion and designated it the Lake Chelan National Recreation Area. Although conservationists were unhappy with these changes, the resulting park (about 500,000 acres) and recreation areas represented what one of them calls "an artful compromise.... *Theoretically* you could log in the recreation areas, but it was artful in that, *practically*, it can't be done. Jackson gives a minimum to each side. I like him not for his instincts so much as for his effectiveness. And when you get right down to it, he does more than he needs to."

Because neither side got all it wanted, Jackson remains in a commanding position. If the conservationists seek legislation enlarging the park, the timber and commercial interests will need his help, and vice versa should the latter want to begin logging or mining in the recreation areas. In the meantime both sides must continue to court him, and he will keep getting votes from one group and campaign contributions from the other. Unquestionably, he engineered a workable compromise in the Madisonian tradition, but whether or not it was good statecraft is another matter.

It would be no exaggeration to call the National Environmental Policy Act the single most important piece of environmental legislation passed by Congress. It not only established for the first time a national policy and the means to carry it out; the law also compelled the various parts of the federal government to take into account the impact of their activities upon what had hitherto been considered "free" resources: the land, air, and water. Moreover, it required the normally secretive federal bureaucracy to make its assessments public and thus enable concerned citizens to add their judgment to determinations of what is or is not in the public's interest.

The federal government owns millions of acres of mountains and forests and administers these lands in accordance with congressionally enacted statutes. In theory, the government is supposed to protect "the public interest," but what is that other than a compromise worked out among various competing interests? It is no accident, for instance, that the Forest Service comes under the Agriculture Department, rather than Interior, because trees are simply crops to the timber companies which lobbied hard to have that point of view written into the law. They argue, of course, that harvesting trees provides jobs for people and results in houses, again, for people. Is this not as much in the *public* interest as leaving them uncut for the aesthetic pleasure of a few hikers?

Questions such as these have typically been resolved by allowing timber companies to harvest some of the trees while putting others beyond their reach in specially designated wilderness areas or national parks. This compartmentalized approach may have appeared workable when we were not so populous a nation and our natural resources seemed unlimited, but it is clearly no longer a responsible policy, if indeed it ever was. Clear-cutting forests can lead to soil erosion, which, in turn, pollutes streams and destroys spawning grounds. Mining and refining of ore can leave carcinogenic residues in the air we breathe and water we drink. As long as the Forest Service could legitimately claim that what happened to the salmon was beyond its legislated purview and the Bureau of Mines could strike a similar pose with respect to, say, air pollution far downwind of ore smelters, the federal government would remain incapable of exercising intelligent stewardship over the resources it is supposed to protect, or permit to be used, for the common good.

In 1965 the Department of the Interior drafted an ecological research and surveys bill, but interdepartmental politics prevented it from doing more than passing it on, without endorsement, to interested legislators. The Agriculture and Commerce departments dismissed this measure in a joint letter to the Bureau of the Budget, noting: "At the present time the Department of Interior has important but limited concerns with the natural environment." Considering Agriculture's close ties with the timber industry and Commerce's adherence to the business community's antiquated notion that land, air, and water are free, their opposition came as no surprise. Yet, as Terence Finn points out, "the bill established the political credibility of ecology and began the process of developing in Congress the recognition that man is dependent upon natural resources which themselves are interdependent."*

William Van Ness became special counsel to the Senate Interior Committee in 1966 and soon thereafter began looking at environmental questions. His inquiry culminated in a long

* I am greatly indebted to Terry Finn who permitted me to use his Ph.D. dissertation on how NEPA became law. I have relied heavily on his good work in this chapter.

memorandum and a draft of an omnibus bill he called "The Environmental Quality, Research, Planning and Coordination Act," which he sent to Jackson in January of 1967. He argued that "the sum total of environment-affecting actions must at some level of government be assessed and evaluated in qualitative terms" but pointed out that there was no institutional structure which made such ecological assessments.

Jackson thought enough of the memorandum to have it printed in the *Congressional Record,* but he chose not to sponsor the bill his aide had drafted. In fact, he did not even allow it to be printed with the memorandum. Although the concept interested him, he did not feel it was then worth a major legislative effort. Van Ness persisted, and by the end of the summer Jackson was giving speeches on the subject.

Van Ness had also "warned" Jackson that if Interior did not assert its jurisdiction over environmental legislation "some other Congressional committee will come forward with a similar proposal to deal with the problem of environmental quality." This danger may have been the key factor in Jackson's ultimate decision to act. The year before, Senator Edmund Muskie of Maine had proposed the Senate create a Select Committee on Technology and the Human Environment, but Jackson exerted his influence in the Government Operations Committee and the proposal died there. Muskie, however, had another base from which to operate as chairman of the Public Works Subcommittee on Air and Water Pollution. Although he could probably have pre-empted Jackson on environmental matters, Muskie seemed less interested at that time in the sort of environmental overview mechanism Van Ness had in mind than in writing comprehensive measures to control specific pollution problems.

In 1968 Jackson was no longer reluctant to push environmental legislation, and he eagerly sought ways to build a public constituency for a bill he had introduced in December of 1967. He asked environmentalist Lynton Caldwell to write a special report which would encapsulate the issue in terms the general public could understand. When Caldwell's report was subsequently published by the committee, Jackson wrote in the introduction: "Declaration of a national environmental policy could . . . provide a new organizing concept by which governmental functions could be weighed and evaluated in the light of better perceived and better understood national needs and goals."

Although Jackson had originally intended to hold hearings on the bill, that course of action could have raised potentially serious problems. Using Caldwell's report and earlier studies, he had been building a favorable case for a national environmental policy and the means to execute it, but the Johnson administration (in the form of several cabinet officers) was certain to testify against it. There was also a growing jurisdictional problem because the Senate Parliamentarian had already assigned to the Public Works Committee, for instance, several bills concerning environmental issues. Thus the normal course of action, hearings on his proposed bill, seemed likely to weaken rather than strengthen the case he had been building.

Although the unusual suggestion to hold a House-Senate colloquium on the environment originated with a House subcommittee chairman faced with similar jurisdictional problems, Jackson quickly embraced the idea. The result was a one-day session which added to the largely favorable commentary in support of a national environmental policy. Yet no one had really addressed the matter of *content*. Should the policy establish the government as a watchdog which could bark but not bite when it saw an environmentally unsound project? Should oversight powers extend to private as well as government projects? The colloquium did not directly address such questions, but the white paper which followed did make tentative steps in that direction. On balance, then, the event was more valuable as a "consensus-building operation" (Van Ness's phrase) than in deciding what the content of an environmental policy ought to be.

The hard battles over the specific elements of that policy were yet to come, but by early 1969 those who favored such a measure seemed to have tacitly agreed on its general scope. Its major provisions would include a statement setting out in general terms a national policy on the environment, an "action-enforcing mechanism" to carry out that policy, and a federal agency or agencies to oversee it. The bill Jackson had introduced in 1967 really contained only the last of these.

Although the Johnson administration had opposed the bill, it was in the uncomfortable position of objecting to an increasingly popular idea without suggesting a constructive alternative. President-elect Nixon, however, seemed to grasp the *political* significance of the issue and solicited ideas for the new administration to consider. He responded in May of 1969 with an executive order establishing a cabinet-level Environmental Quality Council. He attempted to portray it as paralleling in importance the only other such panels: the National Security Council and Urban Affairs Council. The reaction in Congress and the media, however, was overwhelmingly negative because the EQC was seen as a ploy to undercut growing congressional support for an independent environmental body which would oversee a legislatively formulated policy. The House Appropriations Committee turned this sentiment into action by cutting from the proposed budget all funds the White House had requested for the EQC and its advisory committee.

In February of 1969 Jackson introduced a new bill (S. 1075) similar to the one he had introduced in the previous Congress. The hearings in April took just one day, but it was a fruitful one because he managed to get administration witnesses to agree with him on the need "for a strong declaration of congressional policy on the environment so that the executive branch will know its charter and can have a stronger arm." At that time he referred to his measure as "a working paper" because it did not contain a "strong declaration" of environmental policy, but when he later drafted that policy statement, he used the endorsement in principle of the administration's witnesses to strengthen the case for his bill and weaken what little support existed for Nixon's EQC.

The news media did not closely follow the bill, and environmental matters in general did not get significant press coverage until the first "Earth Day" the following year. This lack of attention probably helped rather than hurt Jackson in his efforts to move the bill through the legislative process. No one in the press wrote in detail about the implications of the environmental impact statements in the amended bill, and the White House simply failed to foresee the far-reaching consequences of such statements. Judging from his public remarks, even Jackson seemed unaware of what he had wrought. Thus agencies such as the Corps of Engineers or Bureau of Mines, which would surely have opposed the provision had they been aware of its far-reaching implications, did nothing. The White House was ultimately faced with this choice: it could either continue its mild opposition to the bill, based on the President's formulation of his Environmental Quality Council, which had virtually no outside support, or it could try to strike a deal with Jackson. It chose the latter.

Jackson had been close to the Republican administration from the day President-elect Nixon asked him to be Secretary of Defense. With the Democrats in control of Congress, the White House needed allies in the opposition party, particularly for its upcoming battle in the Senate over the Safeguard ABM system. John Ehrlichman, who was then White House counsel, had practiced law in Seattle and was acquainted with Jackson. After a few weeks of negotiation they apparently reached a modus vivendi. The administration would continue its *pro forma* opposition to the National Environmental Policy Act, but it would exert no private pressure on Republican legislators to try to water down or kill the bill. (I do not know what the administration got in return, but Jackson subsequently led the White House's fight for Safeguard and won by a single vote.)

The executive branch had been neutralized, but the dukes and barons of Congress were another matter. The jurisdictional battle, which had been temporarily averted by the joint colloquium in 1968, could no longer be avoided. The Senate Public Works Committee had handled pollution-control legislation since 1899, and Muskie's Subcommittee on Air and Water Pollution had since 1963 heard from more than 1,100 witnesses and compiled a hearing record of nearly 16,000 pages. (By contrast, the hearing record for NEPA was 120 pages.) Muskie had declined an invitation to testify on NEPA in April because the bill as then drafted seemed to present no serious conflict with his more precise legislation. In June the Interior Committee, meeting in closed session, produced a much-amended version of S. 1075. This revision and some second thoughts on the part of the Public Works staff culminated in Muskie's introducing a comprehensive environmental bill of his own. To emphasize his reputation as "Mr. Environment," he presented the bill with thirty-nine cosponsors.

On July 7, Jackson met with the chairman of Public Works, Senator Jennings Randolph of West Virginia, but each man left with a different understanding as to what had been agreed to. On July 9, Interior reported S. 1075 to the Senate, but the revised bill and accompanying report were not made available. The following morning, during the period set aside for routine legislation, Jackson brought up his measure when only a handful of senators were on the floor. "We have had it under consideration for some time," he said, "and the bill was given the unanimous support of the committee." The ranking Republican on the Interior Committee agreed; there was no debate; and within five minutes the Senate—or, more precisely, seven senators—passed NEPA by voice vote.

Muskie was outraged by Jackson's maneuver. The "consent calendar" on which NEPA was brought to the floor is supposed to be used to expedite noncontroversial bills, such as relief for war widows, and the fact that Randolph and Jackson met at all indicated the measure was indeed controversial. That this action was taken without warning heightened suspicions that Jackson had intended to deceive Randolph and Muskie and—most insulting—thought he could get away with it.

From Jackson's standpoint swift passage meant that potential opponents of the bill, particularly in the executive agencies and the business community, would not have sufficient time to organize against it. This, however, seems to have been a minor risk, because with the ABM coming to a vote in August the White House would certainly have discouraged such a challenge on a seemingly unimportant bill rather than antagonize Safeguard's principal defender. So the stage was set for a confrontation between Jackson and Muskie.

It is no secret among Senate observers that the two men do not get along very well. Indeed, it was widely believed that Jackson was prepared to give up his chairmanship of Interior to take that of Government Operations to keep Muskie from the chair (a move that became unnecessary when the senator from Maine was chosen to head the new Budget Committee). But, while there were personal factors at work, the struggle over NEPA had substantive roots as well.

Jackson believes in concentration of power, and much of his legislative work has entailed substantial shifts of power from Congress to the President. NEPA was no exception, and Terence Finn's assessment bears this out:

> Senator Jackson believed that pollution would be abated by making those agencies responsible for the degradation of resources sensitive to environmental quality. He thought that Federal agencies were administered by reasonable men who would respond to a mandate or a procedure requiring consideration of environmental values. Jackson wanted to internalize these values in the Federal government. He believed that environmental quality would be achieved only with the cooperation of the Federal agencies. He did not believe an environmental overlord, review board, or regulatory council was either desirable or necessary.

Muskie had an entirely different point of view, and he spelled it out in a speech on the floor of the Senate.

> The philosophy of air and water quality legislation has been first to develop the criteria which indicate the effects of pollutants on the various aspects of the public health and welfare and then to apply available, feasible control technology. . . .
>
> The concept of self-policing by Federal agencies which pollute or license pollution is contrary to the philosophy and intent of existing environmental quality legislation. In hearing after hearing agencies of the Federal Government have argued that their primary authorization, whether it be maintenance of the navigable waters by the Corps of Engineers or licensing of nuclear power plants by the Atomic Energy Commission, takes precedence over water quality requirements.
>
> I repeat these agencies have always emphasized their primary responsibility, making environmental considerations secondary in their view.

Muskie and Jackson differed over several parts of NEPA, but their dispute over the section concerning environmental impact statements was central. Jackson regarded it as the "teeth" which would compel government agencies to consider how their projects would affect the environment, but Muskie saw it as a possible "loophole" which agencies might interpret as freeing them from specific antipollution legislation as long as their statement showed they had considered the environmental consequences of their actions. Another problem was the vagueness of the section. Where the impact statements were to be sent or their format was not spelled out. What Jackson was counting on was that the very process of writing such statements and putting their names to them would induce federal officials to refrain from ever starting projects which would seriously damage the environment. Muskie's philosophy required a different strategy. He wanted Congress to set precise pollution standards so there would be no ambiguity about what was or was not acceptable when the government or courts interpreted the law. Without a compromise on this and related issues, Muskie was prepared to block S. 1075 when it returned to the Senate following action in the House. Given the broad cosponsorship of his bill, he stood a good chance of doing just that.

To strengthen his position Muskie asked the Public Works Committee to incorporate his bill on the environment into its comprehensive measure on oil pollution, which it did by unanimous vote. He then wrote to the thirty-nine cosponsors of his original measure and asked their support for the new legislation, noting pointedly: "I do not intend to seek unanimous consent action on this legislation because I feel that the matters covered in this bill . . . deserve discussion and debate by all members of the Senate."

Jackson's and Muskie's bills were finally on a collision course. The Senate leadership naturally wanted to avoid a confrontation; so both men were prevailed upon to seek a compromise each could live with. After two and a half weeks of contentious wrangling, they decided, on the eve of the vote on Muskie's measure, to hammer out their differences.

The result, surprisingly, was that Jackson's bill was much strengthened. Most legislative compromises result in a weaker bill, but in this instance Muskie was out to plug loopholes. And plug them he did. New language was added to Jackson's bill explicitly stating that the filing of environmental impact statements did not relieve a federal agency of its "specific statutory obligations . . . to comply with criteria or standards of environmental quality." Moreover, before statements could be written, "the responsible Federal official shall consult with and obtain the comments of any Federal agency which has jurisdiction by law or special expertise with respect to any environmental impact involved." All comments, favorable or not, had to be attached if the impact statement was subsequently written. Statements also had to include "alternatives to the proposed action," and, most important, they had to be made public.

There were other changes having to do with the composition and responsibilities of the newly created environmental panels, but these were of comparatively minor significance. What was important, said Jackson, was that both bills "will give the nation an environmental policy as well as appropriate governmental structures in the executive branch to implement the policy." President Nixon signed the National Environmental Policy Act into law on January 1, 1970. It was, fittingly, the first new law of the decade.

NEPA is far from perfect. Although the requirement that federal agencies make environmental impact statements public paved the way for public-interest law firms to challenge their adequacy in court and often delay controversial projects, citizens can only challenge an agency's statement, not the project itself. This is an important distinction.

Government officials tend to be less than candid about negative aspects of their own programs, and this tendency has led more than one to write an inadequate assessment of the probable impact for fear of adverse publicity. Such bureaucratic caution will hopefully kill unsound projects before they get started, but what will happen when the various agencies finally catch on and decide to risk public opprobrium by being completely candid? As long as an agency honestly assesses the probable loss of life or deleterious effects on health, it can then claim that, say, national security or the need for petroleum justifies the anticipated costs. Unless such projects violate specific environmental quality standards, such as those written by Muskie's subcommittee, the public will be unable to stop them with NEPA.

Nonetheless, in spite of its limitations, NEPA is a giant step forward. The government has always made life and health decisions for its citizens, and the "process"—if so orderly a word applies—by which they have been made in the past had largely been kept secret. NEPA has forced the government to make public and explicit the anticipated costs of its decisions with respect to the environment and the method by which they have been calculated. Without Jackson there would have been no bill, and government decisions affecting the environment would have remained behind doors marked CLOSED TO THE PUBLIC.

CHAPTER

11

Generalissimo Jackson

YOUNG BOYS who know nothing of war and old men who never served in one often have in common a fascination with weapons and warriors. If a "bellicosity index" were compiled on male members of Congress, I suspect there would be an inverse relationship between distinguished war service and vociferous jingoism.

Take two of the recent chairmen of the House Armed Services Committee. When the *Pueblo* spy ship was captured by North Korea in 1968, Representative L. Mendel Rivers of South Carolina, when asked what course of action the republic should take, shouted with rage: "Retaliate! Retaliate! Retaliate!" When Representative F. Edward Hébert of Louisiana succeeded to the chairmanship after River's death, he boasted: "I am the loudest of the hawks." Neither man ever spent a day of his life in uniform.

When Japan attacked Pearl Harbor, Jackson was a twenty-nine-year-old freshman representative. Soon thereafter, he and his Everett neighbor Jack Dootson tried to sign up for officer training in the Navy. Dootson was accepted and later became a naval aviator, but Jackson was turned down because of color blindness and poor eyesight. "He used to do eye exercises to try to strengthen them," says John Salter, but he was never able to pass the high standards then required for a commission in the Navy. There was no color vision requirement for enlistment in the army and eyesight standards were lower, but Jackson did not rush to sign up. "I wanted to go in the service," he recalls, "and the question basically was whether or not I should seek a commission."

As a member of Congress, he was legally exempt from the draft, but the fact that he was a seemingly healthy civilian could have become a political liability. Although he now says, "I never encountered that as a real issue at all," he acknowledges that his Republican opponent, "Payson Peterson tried to make a point of it." That Peterson did not succeed was evidenced by Jackson's getting 60 percent of the vote in his reelection efforts in 1942 and 1944.

Jackson ultimately decided to volunteer for the draft twenty months after the attack on Pearl Harbor. The Seattle *Post-Intelligencer* reported his induction on the front page and quoted the new private as saying: " 'I want to be a soldier in the army of the United States. I hope I will be permitted to be a doughboy soldier. I want to go into the infantry. . . . My only request was that I be allowed to go into combat service as soon as possible after my basic training. I think it is important that members of Congress have some knowledge of the views of the millions of men who will be returning from service.' "

His motivation was undoubtedly sincere, but the timing of his decision to volunteer for the draft may have been influenced by the Selective Service announcement that month that fathers would be drafted beginning October 1. Because President Roosevelt had granted other legislators (notably Lyndon Johnson and Warren Magnuson) leaves of absence to serve in the armed forces, bachelor Jackson would have been hard pressed that fall to rationalize his decision to stay in the House of Representatives once family men were being conscripted.

There are no indications that Jackson sought or received any special treatment as an enlisted man. Indeed, when some of his constituents wrote to the War Department to complain that their representative was more valuable in Congress than in the Army, the department replied that it had no Private Henry M. Jackson. Wrote columnist Drew Pearson: "Jackson had entered the army so quietly that the public relations office in his camp was not even aware that they had a congressman in their midst."

Jackson's career as a soldier ended after five months of active duty. (He later became an officer in the Army Reserve.) "Half the time he was in the Army," says Salter, "he had an infection in his foot which kept him in the hospital."

Jackson has a different recollection: "I had suffered an injury to my big toe which kept me in the hospital a week. I had lost time and went to another training company and was processed out shortly thereafter. The unit itself—the ones in the company—were not sent overseas for a couple of months after that. Most of them went overseas in the latter part of March or April."

In January of 1944, Roosevelt rescinded the indefinite-leave policy which had permitted congressmen to serve on active duty without losing their seats. Jackson could have remained in the Army had he wished, but he chose to return to Capitol Hill instead. When he announced his decision, however, he put a different construction on Roosevelt's order. "I am not leaving the service voluntarily but under the President's orders," he was reported to have said. "I want to serve where I can do the most good, and if the President orders me back to Congress, I have no alternative." (He had an alternative, of course, but it would have meant resigning his seat and remaining a "doughboy soldier" who would "go into combat service as soon as possible. . . .")

How did his short stint in the military affect him?

"I think he has an inferiority complex," says a former political associate. "He was a draftee who served briefly in the military, and I think he has always felt in awe of generals and brass. . . . When someone in a big uniform talks, he listens. His anti-Soviet feeling may go back to his lack of any real military service."

His close friend and law school classmate Stanley Golub disagrees: "Sometimes he introduces me as Stan Golub, Silver Star, Purple Heart. But I never had any feeling he has a complex about it [his lack of wartime service]. I have found the military men he respected had Ph.D.'s in some science. When he talks about military men, he talks about their academic, rather then military, record. Every time I've met a military officer with him, he's mentioned his academic background."

John Salter avers: "I don't think his lack of military service influenced his military views the way Buchenwald and the Nazi invasion of Norway did."

One cannot *prove* that Jackson's "militarism" arose from feelings of personal inadequacy or out of political necessity. His friends certainly do not think so, and his adversaries almost certainly do. Whatever his motivation, following World War II the young congressman became interested in military affairs, and even though he had only limited legislative responsibilities in the area, he began to speak out.

Although he has been flexible in most areas of domestic legislation, Jackson has been a cold war ideologue in international affairs for the past three decades. Although he has updated his position somewhat—he now concedes that communism is not a monolithic force—his speeches still ring with the rhetoric of the 1950s. Even more striking has been his reiteration of certain themes.

His "magic periscope" (Senator Thomas McIntyre's phrase) always seems to sight a new, potential Soviet threat on the horizon. These threats periodically reappear in slightly different form. In 1958 it was Soviet diesel-powered submarines on the surface one hundred miles off our coasts, but in 1973 it was nuclear-powered ones underwater four thousand miles away. Although this type of threat can never be entirely eliminated because technological improvements keep moving it farther out to sea, each time Jackson raises the danger signal he has a legislative panacea to counter the threat—until the next time he needs it, that is.

How much is enough? Instead of trying to answer that classic military question, Jackson has consistently ignored it, preferring vague formulas such as: "I would far rather we err on the side of too much than too little." One consequence of this attitude is that he has almost always supported whatever the Pentagon wants.

Jackson has never been an innovator on defense issues. He supports the latest concepts and doctrines of the military and abandons them only after they have proven too costly or ineffective. He then picks up whatever new ideas and jargon the admirals and generals are bruiting about.

Jackson relies almost exclusively on the armed services for his assessments of Soviet forces and possible threats. He regards Pentagon reports stamped "top secret" the way Moses did the stone tablets. He assumes anyone who does not have access to such documents is insufficiently informed to make intelligent judgments on military affairs. His faith in the truth of that which is classified borders on the religious.

His deep-seated distrust of the Soviet Union and anti-Soviet reflex cause him to assume the worst possible Soviet motives even when the objective data might yield multiple interpretations. This has frequently led him to misassess the strategic situation and recommend much higher levels of weapons and forces then were actually required.

Because the public record is so extensive, I have selected three of the more noteworthy years from the 1950s to point out some of his early attitudes and then tried to trace their development into the present decade. While this survey falls far short of being comprehensive, it should provide one with a grasp of Jackson's thinking and approach to military affairs.

1951

Jackson had decided to challenge Senator Harry Cain in 1952 and needed to balance his liberal voting record in the House with a hard line on the Soviet Union. Although he did not side with those who thought communism a grave internal threat, he vigorously supported Truman's anti-communist policies abroad. He also saw those policies resulting in economic benefits for the Pacific Northwest, which he predicted would become "one of the principal arsenals of defense for the United States just as it was in the last war": "The present plans of the Army, Navy and Air Force call for heavy outlays of funds. This means that many plants will be converting from peace time to all-out defense production."

In a speech in Seattle that May, he warned: "The United Nations right now lacks the military strength to wage global war. . . . We are not strong enough to meet an attack by the Soviet Union on a global basis." To meet this challenge, he advocated the United States increase its military strength from 3.5 million troops to 6 million, plan a 150-group Air Force instead of "the 95 now on paper," increase guided-missile and submarine programs and double the investment in atomic energy.

After a Soviet atomic test in October, he said, "Falling behind in the atomic armaments competition will mean national suicide. The latest Russian explosion means that Stalin has gone all-out in atomic energy. It is high time that we now go all out." To accomplish that goal he suggested that the proposed atomic energy budget of $1 billion be increased to $6 to $10 billion.

In a speech on the floor of the House, Jackson used a tactic he has often repeated: invoking secrecy rather than logic to buttress his case. "As a member of the Joint Committee on Atomic Energy, I have access to the intelligence reports on the status of Russia's atomic project. National security forbids me . . ."

So much for open debate.

1956

In January Jackson saw the ship of state approaching Armageddon if the Soviet Union won "the next critical race for discovery." I have quoted his Senate speech on "ballistic blackmail" at length because it was his most important until that time. Moreover, his rhetoric and thinking have changed little since then—so little that Jackson himself referred to this speech as recently as the SALT hearings in 1972.

> In my judgment there is the danger that the Soviets may fire a 1500-mile missile before the end of this year—1956.
>
> Some people may minimize the importance of such an achievement. They may say that the Soviets, operating from their present bases, could not reach the American heartland with a 1500-mile missile. They may contend that ballistic missiles will endanger this country only when the Kremlin achieves a weapon of true intercontinental range.
>
> This is not the case. The existence of a 1500-mile Soviet ballistic missile would cancel out our one vital advantage over Russian air-atomic power—our system of advanced overseas airbases. Virtually all of our overseas SAC [Strategic Air Command] bases are within

easy striking distance of a 1500-mile missile. Such a missile could level those bases in a matter of minutes. . . .

A Soviet 1500-mile missile could turn our strategic thinking upside down. It might well compel us to write off our overseas bases as virtually useless. A Russian 1500-mile ballistic missile could force American airpower to retreat 5000 miles from the Soviet Union.

We need not assume that Moscow would actually use a 1500-mile missile to start an atomic war. The mere existence of such a weapon in the hands of the Kremlin, at a time when we did not have it ourselves, could radically upset the balance of power.

Mr. President, we and our free world partners may soon face the threat of ballistic blackmail.

Jackson then went on to describe the sort of nuclear scenario subsequently exploited in potboilers, such as *Seven Days in May*, which peered into the atomic abyss:

I invite you to put yourself in the place of a governmental leader of France or West Germany or England or Pakistan or Japan. Any of these nations could be devastated by a 1500-mile missile launched from Communist-controlled bases. Imagine that Soviet Defense Minister Zhukov has just invited the military attachés of the free world to meet at a missile site near Moscow. Imagine Marshal Zhukov then explaining he is about to press a button which will fire the world's first 1500-mile ballistic missile. Marshal Zhukov might say that this demonstration missile carried only a TNT warhead. But he would undoubtedly add that a hydrogen warhead could be substituted. Standing in a concrete blockhouse for protection, the military attachés would see the missile launched. Some 1500 miles away—perhaps in the wastes of Soviet Central Asia—another group of free world observers would be assembled. Mere minutes later they would witness the crashing explosion of the missile at the end of its journey.

Picture what might happen next. On the wall of the concrete blockhouse would be a huge map, outlining in vivid red the range of the Soviet missile. This range would embrace all of western Europe, all of north Africa, and the Middle East, most of South and Southeast Asia, the Philippines, Formosa, Okinawa, Korea, and Japan. . . .

Caught in this bind, our most redoubtable supporters might

falter. It is well-nigh certain that crucial allies would be forced into neutralism, or even into tacit cooperation with Moscow. . . .

Soviet victory in this race for discovery would be shattering to the morale of our allies, and to our own self-confidence. For the first time, Moscow would have beaten us in a crucial scientific-industrial race. No longer would America be acknowledged as the unquestioned industrial and technical colossus of the world. Our trump card would have passed to the Kremlin, and the reverberating effects on our relationships abroad would be incalculable.

In retrospect, it is clear that Jackson had piled gross misassessment upon erroneous assumption. Not only was there no missile gap, the Soviet Union's 1,500-mile missile did not compel the United States to retreat from Europe, and no allies were "forced into neutralism" or "tacit cooperation with Moscow." What he did not realize then and, alas, fails to realize now are the *limits* of nuclear power.

The danger of mutual annihilation has made the United States and the Soviet Union more cautious—not more bold—in dealing with one another, particularly when important national interests are involved. This danger makes *unusable* all nuclear weapons, even the so-called "precision" warheads Jackson is now enthusiastically boosting. The latter are not necessary to deter an attack on the United States or a close ally because we already have a large enough strategic and tactical arsenal to accomplish that goal. Moreover, their threatened use in another area of the world would be neither believable to an adversary nor, I am sure, tolerable to the American people. We have learned since Hiroshima and Nagasaki that nuclear weapons have no purpose but to deter war. To initiate their use when so many nations have them is to enter a world where prediction and control are impossible. Nonetheless, Jackson still retains an almost mystical faith in the power of the nuclear weapons to accomplish political goals, such as restoring "the balance of power." He believed that in 1956, and he has not changed his mind.

Having enunciated the threat, Jackson apparently felt it necessary to propose a solution. He did this in May with an article in the *New York Times Magazine* entitled "Toward a

Superior 'Force in Being.' " It was a call for nothing less than a massive mobilization of the nation's resources.

> "Force in being," as I understand the phrase, describes the actual military strength available to us for immediate use—as opposed to the latent resources on which we can draw tomorrow, the next day, or sometime in the future. . . .
>
> To recognize and exploit vital "breakthroughs," with heavy applications of men and money, requires the finest organizational teamwork and the highest administrative skill.
>
> The concept of a superior "force in being" calls, in addition, for production techniques which match the effectiveness of our scientific effort. Once our scientists have devised an important, perhaps crucial, weapon, we cannot hesitate to produce it in such numbers as to create a genuine deterrent. . . .
>
> We will never be able to maintain a superior "force in being" as long as dynamic weapons are stalled on production lines by overcautious and archaic administrative methods. Discussing our production failures, Admiral [Hyman G.] Rickover points out that the "money we try to save by being too careful not to make mistakes, is frequently offset by the lengthening of our lead time." In the long run, such economy can be both false and fatal, for the margin by which we lead the Russians in placing advanced weapons in mass production may also be our margin of survival.

Nowhere in the article did Jackson discuss *which* sorts of "breakthroughs" ought to be exploited and *how* the government should make such determinations. His philosophy seems to have been: If it looks as if a new weapon might be better, build it regardless of need or price.

Another costly notion he advocated was what the Pentagon later called "concurrency": starting production of a new weapon before it has been thoroughly tested. As we have since learned with the F-111 fighter, C-5A transport, and several other programs, huge "cost overruns," not better weapons, are the inevitable progeny of concurrent development and production of unproven concepts.

Jackson is more comfortable with abstractions than reality. Although he has had many opportunities to visit the Soviet Union, he made his only trip in 1956, reinforced his preconceptions, and never returned. After that trip, he wrote a series of articles for the Seattle *P-I*, and in one of them he described how the Soviet Union was using foreign aid to convert uncommitted nations into allies.

> The Soviet Union has paved the streets of Kabul, the capital of Afghanistan, and won another satellite.
>
> It isn't that simple, of course.
>
> But the paved streets of Kabul, and the other things the Soviet Union has done in Afghanistan, points up the fact that the Soviets know how to go about winning friends among the underprivileged areas—and then moving in to take over completely.

Jackson then went on to note that the United States had refused to pave the streets, and for want of asphalt Afghanistan was lost behind the iron curtain. But he was even more disturbed about a road which was then being built: "It will give the Russians a military highway right up to the border of Pakistan—and present the Free World with another grave threat. Thus the Soviets use their foreign aid to carry out their goal of world domination."

Jackson's perception of the uncommitted nations was a rather simple one: they were commodities to be purchased for the cold war. Thus the task of foreign aid was equally simple: get there with dollars before the Russians send in their rubles. Missing from his thinking was any appreciation of nationalism and how that very important factor would lead to such nations' making independent determinations of what was or was not in their own interest. As we have since learned—sometimes painfully—the United States has not been very successful buying allies.

1958

Jackson was running for reelection; so his pronouncements on defense once again were closely tied to federal payrolls in Washington State. In January he said, "The Air Force needs a fleet of 1800 Boeing Airplane Company jet bombers and tankers." He then suggested that the service increase its order for 603 B-52 bombers by 300, and buy 900, rather than 400, KC-135 tankers. Although the B-52s were being built in Wichita, Kansas, he opined that they could also be built at the plant in Renton, Washington, along with the KC-135s.

The following month he foresaw a grave threat at sea: "Soviet submarine commanders could surface 100 miles out, take a radar fix and hit one-third of the US population with frightening accuracy." To counteract this threat he advocated building one hundred Polaris submarines by the earliest possible date. (Forty-one were ultimately constructed.)

Here again Jackson grossly overestimated what the United States actually needed in air and sea power to deter the Soviet Union. Fortunately, he went unheeded. Equally disturbing, however, was his muddled strategic thinking. Missile-firing submarines are a threat to targets on land, not each other. Building more submarines thus would not have countered the Soviet fleet; it would simply have added more missiles to our arsenal than were required for deterrence. Yet, he would use that same sort of argument again in his 1973 fight for Trident, the successor to Polaris.

Although Jackson did not give up the numbers game after John Kennedy became President, he began to focus more attention on geopolitics than on military hardware. This seems to have been a deliberate choice, perhaps taken to avoid seriously conflicting with the defense requests of a Democratic President. So he began to speak on problem areas such as the Middle East and, later, Southeast Asia (the subjects of the following two chapters). He had his differences with JFK, most notably over the partial nuclear test-ban treaty, but by this time the strategic programs of the United States for bombers, submarines, and missiles had been set—spurred unnecessarily high, in part, by Jackson's frequent public assertions that there was a missile gap between the United States and the Soviet Union. The aerospace industry was in full boom, and it would have been premature to begin agitating for weapons not yet off the drawing board. Later on, when Vietnam began consuming even larger shares of the budget, the Pentagon was forced to postpone the costly strategic programs it would subsequently propose under President Nixon. It was not until the debate over the Safeguard antiballistic missile system in 1969 that Jackson resumed his role as hardware salesman for the military.

Nineteen seventy-two was an immensely frustrating year for Jackson. His power in the Senate had never been greater; yet he could not translate it into votes in the presidential primaries that spring and suffered one humiliating defeat after another.

The strategic arms agreements signed in Moscow that May by President Nixon and Communist party General Secretary Leonid Brezhnev were particularly bitter pills to swallow. Jackson had heavily invested his personal prestige and political capital to win Senate passage of Safeguard, only to have his hard-fought victory negated by the ABM treaty. Moreover, administration witnesses at the hearings on the SALT agreements refused even to discuss what data they had used to estimate future Soviet force levels. He took this as proof of the administration's ingratitude, and at one point in the hearings he fumed: "Mr. Ambassador, when the administration wanted my help, on getting the ABM through Congress, it didn't hesitate when I asked about the consequences of the Soviets developing a missile as accurate as our Minuteman."

Nixon had facilitated Jackson's rise to power in the Senate and may have thought he could just as easily diminish it, but Jackson had two strong bargaining levers. One was his amendment interpreting the offensive-arms limitation agreement; the other was the Trident ballistic-missile submarine.

The year before, the administration had asked for $105 million for research and development of the Trident 1 missile and Trident submarine, but in 1972 the price tag shot up to nearly $1 billion. Secretary of Defense Melvin Laird justified the tenfold increase as a "signal to the Soviets . . . in the face of a growing Soviet threat." Yet, when that threat was restricted a few months later by the SALT accords, Laird did not return Trident to its original schedule. So the accelerated Trident program was certain to come under challenge in the Senate, and the White House needed all the help it could get.

Jackson initially believed the accelerated program was unwise, and when Senator Lloyd Bentsen of Texas moved to return the submarine to its original schedule (launch in 1981 instead of 1978), Jackson made a surprising show of independence and supported Bentsen. The motion, however, failed to carry in the Armed Services Committee on an 8-to-8 tie.

A few weeks later, Bentsen took his opposition to the floor, but just minutes before the vote on his amendment, Jackson announced he had changed his mind and voted against it. Had this dramatic flip-flop occurred on a minor issue, it would merit only passing mention, but Trident was, and is, the nation's most important strategic arms program. Jackson has frequently misassessed a military situation, but he has a well-earned reputation for methodically studying important defense issues. It was inconceivable to Senate observers that Jackson would have broken with the Pentagon to support Bentsen's committee motion on a whim. Why, then, had he so suddenly switched?

This is what Jackson told the Senate:

> My chief concern has been one expressed by other Senators: that commitment to the procurement of long lead time items this year could lead to a premature freezing of the design of the Navy's follow-on submarine system. After lengthy discussion with responsible officials, including Admiral Rickover whose judgment has over and over again proved of great weight and value in these matters, I am persuaded that whatever merit there is in this argument is more than balanced by the urgent need to press ahead with programs essential to our deterrent posture.

Jackson's new position on Trident was based less on any specific rationale than on the general proposition he had so often embraced: too much defense is better than too little. It was also vaguely reminiscent of his 1956 advocacy of a "superior 'force in being.' " He wanted immediate exploitation of the new weapon even though there was no immediate need for it. He was once again quite willing to risk tax dollars on the discredited policy of "concurrency" by authorizing nearly $1 billion for a submarine which did not even have engineering blueprints.

A Jackson aide who had privately called the accelerated Trident program "a crock of shit" before his boss switched sides subsequently tried to convince me that the senator had decided to vote against the Bentsen floor amendment only after many long and lonely hours of carefully weighing the arguments of each side. To put it mildly, I was not convinced. Jackson is a hard-nosed politician who does not give away his votes. If he reversed himself on so important an issue in so short a period of time, it is a safe bet there was a quid pro quo. What did he get in return?

In February of 1973 the Navy announced that Trident would be based at Bangor, Washington. The decision was a complete surprise because service spokesmen had previously indicated the new base would be on the Southeast Atlantic coast. Construction cost was estimated at $550 million, and the federal payroll at the base would pump an additional $100 million into the stagnant economy of Washington State. Although many speculated this was Jackson's payoff, his aide asserted to me: "Scoop didn't really want the base at Bangor because of the boom-and-bust phenomenon, but he couldn't come right out and say that, of course." It was an elegant pose but just a bit too elegant to be convincing.

Another possibility is that Jackson agreed to support the accelerated Trident as part of a complicated deal involving his amendment to the offensive arms limitation agreement. In fact, the Nixon administration did support the amendment—though not Jackson's interpretation of it—and his faint praise for the Democratic party's candidate for President that fall may simply have been an extra dividend; it was certainly not the first time Jackson had split the Democrats to Richard Nixon's advantage. In the end, Jackson maintained his preeminence in the Senate on strategic affairs, and Nixon harvested favorable publicity for SALT and, most important, the electoral votes of forty-nine states.

Jackson was now committed to the Trident acceleration. So when Senator Thomas McIntyre of New Hampshire challenged it in 1973, Jackson led the counterattack for the White House. Facing the public gallery, both arms pumping up and down like a football referee playing to the grandstand, he began the debate with distortions and non sequiturs. Here are two examples.

—"Our present missile submarines," he asserted, "have a life expectancy of 20 years, and the last thing we want to do is have submarines that might collapse from structural failures." This was a blatant misrepresentation of the facts, and Senator Howard Cannon of Nevada quickly set the record straight: "The Department of Defense now says the Polaris-Poseidon has a life expectancy of 25 years." Nonetheless, in the days that followed, Jackson continued to imply that a pinch-penny Congress would be sending sailors to their doom in obsolete submarines.

—Although the size of the Soviet submarine fleet relative to the American is irrelevant because the two boats do not have one another for targets, Jackson ominously noted that "the Soviets already have in the water more than three Tridents" and upped the figure to five a few days later. Not only had he attempted to fuzz the numbers, he also glossed over the fact that the Soviet Union's so-called "Tridents" were actually modifications of an older class of submarine which now had 12 instead of the original 16 missiles. These boats are quite noisy, thus making them susceptible to acoustic detection, and their missiles have only single warheads. Compare that to the quiet Trident's 160 individual warheads.

Jackson knew the vote would be close so he asked for a rare secret session of the Senate so he could discuss classified information. About seventy senators attended, and he was at the ready with his secret briefing charts. "Jackson's purpose," one senator told me, "was to scare hell out of the Senate." But he apparently told the upper chamber little it did not already know; indeed, his real purpose was probably boosting attendance. While he was going over one "top secret" chart on Soviet missile strength, this senator told me he was looking at the identical information in an unclassified publication.

In the days before the vote, Jackson had the resources of the Pentagon and its allies at his disposal, and he skillfully exploited them. He arranged for several undecided senators to meet personally with the Secretary of Defense and Chief of Naval Operations. Senator Lee Metcalf of Montana was reportedly visited by Admiral Rickover and AFL-CIO lobbyists who apparently persuaded him to support Trident even though he had voted against it the year before. Jackson played upon the vanity of Senator Joseph Montoya of New Mexico by arranging for him to be honored by the "Old Crows," a group of electronic warfare experts, the night before the vote: he too abandoned his previous opposition and voted for the accelerated Trident. It was close, but when the vote was tallied on September 27, Jackson and Trident came out ahead, 49 to 47.

Ironically, the Pentagon decided in 1974 that Trident was being built with undue haste. Although the first boat remained scheduled for 1978, the Navy decided to build three boats every two years and restored its original plan to deploy Trident 1 missiles on late-model Polaris submarines. These changes were precisely what Senate critics such as Bentsen and McIntyre had advocated and Jackson had so successfully opposed. So, once again, his position on an important military program proved to be a potentially expensive misassessment.

"The free world is being tried in a life-and-death contest that is novel in nature and therefore unprecedented in the demands it makes on its leaders. We are at war, and precisely because the guns are not being fired, we need leaders who can teach us the necessity and the art of waging the war that looks like a peace."

Orwell did not write those words in *1984*: Jackson did in 1960 for an article in the prestigious journal *Foreign Affairs*. He has never been much of a wordsmith, but his "war is peace" formulation was more than just a poor choice of language. It revealed a mind in which perception and thought were, to put it charitably, confused.

Jackson believes he is an internationalist and regards those who oppose his cold war outlook as isolationists. His brand of internationalism is more properly called "interventionism" because it is predicated almost entirely on military power. As his statements cited in this chapter indicate, he can reduce the most complex international issue to a matter of arms and their threatened or actual use. Although the word has emotional overtones, he may properly be called a "militarist" without stretching the definition.

For most of his career, Jackson has equated nuclear superiority with the nation's security. In 1949 he called atomic energy "the one main barrier we have to stop Soviet Russia from reaching the shores of America." In 1956 he spoke about "the threatening achievements of the Soviets in the development and production of new weapons" and warned that their goal remained "ultimate world domination." He held the same view in 1963 when he predicted dire consequences should the Soviet Union draw even in the nuclear arms race: "I am confident that if the Russians should obtain parity or equality with the United States—I am talking about nuclear or thermonuclear parity or equality—they might risk a surprise attack on the United States." (Now that the Soviet Union is our nuclear equal he claims to have abandoned the goal of nuclear superiority in favor of "essential equivalence.")

"The true champions of peace," he said in 1965, "are those who understand that power must be used, with restraint but also with assurance, to keep the peace, or to restore it." Preparedness, then, was, and remains, the only road to peace, and in an unwitting allusion to Mao Tse-Tung's aphorism, "political power grows out of the barrel of a gun," he warned against detente: "And today, if the Russian bear looks tranquil, we must remember he is looking down the barrel of NATO—and not into a barrel of happy pills."

Jackson had tempered his view somewhat by 1967 in that he admitted the possibility of cooperation with the adversary as long as the United States kept its powder dry: "In relations with the Soviet Union the free world must pursue two consonant courses of action: to work with them where interests converge, and at the same time to maintain the strength and the resolve to discourage peace-upsetting moves by them." But he still predicted peril if the Soviet Union was able to match our nuclear firepower: "As I see things, international peace and security depend not on a parity of power but on a preponderance of power in the peace-keepers over the peace-upsetters."

Ironically, the following year, Jackson himself sounded like a would-be "peace-upsetter." After North Korea seized the U.S.S. *Pueblo,* he loudly rattled the nuclear saber, and the media in his home state widely reported his apocalyptic vision. On the front page of the Bremerton *Sun* he was quoted as saying: "The US is so close to the use of nuclear weapons it's not funny. . . . I don't want to see the use of nuclear weapons. But the only way it could be avoided would be through a massive infusion of ground troops in South Korea by someone. And we just don't have the troops."

Such comments led *Argus,* a respected Seattle weekly, to observe: "Irresponsible and inflammatory statements by individual senators, particularly those as hawkish as our own Senator Jackson, only provide more sparks which could ignite the tinderbox."

In a reply the following week, Jackson angrily denied he had been irresponsible and tried to set the record straight. Instead, he simply confirmed that he had indeed been raising the specter of nuclear war:

> My statements concerning nuclear weapons were in response to specific questions from the press asking whether I foresaw the use of nuclear weapons in a conflict over the Pueblo seizure. My answer was "*no*" with the qualification that if an all-out invasion of *South Korea* by *North Korea* were to occur, then stopping that invasion required the use of *tactical* nuclear weapons—a step the US was prepared to take. That the North Koreans know this and believe it is an important deterrent to their re-invading South Korea.

"Arrogant" is an adjective critics frequently use to describe Jackson, and it does not seem an unfair characterization. But his is not the self-assured sort of arrogance one finds in individuals of superior intellect; it is that of the closed-minded fundamentalist who firmly believes that what he knows is all there is to know. It most frequently manifests itself as intolerance, as when he turns away probing questions with a put-down. One Seattle editor told me of an instance when he asked a particularly detailed question about a defense issue. Instead of answering, Jackson haughtily dismissed it: " 'You don't know the facts: they're classified.' "

Because of his nearly absolute faith in the military's secret assessments of Soviet forces and intentions, he has consistently overreacted to supposed threats. Had this nation built the military forces he has recommended over the years, we would now have more than twice as many planes, submarines, and men under arms and a price tag to match. Instead of a military budget about to exceed $100 billion, we would be spending on the order of $150 to $200 billion a year. It is unlikely our economy could have supported such a nonproductive burden.

As we are painfully discovering, our economic resources are not infinitely expandable; they are limited. Money must be spent on defense, but it must be spent judiciously. Squandering it simply on the proposition that we ought to "err on the side of too much [rather] than too little" not only wastes billions of dollars, it begs the most important question government must answer: How much is *needed* for defense?

Jackson, alas, has never tried to answer that question; he simply gives his uncritical support to whatever the armed services request. It is not that the nuclear forces of the Soviet Union present no danger to this country: they do. But the challenge of government is to minimize that danger, and all Jackson seems to be able to do is redefine the threat to rationalize the Pentagon's most recent weapons programs. Thus he exploited the presence of Soviet submarines one hundred miles off our coasts to peddle Polaris in 1958 and used a similar, if more distant, threat to sell Trident in 1973. If either of these American boats had eliminated or reduced the Soviet submarine threat, his position might have had merit, but they did not. The threat remains, and Jackson will probably recycle it whenever he needs to do a new sales job. The obvious consequence of his "reasoning" is that the United States will constantly need more arms than it has, and because the threat will always be there, we will never have enough. The expensive nuclear arsenal we have built and continue to augment has not made this nation and its interests one whit more secure, nor can it. So we keep adding more weapons to our arsenal to match real or imagined Soviet increases, and the Soviets do likewise. They, too, have their Scoop Jacksons.

CHAPTER

12

Vietnam: "We Must Pay the Price"

THE CAMERA closed in. CBS reporter Mike Wallace thrust his question like a rapier: "Were you wrong on Vietnam?"

Senator Jackson, the target of an interview on "60 Minutes," flinched. "No. No," he said.

Wallace thrust still deeper: "You were—you were a bitter-end hawk on Vietnam."

Jackson: "No! Now let's just take one quick comment—make one quick comment on that. My position—bear in mind Jack Kennedy and those who were associated with him made that commitment out there—my view on Vietnam was a very simple one. I was violently opposed to a protracted conflict. Either bring this conflict to an early conclusion or get out. I opposed the Johnson formula and the advice he got from his military advisors. I said it was wrong; it wouldn't work.

"Why did I hold on to the end? So that we could get our prisoners back and get out of there. Now that's what I did. And the others were just saying, 'Look, you've got five hundred thousand men. What do you want to do? Cut all appropriations off and just leave them there? Why, of course not. I'm at least honorable enough that having been involved out there—and listen. They were all—were in there, including [Senator J. William] Fulbright—supported the Tonkin Gulf Resolution.

When it got a little . . . rough for them . . . you'll find that a lot of these guys just jumped ship. Now, I don't jump ship easily."

It was a less-than-candid response. While it was true that President Kennedy had committed several thousand American military "advisers" to South Vietnam, he did not spread the war to North Vietnam, Laos, and Cambodia. He did not send a half-million-man army into Southeast Asia and turn what had been a civil war into a test of American arms. He did not put escalation theory into practice by launching American bombers over North Vietnam, and he was not the commander in chief when the first American pilot was taken prisoner of war. Either Jackson did not understand the limits of Kennedy's policies in Vietnam or he intentionally misrepresented them; the commitment he had supported was begun by President Johnson and continued by President Nixon. Moreover, he was among the few diehards who were still voting to bomb Cambodia after the last returning POW had been given a hero's welcome.

Jackson no longer takes the initiative to talk about Vietnam. He would rather forget that long, tragic episode and, I suspect, so would most Americans. Indeed, when he mentions the war at all, it is because he has been prodded by a reporter, but as his answer to Mike Wallace made plain, he does not squarely face such questions. He would rather wrap himself in the shroud of a martyred President or represent himself as a humanitarian who was principally concerned about the welfare of captured American pilots. That is the image he would like to project. But reality is another matter.

Although no politician in his right mind would now want to be closely identified with America's discredited policy in Vietnam, for a decade Jackson was one of its most enthusiastic advocates. His faith in the power of the military to "restore the balance of power" in Southeast Asia knew no limits, and he accepted as dogma the Pentagon's transmogrification of the limited-war theories dreamed up in academia by so-called defense intellectuals. Generals would speak of falling dominoes in Asia should Vietnam be "lost" to the communists, and Jackson believed. They said escalation would "turn the screw" on Hanoi and force her to sue for peace, and again he believed. When reality later shattered his faith in these abstractions, his evangelical ardor cooled noticeably, but he could not bring himself to admit he had been wrong. Because Vietnam gave the United States an opportunity to match its theories and weapons of limited war against the communists', a general would later refer to it privately as "our Spain." To Jackson, it was a "most serious test of our national character and democratic processes."

Jackson viewed the struggle in Indochina from the perspective of the cold war: a skirmish in the global battle between the forces of light and darkness, the free world versus the communists. His simplistic point of view can be traced to 1954, when the United States was considering sending massive aid and possibly troops to the beleaguered French in their foredoomed attempt to retain control of their colonies in Indochina. Of course, every member of Congress was then an anti-communist, but not all of them saw Indochina in black and white. John Kennedy and Henry Jackson, for example, were freshman Democrats with similarly liberal voting records, but though both were cold warriors, Kennedy grasped the complexities of the situation in Indochina and the difficulties involved in fashioning an American policy there. Jackson, on the other hand, was impatient for President Eisenhower to formulate some policy—*any* policy—so he could support it.

On April 6, Kennedy gave a major speech about Indochina on the floor of the Senate. Afterward, Jackson joined him in a colloquy which showed just how different their perspectives were.

"I am frankly of the belief," said Kennedy, "that no amount of American military assistance in Indochina can conquer an enemy which is everywhere and at the same time nowhere, 'an enemy of the people' which has the sympathy and covert support of the people." He properly blamed the deteriorating situation on the French for their failure to prepare their colonies for independence.

Jackson commended Kennedy for his "brilliant analysis of the problem we face in Indochina" and suggested that "the genius of our policy must be to give full expression to the basic desires and wishes of the people of that area. I believe that their deep-rooted desire is for freedom." Having said that, however, he turned preacher. "In my opinion, the Congress of the United States, Democrats and Republicans, have a responsibility to support the administration in trying to save Southeast Asia."

Kennedy reacted to this notion of a crusade by remarking that Indochina could not be "saved" unless neighboring nations were willing to shoulder some of the burden. In words which proved prophetic, he warned: "For the United States to intervene unilaterally and to send troops into the most difficult terrain in the world, with the Chinese able to pour in unlimited manpower, would mean that we would face a situation which would be far more difficult than even that we encountered in Korea. It seems to me it would be a hopeless situation." Whether the French withdrew immediately or the United States sent its troops "unilaterally in support of the French on the current political basis," the result in the long run, he said, would be the same. "Both policies would end in disaster."

Jackson was not on the same wavelength as his colleague: so, as he does so often when confronted by a new situation, he fell back on his past experience. He recalled that "when Greece was about to fall" President Truman "came before Congress and recommended a policy, which later became known as the Truman doctrine. He outlined what he expected of Congress and Congress promptly responded. Greece was saved." To Jackson, then, the solution seemed as simple and straightforward as the script in a Western movie. The sheriff (President) would deputize a posse (Congress), and together they would mete out justice to the outlaws (communists).

Kennedy brought him up short, however, by pointedly noting that, in Greece, "we went to the assistance of a regime or a government which had the wholehearted support of the people against the communist guerrillas." Was Jackson, he seemed to be asking, trying to equate Greek *nationalists* to French *colonialists*?

Jackson must have sensed he had overstated his case, and he protested that he did not want his remarks "to be construed as asking that our people intervene on behalf of French colonialism." His apparent appreciation of nationalism and the desire of the Vietnamese for independence was short-lived, however, and a few minutes later he concluded with an even stronger restatement of his original theme. "The reason why we are concerned in Indochina, above everything else," he stressed, "is to prevent Indochina, and with it all of Southeast Asia, from falling into the hands of the communists."

Jackson toured Asia during the 1955 Christmas congressional recess, and upon his return he advocated the United States draw a definite "defense line" in the Far East. "If we do not stop aggression," he said, "we might as well sign a quitclaim deed to the balance of Asia." It was a revealing choice of words. Asia, in his mind, was "ours"; we held the deed and must stand ready to defend our property. To accomplish this he suggested we establish an Asian version of NATO based on the premise that "a trespass on one is a trespass on all." The task, then, was clear: "We have to do in Asia what we have been able to do successfully in Western Europe—that is, put up an effective no trespassing sign—and back it up with all the resources of the area, plus our own."

Jackson was not only willing to draw the line in Asia, he was prepared to accept the consequences should it be crossed. So, five years later, when a recently inaugurated President Kennedy decided to send one hundred more Special Forces to Vietnam, Jackson's support was unequivocal. If additional American soldiers were needed, he declared, "we must pay the price." Of course, the price then seemed small, but even as it grew, his determination that it be paid never wavered.

In 1963 Jackson called the Army the "key to victory in Vietnam," and he was optimistic that "with a few more shoves, we might get a bandwagon rolling. Little successes can lead in this situation to more and bigger victories. Confidence in the government [of South Vietnam] could grow rapidly once it is evident that the government is beginning to get the upper hand." Sensing success within reach, he suggested it was then "a psychologically opportune moment to step up the scale and intensity of our programs in all reasonable ways."

Again, his choice of language was indicative of his perception and mental processes. The idea of a "scale" of warfare which has discrete levels of "intensity" is central to escalation theory. Although defense intellectuals had written about escalation ladders strictly as metaphorical devices, the military, with little thought, put metaphor into practice. I still have vivid memories of a supremely confident Air Force general explaining to a group of junior officers how we would succeed in Southeast Asia. All we had to do was go one step higher on the scale of intensity than the North Vietnamese and victory would be ours: superior technology and firepower would carry the day. I suspect that Jackson received similar briefings and believed them.

Although he no longer talks about escalation theory, Jackson was once among its true believers. "The more limited one's objectives," he said in 1965, "the more limited is the power that has to be brought to bear in achieving them. This point has relevance today in Vietnam. . . . Our goals are limited, and because they are, I believe that we will be able to achieve them with a limited use of American power."

In another speech that year, however, he acknowledged that the war had resulted from several factors. "Politically, economically, psychologically, and militarily, conditions developed which made South Vietnam ripe for communist exploitation and violence." Yet, when it came to finding a solution, he focused on just one factor: the military. "There is a direct relation between the decline in the political situation and the deterioration in the military situation—and nothing will so transform the politics of South Vietnam as a string of military successes."

If escalation held out the promise of ultimate victory, that did not necessarily mean it would come immediately. Unlike Secretary of Defense Robert McNamara and General William Westmoreland, who kept seeing light at the end of the tunnel, Jackson was realistic enough to acknowledge that the war could not be quickly won. "It is wrong to cry 'Wolf, Wolf,' " he said. "But it is equally wrong to predict that victory lies just around the corner when it doesn't, when, in fact, there isn't even a corner visible down the road. To arouse great but unjustified expectations may quiet a few critics today, but it will only sharpen their doubts and disillusion tomorrow." (Compare that to his assertion to Mike Wallace that he had been "violently opposed to a protracted conflict.")

So, even though Jackson's faith in escalation theory was misplaced, he correctly judged that no quick victory was possible. He saw Vietnam as an extension of the long cold war which had begun in Greece and had been going on nearly two decades. "We did not seek this struggle," he said, "but we cannot escape it." Thus, in one sense, he was not fooled about Vietnam. Although he had been overly optimistic at first, he soon came to understand that Vietnam would require a massive investment of men and money. Nonetheless, he saw no reason to change his mind and continued to believe that "we must pay the price."

The failure of Prime Minister Neville Chamberlain to discern Hitler's true purpose and prepare England for war had made a lasting impression on Jackson, who feared that history might be repeated in Vietnam. He also began to see himself as a latter-day Churchill and began appropriating Churchillian phrases, such as "the will to stay the course"—he used that one several times—for the titles of his speeches. Indeed, he drew the parallel so tightly that he later blamed the lack of American progress in Vietnam, in part, on those who opposed the war. "It is not a pleasant fact to recall," he said, "but the truth is that the peace movement of the thirties helped to bring on World War II, not to prevent it. And it is a fact that the well-intentioned advocates of immediate withdrawal of our armed forces from Vietnam should ponder." By the end of 1965 he was recommending that the size of the American troop commitment be doubled.

Beginning in 1966 Jackson started identifying "Red Chinese expansionism" as the real enemy in Southeast Asia. At the World Affairs Council in Philadelphia that February, he explained this abstraction.

> Peking has not tried to conceal its purposes. Red China has helped the Vietcong with material support and political direction. Tibet was gobbled up long ago. India has experienced a military invasion—carefully calculated to lower Indian prestige. Red China supported last fall's abortive communist coup in Indonesia. The move against Thailand has started, there are signs of renewed communist efforts in the Philippines, and guerrilla units have been identified in South Korea. In the end, the spread of Chinese domination could threaten even securely based nations such as Japan.
>
> Hanoi, of course, is not just China's proxy. In part, the North Vietnamese aggression is the result of Hanoi's own ambition and

efforts. But from Peking's perspective Hanoi's victory over South Vietnam would clear the way for its own drive into Thailand and elsewhere into Southeast Asia. Vietnam is a place to demonstrate to the Chinese communists that we can successfully help those who resist subjugation when they become a target of the so-called "war of national liberation."

As these excerpts make clear, Jackson had swallowed the domino theory whole, and he would regurgitate it often in his speeches over the next three years. Indeed, in 1967, he began to assert that

> . . . the Vietnam problem does not make sense except as we fit it into our conception of where we are and where we are going in the world. If the stakes in Vietnam were restricted to Vietnam, we would be concerned and unhappy at the fate of the Vietnamese people, but it is not likely that we would have taken a stand there. For if the struggle had no wider implications, we could not justify the cost of that stand in terms of a clear and present threat to our national interests.

It was a remarkable admission. No longer were we fighting to help a gallant ally, nor were we trying to attain the limited objectives Jackson had alluded to two years before. Even the enemy was different. Instead of flesh-and-blood North Vietnamese and Viet Cong, our target was now an abstraction, "Red Chinese expansionism," and our goal was yet another abstraction, "to create a reliable balance of forces." He was still convinced, these changes notwithstanding, that the United States would ultimately succeed and that "benefits will accrue not only to the non-communist countries of Asia but also to ourselves and to our European allies." He firmly believed that China was intent on exporting "wars of national liberation," and, he said, "I find nothing to encourage me to believe that Peking will refrain from exploiting the weakness of its neighbors—unless it is checked by countervailing power."

In 1969 Jackson underwent a change of mind—and, later, heart—with respect to China. He began tentatively that March when he said "we ought to keep in contact with the enemy to know where he is and what he's up to." But he was not yet ready to suggest a more cooperative relationship. "You don't change a bad character's habits by trading with him," he argued, and to emphasize his point, he added: "We were trading scrap iron to Japan on the eve of Pearl Harbor."

By the end of the year, however, he was striking a more conciliatory note. "While the Peking regime continuously has aided and abetted Hanoi in South Vietnam," he said, "there is evidence that the regime's own military policies remain cautious and of a low-risk nature. The [Chinese] refrain is constantly reiterated: 'We shall not attack unless we are attacked.' " Thus, within the space of a year, the threat of "Red Chinese expansionism," which had been his principal fear in Vietnam, evaporated into thin air.

Jackson never looked back, and five years later he made his first visit to the People's Republic of China and returned to report that "the center of Chinese concern is what they perceive to be the unreliable and expansionist nature of the Soviet Union." When he was asked on NBC's "Meet the Press" if it was not inconsistent for him to advocate trade sanctions against the Soviet Union because of its restrictive emigration policies while promoting greater trade with China, which has similar policies, he cagily replied: "The Russians are asking for economic help. The Chinese are not. . . . The Chinese are paying cash on the barrelhead. The Russians are not. They are asking for long-term credits, and I think we have a right to attach conditions when long-term credits or subsidies are being asked for."

In his 1974 report he recommended that the United States "move toward diplomatic recognition of the People's Republic of China." He accurately traced his change of thinking to 1969 "when developments in China—coupled with the demonstrable growth in Soviet conventional and strategic power—suggested the appropriateness of a new American approach to Peking." At that time, he recalled: "I advocated that we attempt to put our relations on a less-rigid footing."

Jackson's present position on China indicates he is capable of growth, and that is a commendable trait in a politician many consider an ideologue. But his change of mind about China also raises serious questions. If we were fighting in Vietnam, as he repeatedly said until 1969, to thwart "Red Chinese expansionism," why did he continue to support that war long after he concluded the Chinese threat no longer existed? If, as he said in 1967, "the fate of the Vietnamese people" was not reason enough for the United States to "have taken a stand there," for what cause did another twenty thousand American servicemen die?

If we accept Jackson's remarks prior to 1969 as honest statements of his reasons for supporting the war in Vietnam, then we are forced to conclude that the intellectual underpinnings for that support gave way when he concluded China did not intend to expand into Vietnam. Once the specter of China taking over one country after another in Southeast Asia vanished, so did any plausible reason for believing in the domino theory. To put it mildly, these were important changes. Yet, paradoxically, Jackson's voting record after 1969 indicates no change at all in his support for the war. Although he did vote for an amendment prohibiting funds for military operations in Cambodia after June 30, 1970, it was largely a symbolic gesture, because President Nixon had already promised that all American forces would have concluded their "incursion" into Cambodia by that date. On other war-related issues, such as cutting off funds for defoliation in Vietnam that August, Jackson continued to fly with the hawks.

In 1971, however, he began to back-pedal away from his once-vociferous support of the war although he still voted with the Nixon administration. Without Chinese expansionism and the domino theory to fall back on, his answers to questions about American policy in Vietnam seemed more and more the product of a visceral sort of chauvinism. We can't "cut and run" was a frequent retort. Another was his prediction that a "horrible slaughter" would follow should Congress compel the withdrawal of American forces. But, when a combat veteran of that war visited his office and challenged him on that point ("I contend there's been a horrible slaughter already"), Jackson quickly tried to turn the discussion to the educational benefits of the GI bill. He was no longer the self-assured cold warrior where Vietnam was concerned, but he could neither bring himself to denounce the administration's war policy nor offer a serious alternative of his own. He just went along.

"I have supported my President, both Mr. Johnson, Mr.

Kennedy before him, in this regard, and now Mr. Nixon, in his efforts to bring about a sensible solution to this problem," he said in 1971 on ABC's "Issues and Answers." "I believe the President must be given enough leeway here, enough flexibility to bring this war to a conclusion as fast as possible without tying his hands so that he must do certain things by a certain time. If that is the position, then we should announce that we are going to leave [the] Paris [negotiations], we should announce we are not going to do anything about prisoners of war, and we should leave tomorrow."

Bereft of any plausible reasons to justify continuing the war, Jackson avoided any substantive discussion of Vietnam and, instead, began to focus his wrath on critics of the Nixon administration's policies. Jackson is an emotional man: a fact he tries to conceal. For example, when he returned from a trip to Vietnam in 1965, the Seattle *Times* reported: "Jackson broke down and paused when he described a visit to a civilian hospital where an elderly surgeon prepared to give his own blood to a nine-year-old girl maimed by the Viet Cong and then to operate on the child. 'I'm sorry,' " he said after regaining his composure. " 'Please excuse me.' " (The military often arranged for visiting congressmen to see evidence of the enemy's brutality to reinforce political support for the war; the tactic worked particularly well on those legislators who had never served in combat.) So, when he later began to attack critics of the war, he may well have connected them in his mind with the dead and maimed he saw in Vietnam. His remarks to a labor group in New York were not untypical: "Our party has room for hawks and doves, but not for mockingbirds who chirp gleefully at those who are shooting at American boys."

Emotional outbursts such as these were relatively few; for the most part, he simply avoided the subject. During the spring of 1971, for instance, he gave major foreign-policy speeches in three cities but relegated his mention of Vietnam to a single paragraph in each and then delivered lofty pronouncements on American policy in Europe, the Middle East, and China.

When General Nguyen Van Thieu was elected president of South Vietnam with no other candidates on the ballot, Jackson seemed genuinely outraged, and many careful political observers thought he was about to break with the administration on the war. But he did not, and even after he declared himself a presidential candidate later that year (1971), he continued to avoid any substantive discussion of Vietnam. When reporters pressed the issue, he would serve up a bromide: "It seems to me you ought to give the President a little elbow room." Or, "I think what has to be done here is to get our prisoners back with the withdrawal of all of our forces . . . [hold] an election [in South Vietnam] that will be under international supervision."

Jackson had plenty of ideas about limited war when the United States became involved in Vietnam, but he never had a plan for peace. Yet, when some of his political allies in Washington State tried to discuss with him the war and possible paths to peace, they were coolly rebuffed. His close friend Stanley Golub, who could talk to him about Vietnam, seemed to elicit little of substance. "I always considered it a civil war," says Golub. "He [Jackson] thought the result in South Korea was good. . . . He was concerned about the loss of life in Vietnam, but he felt a 'Korean stalemate' would prevent [communist] expansion."

Jackson stood by Nixon on Vietnam to the bitter end. Occasionally he would voice a doubt about a particular aspect of the President's policy—in muted tones, to be sure—but he never turned such doubts into meaningful votes against the war. On May 31, 1973, after all American POWs had been repatriated, an amendment to end the bombing of Cambodia came before the Senate. At last the doves found a majority, and the measure passed, 63 to 19. Jackson, however, remained an unrepentant hawk.

Finally, in the spring of 1975, when the government of Nguyen Van Thieu was being overrun, Jackson broke with the past and forthrightly opposed sending more aid to South Vietnam.

Vietnam cost this nation more than fifty thousand dead. There are no reliable estimates of the number of Vietnamese who were killed—hundreds of thousands certainly, perhaps a million. Also left in the rubble were the limited-war theories Jackson had so enthusiastically espoused. Billions of bombs and shells failed to make escalation decisive, and the domino theory collapsed once China's limited regional ambitions were understood. Jackson's neatly black-and-white globe where the free world battled communism proved a simplistic delusion now believed only by extreme right-wingers. But rather than face reality, Jackson retreated behind a wall of mindless platitudes and chauvinistic rhetoric and waited for the problem to disappear.

Jackson, by all accounts, is not an introspective man. He is not the sort of person who lies awake at night questioning his beliefs and confronting his misjudgments. As more than one of his friends told me: "He cannot bring himself to say: 'I was wrong.' " That is certainly the case where Vietnam is concerned. Politicians are naturally reluctant to admit mistakes, and in minor matters that trait would merely be objectionable. But when war and peace are at issue, such hubris in a President could be fatal to millions.

When the United States began to increase its combat forces in Vietnam, Jackson invoked the memory of Great Britain's wartime leader as well as Churchillian rhetoric to stir the nation into accepting the challenge of Vietnam. "We did not seek this struggle," he said, "but we cannot avoid it." He was wrong on both counts.

This nation was led into Vietnam by men who, like Jackson, did not question America's global crusade against communism, but when it became evident that whatever we might gain by force of arms could not possibly be worth the price, they lacked the strength of character to admit their mistake. Such men know how to start wars but, alas, not how to stop them. "We must pay the price," said Senator Jackson. And we did.

CHAPTER

13

Is He Good for the Jews?

DURING THE Diaspora Jews lived and prospered in many countries but always with an eye sensitive to changes in the political climate. Their religion, culture, and language set them apart from the communities in which they lived and from the leaders who made the law and commanded the army. Their seemingly disproportionate wealth and influence, real or imagined, made them frequent targets for the frustrations of the majority and the calculations of political opportunists. So, when a previously unknown politician gained power, speculation about how he would approach commercial or even martial affairs was subordinated to a single question: Is he good for the Jews? The death of six million Jews in the holocaust, the present plight of Jews in the Soviet Union and certain Moslem countries, and the precarious existence of the State of Israel have only served to reinforce the validity of that question for many people.

Since 1970 no member of Congress has tried harder to assist Israel and Soviet Jewry than the junior senator from Washington. Rabbi Mitchell Wohlberg of Beth Sholom Synagogue in Washington, D.C., no doubt spoke for many American Jews when he said, "We have a hero and his name is Henry Jackson. More than any other leader on the American political scene, Senator Henry Jackson has been there in our times of trouble and pain."

The event which catapulted Jackson into the leadership

role only a non-Jewish member of Congress can credibly fill was an amendment to the Defense Procurement Act which he proposed in 1970 and the Armed Services Committee adopted. It made an essentially open-ended commitment to fulfill Israel's need for military weapons. This was its key sentence: "In order to restore and maintain the military balance in the Middle East, by furnishing to Israel the means of providing for its own security, the President is authorized to transfer to Israel, by sale, credit sale or guaranty, such aircraft, and equipment appropriate to use, maintain and protect such aircraft, as may be required to counteract any past, present, or future increased military assistance provided to other countries of the Middle East."

Senator J. William Fulbright, then chairman of the Foreign Relations Committee, opposed Jackson's provision because he believed it usurped his committee's jurisdiction over the Foreign Military Sales Act. When he countered with an amendment to try to reassert that jurisdiction, Jackson warned the Senate that its adoption "would deprive Israel of the support she needs both to strengthen her hand in the current negotiations and to protect herself from Soviet ambitions in the Middle East." The effect of this amendment would have been to restrict military aid to Israel to the statutory limit of $250 million under the Foreign Military Sales Act, a level Jackson called "woefully inadequate." When the issue came to a vote on September 1, 1970, Jackson won by an overwhelming margin, 87 to 7. His provision gave Congress the authority to increase military aid to Israel beyond the statutory limit, and a subsequent appropriations bill provided $500 million for that purpose. Getting Congress to spend an additional quarter of a billion dollars without even a *pro forma* hearing on the matter was quite a legislative feat.

Since then, Jackson has annually led Senate efforts for increased aid to Israel and tried (unsuccessfully) to use an amendment to liberalized trade legislation to induce the Soviet Union to permit more Jews to emigrate to Israel. He is now so closely identified with these issues that Jamil Baroody, the loquacious Saudi Arabian ambassador to the United Nations was moved to ask: "Who is this Senator Jackson, who hails from a distance of 6000 miles away from the Middle East, to be the arbiter of the people of Palestine, when he gives the impression that he is more Zionist than the Zionists, more Jewish than the Jews?"

Jackson's standing and image as a "defender of Israel" are clear and unambiguous. He believes fervently in that nation's cause and in the need to help Jews who are persecuted throughout the world. "No one could smell it if it were a phony position better than I," says Stanley Golub. "And I know it isn't."

How did he come to this position? Some friends suggest he inherited the traditional Scandinavian concern for social justice from his parents. Golub, for example, tells a story the senator himself has often related about young Jackson and a "Jewish peddler who had a pushcart. . . . Kids used to follow him around and call him by anti-Semitic names." When he told his mother about the incident, she "gave him a lecture on the subject, telling him how wrong it was. He [later] had Jewish friends in Everett, but that didn't mean much in terms of votes. It's not a self-serving position."

Another incident during the Everett years involved a group called the "Silver Shirts." In a seven-page document ("The Jackson Record on Israel: The Origin and Background of One Senator's Stand") which was written by a graduate student but typed and distributed to reporters by Jackson's office, an article from the *Jewish Daily Forward* is favorably quoted:

> His political career began in 1936 at the age of 24, when he headed the first Voters League for the re-election of President Franklin D. Roosevelt, in his home town of Everett, Washington, after graduation from the University of Washington law school. Two years later, he was elected prosecutor of Snohomish County. Though there were only a handful of Jewish families in the whole county at the time, Jackson was instrumental in running out of town the notorious "Silver Shirts," a fascist grouping of the 1930s, because he abhorred their activities which included the molesting of a Jewish family in the area.

My research in the files of the Everett *Daily Herald* turned up no contemporary account of the event; so the source of the

Forward's account was probably either the senator or his staff. Indeed, Jackson sometimes uses a similar characterization ("I ran them out of town") when he tells Jewish audiences about the Silver Shirts. However, when I asked him and two of his friends from Everett about the incident, I was given more equivocal interpretations of what transpired.

This is how Jackson describes the episode: "The Silver Shirts had been operating in our county and in Everett. . . . They had a small but vicious group in our county. We had a small Jewish community: ten or twelve merchants. . . . What happened, as I recall . . . was that they had the swastika painted on their storefronts or their homes, and we had every reason to believe that it was the Silver Shirts. They had a meeting in Lombard Hall, across from the labor temple. . . . We heard about the meeting, and Mr. [Phil] Sheridan and I went down there and warned them about existing state law, which was very broad at that time, about inciting to riot and to engage in a course of conduct that could be injurious to the rights of others. . . . I said that the first instance this occurs again I am going to bring action under the criminal statutes against all those involved. That was the end of their operation in the open—they had an open meeting—whether they met in cell groups I don't know, but that ended their overt activity. . . . There were leaflets [after that], but there were no threats against the merchants at that time, and they were cearly threatened [before]. . . . I can't recall specifically whether they put the swastika business on there with soap or paint . . . but all the elements of fear and what-not were there."

Phil Sheridan, who was one of Jackson's deputy prosecutors, has a slightly different recollection: "We had a little incident. We don't have a large Jewish population, but there are some substantial merchants. We had some complaints of subtle threats, and we did learn that a meeting was being held in Lombard Hall—anyone could rent it. Jackson went to the meeting and told them he'd not tolerate any intimidation of others. . . . He did not put it provocatively but gave them a lecture on the Fourteenth Amendment, told them the law and the consequences. I think I recall that one complaint may have been a swastika on a porch or soaped on a window. The collation of evidence indicated these people. Jackson laid it out in a matter-of-fact way."

John Salter, who managed Jackson's successful campaign for prosecuting attorney in 1938, has a much different recollection: "We went to several meetings; a cell was quite active. Some of the older ones were Ku Kluxers. We used to get in confrontations with them. In Everett they were not evil people, just misguided. So, we'd ask questions or say things contrary to what they were being told. Three or four of us sat out in the audience and needled them. There were no swastikas on houses or stores. These were mostly older people, not younger ones. They were not marchers. They had no uniforms: they were too poor to buy them. They'd call Roosevelt a Jew and say all Jews are communists. All I can recall is that they just met."

This episode occurred in 1939; so one must take into account dimming memories. But the facts involved are of less interest than the differing perceptions of these three friends. To Jackson it was nothing less than an epic encounter between good and evil, the fair-minded prosecutor standing up to "a small but vicious group." Sheridan, who is now a judge in Snohomish County, recalls that Jackson made his presentation to the Silver Shirts in a "matter-of-fact way." Salter, who was Jackson's top political operative for many years, paints a rather pathetic picture of a reactionary fringe group who "were not evil people, just misguided" and "had no uniforms [because] they were too poor to buy them."

Jackson is fond of quoting Orwell's observation about dictatorships where "yesterday's weather can be changed by decree," but reinterpreting past positions to demonstrate visionary qualities or depth of sincerity is a trait common to politicians in every land. Political writers can often set the record straight by a more disinterested reading of what a politician asserts he did or did not do. but the mind tends to telescope events which took place over many years and interpret them in the light of the immediate past. That tendency, reinforced by an editor's deadline, has resulted in more than one writer's uncritically accepting a politician's revision of history. That is precisely what has happened with

Jackson's reinterpretation of his record of nearly forty years on issues of particular concern to American Jews.

The varying accounts of the Silver Shirts episode present comparatively minor discrepancies, but they seem to indicate that Jackson is attempting to change yesterday's record by decree. The discrepancies become serious when he recounts what he thought and did in the 1940s, perhaps the most fateful decade for the Jewish people since the Diaspora. When he spoke at Yeshiva University in New York City in June of 1973, he gave this dramatic account of his awakening: "I was at Buchenwald three days after its liberation in 1945, when it was still an occupied camp. I knew then in my gut what before I had known only in my head—that the holocaust is the central political experience of our time and that it must never happen again." That theme is repeated with minor variations almost every time he addresses a Jewish audience, and it has gone unchallenged by political reporters in every recent evaluation of his record I have seen.

If in fact Jackson believed "that the holocaust is the central political experience of our time," he did remarkably little to show it. Putting a written statement in the *Congressional Record* or making a short speech on the floor of the House after he returned from Europe would have communicated his concern to others. Instead, he said and wrote nothing about Buchenwald and the holocaust although several of his colleagues who made the same visit did. What one finds reflected in the pages of the *Record* of 1945 is a Representative Jackson heavily preoccupied with legislation of interest to the Pacific Northwest. (By contrast, in December of 1973, an aide gave me a packet containing a few of the senator's speeches and reprints from the *Record* of the three preceding years concerning Israel and related issues; it weighed over three pounds.)

Jackson did, however, speak to reporters who accompanied the congressional delegation to Buchenwald, and the *New York Times* reported his remarks: "We heard atrocity stories from the last war which were not verified, but now we have seen them with our own eyes, and they are the most sordid I have ever imagined."

When I mentioned to two of Jackson's foreign-policy aides

that a single sentence in the *Times* hardly indicates that he was as affected by Buchenwald then as he now claims to have been, Dorothy Fosdick's reaction was sharp. "What the hell are you trying to prove?" she snapped. Richard Perle was not so emotional. He told me he thought Jackson had written an article about Buchenwald for the Seattle *Times*, but an inquiry to the library of that newspaper produced only a short clip from an Associated Press story. " 'We must act now while witnesses are available if we are going to ferret out the men responsible for the acts in the camps.' Trials, Jackson said, should be held in the communities where the atrocities occurred, 'so that the German people will know what happened, if they don't already know.' "

These two contemporary news accounts confirm that Jackson was shocked by the "sordid" events which had occurred at Buchenwald and wanted those responsible brought to justice, but that is the extent of his public record on the matter in 1945—no articles, speeches, or legislation. This is hardly what one would expect of a politician who claims he recognized *then* that "the holocaust is the central political experience of our time."

Perle opened a large manila folder, which he refused to let me see, and read from one of the papers enclosed. He told me Jackson had "contributed" to a 1944 book entitled *America and Palestine*. He then read a sentence from that book which he attributed to Jackson: "If I can forward the work of making the Jewish homeland come true, you can count on my efforts in that great humanitarian cause." It sounded quite convincing, but when I asked what else he said, Perle dodged the question in words reminiscent of Nixon's press secretary, Ron Ziegler. "*That*," Perle emphasized, "is the operative quote."

America and Palestine has long since been out of print, but the Library of Congress, a five-minute walk from Jackson's office, had a copy. Jackson, I found, had "contributed" to the book, but so had 317 other House members and 77 senators. The author, Reuben Fink, a Zionist, had solicited their opinions and appended them to his otherwise brief tract. The sentence Perle had read proved to be an abridged version which conveyed something other than the original context. This is the verbatim text of Jackson's statement:

> Through following the developments in regard to Jewish affairs all over the world, I have come to the conclusion that the establishment of a Jewish National Homeland in Palestine would be a great stride forward in the solution of the Jewish problem.
>
> Of course, the destruction of Nazism in all its phases is a necessary prerequisite to the ending of Jewish persecution.
>
> In view of Dr. Lowdermilk's report stating that Palestine could easily support four million more people through land reclamation, the opening of free immigration there would not only mean giving the Jewish people a homeland but would help rebuild the country to a prosperous, happy land for Jew and Arab alike.
>
> If in any way, through my offices as a Congressman, I can forward the work of making the dream of a Jewish Homeland in Palestine come true, you can count on my most earnest efforts in this great humanitarian cause.

There is nothing in this statement which shows the thirty-two-year-old congressman advocated pan-Arabism, but neither is there any evidence he was a Zionist. The term "Jewish National Homeland in Palestine" in the context of the times did not mean a Jewish *state*: it was an intentionally ambiguous formulation similar to the Balfour Declaration of 1917 in which Great Britain promised "the establishment in Palestine of a national home for the Jewish people." His use of the phrase "a prosperous, happy land for Jew and Arab alike" shows he knew how to use such circumlocutions. In short, he supported the establishment of a *secular* state once Britain relinquished its mandate in Palestine. Oddly enough, that is what Yasser Arafat, the head of the Palestine Liberation Organization, ostensibly advocated at the United Nations in November of 1974.

There is nothing sinister or anti-Semitic about his former position. It was the sort of noncontroversial stand the young legislator usually took on national or international affairs. He was a cautious, provincial representative from the Pacific Northwest intent on doing a good job for his constituents and getting reelected. He saw no reason to side with the Zionists in 1944 just as he saw no reason to oppose them when President Truman supported the creation of a Jewish state in 1948. He simply went along with national policy. What is deceptive (to put it charitably) is his ex post facto Zionism and exploitation of the holocaust to explain his conversion. "I've been interested in the State of Israel since I saw Buchenwald after World War II," he asserted at a press conference in Chicago in December of 1973. Then, turning to the Jewish sponsors of his visit, he smiled and said, "When I was a congressman, I had just twelve Jewish families in my district; so you can see I supported Israel to get votes." That night the Chicago State of Israel Bonds organization presented their "Man of the Year" Award to Jackson.

If he is cautious, he is also calculating. He had no reason to oppose Israel once it had been created, but he stood to gain little in his home state by being among its more visible champions. (Anti-Semitism and anti-Catholicism were not isolated phenomena in his native region at the time.) So he made few statements about Israel and the Middle East during the 1940s, and when he did, they tended to be of the noncontroversial sort. When Truman spoke in favor of allowing 100,000 European Jews to immigrate to Palestine in 1946, Jackson backed him up and criticized the British for arresting members of the Jewish Agency for Palestine who were trying to arrange that immigration. The following year he accused the British of making "an unholy mess of the Holy Land" but then remarked that they had "broken faith so many times that neither side can trust them." That phrase "neither side" seems to indicate he still supported the even-handed policy implicit in his 1944 statement in *America and Palestine.*

In 1950, a twenty-four-line squib appeared in the *Congressional Record* commemorating Israel's second anniversary. "Born and nurtured during times of greatest adversity, this Republic has demonstrated to a world torn between two systems of government that democracy is made of stern stuff," wrote Jackson. "In my opinion there is little doubt that the first two years in the life of the Republic of Israel will be brightly illuminated in the pages of the history of man's struggle for a better, more humane life."

The complete Jackson record on Israel and Jewish issues for his twelve years in the House is not much larger than the foregoing quotations. His Senate record prior to 1970 is similarly sparse. Although he signed various Senate resolutions and voted for aid to Israel, he continued to maintain his low public profile. When he spoke about the Middle East, it was invariably in the context of its potential for becoming a U.S.-Soviet battlefield. He would not rhapsodize about Israel's deserts being turned into orchards until much later.

Jackson made his first visit to Israel in 1956; it was one stop on an extensive itinerary which took him to the Soviet Union and the Near East. Afterward, he wrote a five-part series of articles, "My 10,000 Miles Through Soviet Russia," for the Seattle *Post-Intelligencer.* That he saw Israel and the Arab states through the prism of the Cold War is evident from the title of the final installment: "Soviets Stirring Witch's Brew in the Middle East." He had previously called Egyptian President Gamal Abdel Nasser "another Hitler but worse because he is supported by the Soviet Union." In the article, he referred to Israel as "an oasis of civilized progress in the Arab world" but, more importantly, "one of our bulwarks against Nasser." Once the Egyptian leader had been blocked, he predicted "we also will have stopped—or at least seriously impeded—the Soviet Union's bid for control of the Middle East and Africa."

Jackson had also visited Jordan, and his praise for the Arab kingdom almost matched his favorable assessment of Israel. Indeed, he was still even-handed enough to note that "the story of the Soviet Union's treatment of Moslems and Jews within the USSR has not been told to the people of this strategic area." It seems his interest in both countries centered on their role as "bulwarks" against Nasser and, by extension, the Soviet Union. He may well have regarded Israel as an "oasis of civilized progress," but his speeches in that decade focused on her strategic value in the cold war rather than her intrinsic value as a Western-style democracy.

In the following decade the pattern did not change. Jackson would periodically point out the danger of Soviet ambitions in the Middle East, but he rarely talked about Israel per se. He continued to put his name to various resolutions, such as Senator Abraham Ribicoff's in 1963 condemning Soviet persecution of religious persons, but he was usually one of several dozen cosponsors and never a leader.

Even the 1967 war in the Middle East failed to turn him into a vociferous champion of Israel. He criticized the Secretary General of the United Nations, U Thant, in May for "his precipitate action in withdrawing the United Nations buffer [3,400-man emergency force] that has helped keep the peace between Israel and the Arabs for 11 years," the *New York Times* reported. He suggested that the UN "explore alternative ways of maintaining a UN peace-keeping presence in the area." but he made it plain the United States ought to keep its hands off the area. "The Near East is one area in which the major powers are not directly involved and in which the United Nations has had its best chance to prove its peace-keeping capacity," he said. Two weeks later the Six-Day War began.

To understand the true significance of his position one must recall his 1962 speech: "The US in the UN." At that time he downplayed the importance of the world organization and pointedly complained that its affairs absorbed "a disproportionate amount of the energy of our highest officials. . . . The truth is, though we have not often spoken it in recent years, that the best hope for peace with justice does not lie in the United Nations. Indeed the truth is almost exactly the reverse. The best hope for the United Nations lies in the maintenance of peace. In our deeply divided world, peace depends on the power and unity of the Atlantic Community and on the skill of our direct diplomacy."

The implication is clear. The UN might be able to attend to minor peace-keeping chores, but "the power and unity of the Atlantic Community"—meaning the United States—would have to maintain the peace in areas of major importance to this nation. Thus his remarks prior to the Six-Day War imply that the impending Arab-Israeli confrontation was of relatively minor significance to the United States. How else are we to interpret his suggestion that the UN "explore alternative ways of maintaining a UN peace-keeping presence" in the Middle East?

Of even greater relevance is what Jackson said or, rather, did not say after the United Nations failed in "its best chance to prove its peace-keeping capacity." Once war broke out, congressmen began speaking about their concern for Israel on the floor of the House and Senate, to reporters directly and through press releases. Jackson, unaccountably, was silent.

The indexes of the *Congressional Record, New York Times,* Washington *Post* and Seattle *Post-Intelligencer* indicate he made no public comments about the Six-Day War while it was being fought or immediately thereafter. If he had been an obscure freshman representative, one might assume his views were simply not considered newsworthy enough to be printed, but that was hardly the case. Jackson in 1967 was a twenty-six-year veteran of Congress, chairman of the Interior Committee, and a prominent member of the Armed Services Committee. If he had spoken about the war, it would have received extensive coverage. The conclusion is inescapable: he chose not to be closely identified with Israel in that time of need.

Another glaring inconsistency in Jackson's record is his membership in two prominent "social" organizations which have a long history of anti-Semitism. One is Seattle's University Club, an exclusive group of the state's business and professional elite, which has excluded Jews and blacks. Jackson joined in the mid-1950s.

The other is the prestigious Chevy Chase Club located in the Maryland suburb of Washington, D.C. Jackson joined in 1965, and as late as 1970 Jewish guests of members were not permitted to use the club's "public facilities," such as locker rooms and toilets. "I couldn't believe it," recalls a former member. "I wanted to give a wedding reception there, and they told me: 'Fine. Will you be having any guests of the Jewish persuasion?' I said, 'You're damned right I will.' And they said, 'Well, that's fine, love to have them, but there is one thing you know. . . .' Well, they told me my Jewish guests couldn't go to the bathroom. So . . . I had the reception somewhere else." (A club spokesman says Chevy Chase now has a few Jewish members but still no blacks.)

Jackson still lacks sensitivity to racial or ethnic discrimination. Listen, for example, to what he said about the Arab states and people in New Hampshire in October of 1974. Kathy Starbuck, the political editor of The Milford *Cabinet,* recorded these excerpts from the senator's speech in Nashua: "I'm proud of America. . . . We've fed the world. . . . I saw Yamani [the Saudi Arabian minister of petroleum] yesterday. Yes, I had to shake the hand of that sheik. I smiled. We've given them so much, ever since 1946 we've been feeding the world. . . . I want a sense of urgency as if we were in war, *in war*, to mobilize our energy interests and to give to those potentates in the East that we're not gonna be blackmailed and bow down and scrape to any of them. No dirty A-rab sheik is gonna tell us what to do."

It was chilling rhetoric, not too dissimilar from what politicians in another land said about a different branch of Abraham's family some four decades ago.

Since 1970, Jackson's public record on Israel and issues affecting world Jewry has been unambiguous, and he has won singular acclaim because of it. Indeed, the Judaic Heritage Society named him "Man of the Year" for 1974 and had his image struck in silver medallions to commemorate the honor. Yet, for reasons I cannot completely fathom, he is not content with his recent acclaim and in fact has desperately sought to misrepresent the first thirty years of his record in office by falsely tracing his concern for Jews to the Silver Shirts of Everett in 1939 and his concern for Israel to his 1945 visit to Buchenwald. The public record clearly belies such a revision of history.

Call it coincidence or calculation, but the weight of the record makes plain that Jackson did not assume the mantle of leadership on these issues until the year before he declared himself a presidential candidate. Although his 1972 effort sputtered to a halt after a few primaries, he managed to raise more than $1 million, about a third of which came from American Jews. Of the first million he raised for his 1976 campaign, nearly two-thirds came from American Jews.

Politicians by nature avoid controversy, and Jackson is no exception. By assiduously attending to the needs of his home state and avoiding positions which might alienate a significant bloc whose support he needs, he has piled up enormous reelection majorities. He has even ducked important votes in the Senate on school busing and the Equal Rights Amendment and *not* announced his position, as senators who must miss a vote but want to go on record often do. This, then, is not a man who squanders his political capital. He hoards it. And when he does spend it, you can be sure he expects something in return.

Jackson tried to run for vice-president in 1956 and 1960; so he has nursed an ambition for higher office for at least two decades and probably longer. Although American Jews represent about 3 percent of the population, they are an important voting bloc in the largest states and could well be decisive in the all-or-nothing Electoral College. Moreover, as Stephen Isaacs of the Washington *Post* points out: "Demographic data show that, as a group, Jews are the best-educated Americans, the most affluent, the most professional. Further, they tend to be disproportionately active in politics." The traditional estimate is that they account for about half of all major contributions to the Democratic party. As a practical matter, then, their support is indispensable for a Democrat with presidential ambitions.

That data and Jackson's ambitions may have led him to fashion, quietly, a pro-Israel voting record in case the opportunity to run for higher office, which seemed to vanish for good in 1960, suddenly reappeared. With Richard Nixon's narrow victory in 1968 and Edward Kennedy's accident at Chappaquiddick in 1969, the Democratic nomination and the Presidency itself no longer seemed unattainable, and he began to construct a national political base. His amendment which made a half billion dollars' worth of military aid available to Israel and his first visit to that nation in fourteen years followed in 1970. He did not take a leadership role sooner, quite simply, because there were no votes or campaign funds in it for him.

Jackson has done much for Israel, but it was not force of personality which passed his 1970 amendment by an 87 to 7 majority. A survey conducted for the American Jewish Committee by Daniel Yankelovich indicates that more than 70 percent of the American people support Israel's right to exist as a sovereign state: a level which has not changed very much over the past decade in spite of two wars and an Arab oil embargo. With such broad support for Israel and practially none for the Arabs, it is the nation's political climate, rather than a single politician, which has made possible such strong American efforts in behalf of Israel and world Jewry. Jackson is fond of saying that "if there were no Arab-Israeli conflict, the Soviets would invent one." Likewise, it might be said that had Jackson's political ambitions not propelled him into the role of "defender of Israel" another senator would have filled it. After all, Israel had won three major wars and celebrated its twenty-second anniversary before Jackson decided that the road to the White House ran through Tel Aviv.

POWER

CHAPTER

14

The Purge

POWER, real power, works quietly in Washington. It is not heralded by press releases churned out by eager assistants, nor is it displayed in that ritual known as the press conference. It may stem from something written, but more often than not agreements are recorded only in the minds of the protagonists. A nod or a handshake seals the arrangement; nothing more is required because each knows what the other can do should the terms of their agreement be abrogated. The close observer of events often learns *what* power has done but only seldom *how*: the visible effect and its invisible cause. Real power rarely leaves tracks; it does leave scars.

When Richard Nixon resigned the Presidency, he ended the half-century-old debate about whether Ulysses Grant or Warren Harding was the most corrupt President in our history. His own words in the unexpurgated White House tapes were a bloody dagger in his hand, incontrovertible proof of his guilt. Yet one must acknowledge that his first term was not without substantive accomplishments in the field of foreign affairs. Premier among them were the two agreements which resulted from the strategic arms limitation talks, or SALT.

May 26, 1972, may prove to have been one of the most important dates in this century. On that day in Moscow, President Nixon and Communist Party General Secretary Leonid Brezhnev signed a treaty limiting the United States and the Soviet Union to two antiballistic missile (ABM) sites and a five-year agreement freezing intercontinental ballistic missiles (ICBMs) and imposing a ceiling on ballistic-missile submarines and submarine-launched ballistic missiles (SLBMs). It was the most important development in US-Soviet relations since negotiators for President Kennedy and General Secretary Nikita Khrushchev signed the Treaty Banning Nuclear Weapon Tests in the Atmosphere, in Outer Space and Under Water on August 5, 1963.

Kennedy began the process of détente with the Soviet Union in the 1960s, and Nixon broadened U.S.-Soviet relations in this decade; Jackson, however, seems never to have left the 1950s. Throughout his Senate career he has dragged his feet or directly opposed presidential initiatives to bring the arms race under control. In 1961 he joined forces with Senate conservatives in their unsuccessful attempt to kill Kennedy's proposal to create the Arms Control and Disarmament Agency. He threatened to block Kennedy's test-ban treaty in 1963 and Nixon's offensive-arms agreement nine years later. Although he voted for final passage of each of these measures in the Senate, he used the threat of obstruction to exact concessions from the presidential authors of these proposals.

On "Meet the Press" in 1971, Jackson was asked if he was "obsessed" with questions of national security. "Yes, I am concerned about the security of my country," he replied. "I think it is priority number one. My parents, you know, came from Norway. They were immigrants. There was a country that thought they could be neutral. They had a thousand years of freedom. They had clean air, clean water, clean land. They had a fine system of social justice. What good did it do them when the Nazi hobnail boot took over? I believe that we have to maintain a prudent security program. At the same time I have led the fight for arms control."

The last sentence was, of course, sheer fabrication, but the rest of his response revealed much about the senator's thinking. He came of political age during World War II and has been concerned ever since that we learn the lessons of that era; indeed, he often seems unable or unwilling to disenthrall himself from that period and the cold war which followed. Confrontation is his secular religion, "toughness" his first article of faith. The cardinal sin is "weakness," and he seems to regard most arms-control measures as tantamount to, if not exactly, "appeasement."

This cold war outlook distorts Jackson's perception of events. In 1968, for instance, he was one of the principal advocates for President Johnson's Sentinel ABM system. Soon after it was passed by the Senate, the Soviet Union agreed to the American proposal to begin the strategic arms limitation talks. An individual who was then a high official in the Defense Department says, "The Sentinel ABM decision [in the Senate] and Brezhnev's announcement on SALT, which we knew had already been planned, were not really connected." Nonetheless, Jackson asserted that they were and exploited the coincidence to rationalize his confrontational approach to dealing with the Soviet Union. "He has a very consistent set of premises," says the former official, "and he can fit all the facts into that framework. He knows what he belives."

After his election in 1968, Nixon asked Jackson to become his Secretary of Defense and later offered him the State post, but Jackson was reluctant to lose the independence of his Senate seat. Nixon's offers were undoubtedly sincere, but they also served to flatter Jackson and made him more favorably disposed toward the man he had so harshly criticized in the 1960 presidential campaign. (The Nixon-Jackson relationship will be discussed in more detail in the following chapter.) Thus, when the administration faced its first hard fight in the Senate, the President naturally turned to Jackson for help.

Johnson's Sentinel ABM was designed ostensibly to defend American cities against a "thin" Chinese ICBM attack but would have been of no value whatever against a Soviet strike. Indeed, its real purpose seemed to be to defuse the "ABM gap" as a potential issue for the Republicans to exploit in 1968. And it succeeded in that end.

At the same time, however, the thought of nuclear weapons, which could be fired on a few moments' warning, based in the suburbs of Boston, Chicago, and other cities set off large-scale citizen protests no politician could afford to ignore. A few months after he took office, Nixon changed Sentinel to Safeguard and moved it, physically and conceptually, from the suburbs to the Great Plains. Instead of protecting people, it would now defend four Minuteman ICBM sites. The theory behind the switch, simply stated, ran something like this: Safeguard would make Soviet planners more uncertain of their ability to knock out Minuteman in a surprise attack; their greater uncertainty would, perforce, increase deterrence of such an attack. Jackson found the concept as appealing as Nixon had.

The Safeguard ABM debate spanned several weeks in the summer of 1969, with Jackson leading the fight for the Nixon administration. His principal argument was based upon Pentagon data which hypothesized that a massive attack of heavy Soviet SS-9 ICBMs, each armed with multiple warheads, might, at some vague point in the future, be able to destroy 95 percent of the Minuteman force. Although the Soviet Union did not possess the requisite number of missiles and had no multiple warheads, Jackson skillfully used the Pentagon's hypothetical projection to argue that four major ABM sites were necessary to maintain Minuteman's future "survivability." He believed fervently in Safeguard, lobbied hard to convince his colleagues, and managed to eke out a one-vote victory in the Senate.

Because the Soviet Union has more and heavier ICBMs than the United States, Jackson suggested that four U.S. ABM sites and the one around Moscow would be an equitable basis for an ABM treaty, but the Soviets rejected the idea out of hand. When Nixon and Brezhnev subsequently signed the treaty limiting each country to two ABM sites, only one of which could defend Minuteman, Jackson was outraged. He had invested his personal prestige and political capital to win Senate approval of four ABM sites of several hundred launchers each and felt betrayed because only one site with a hundred launchers could now be built to defend Minuteman. So the day the SALT accords were signed in Moscow, Jackson lost no time venting his spleen. "The present agreements," he charged, "are likely to lead to an accelerated technological arms race with great uncertainties, profound instabilities and considerable costs." When the Senate Armed Services Committee met in June and July to consider the accords, Jackson was present for every session; his questions were hard and pointed, and at times he seemed barely able to control his emotions.

"When the administration wanted my help on getting the

ABM through Congress," he said at one point, "it didn't hesitate when I asked about the consequences of the Soviets developing a missile as accurate as our Minuteman." Now, however, he was being denied similar requests for information.

When Ambassador Gerard Smith, the chief of the SALT delegation, told him that a four-site ABM system "would not be strategic arms control; it would be strategic arms buildup," Jackson shot back: "Then why didn't the President tell the country that while some of us were up here fighting for a four-site ABM?"

Sometimes he focused his anger at the SALT delegation: "Our people caved in; let's face it; we were to have a minimum of two hardsite [ABM] defenses. I put them on notice; I said that if you turn around and agree to two sites . . . you are going to end up with one. [Congress had consistently opposed an ABM ring around Washington; thus, the two-site treaty limitation really meant only one would be built.] They knew it, but they went ahead and did it anyway."

Later he complained: "Let's not kid ourselves; they [the Soviets] are just going to sit there; time is on their side. We are the ones coming hat in hand; we are going to have to try to get some modifications of SALT I. If you don't have it now, would you give us some indication of what kind of programs that we could stand for because we haven't stood for anything yet. We have caved in on everything."

Although Jackson generally tries to avoid contentious issues, once he commits himself, he can become emotionally involved in his stand. Military assessments may have played a part, but his anger seemed to stem more from having staked his advocacy for Safeguard on Pentagon data which showed Minuteman potentially vulnerable to a future Soviet attack and now having to face administration witnesses who used the same data to refute his earlier argument. Although more disinterested analysts had disputed his interpretation of the data in the first place, Jackson had ignored them and built his case on the Pentagon's self-serving interpretation. Although he had, in truth, deluded himself, his emotional outbursts indicate he believed the administration had deceived him. Nixon's ABM treaty was not simply unwise; it was a personal affront.

Because the treaty allowed each side identical forces (one site to defend ICBMs, the other to defend the capital), it could hardly be attacked as unfair. The interim offensive arms agreement was another matter. On its face it seemed to give the Soviet Union a decided advantage: 1,618 ICBMs, 62 ballistic-missile submarines and 950 SLBMs; the comparable American figures were: 1,054, 44, and 710. (To reach the submarine and SLBM ceilings, however, the Soviet Union would have to deactivate 210 older, pre-1964, ballistic missiles and the United States 54, thus reducing each side's ICBM total correspondingly.) These numbers were not the entire story, however.

The United States has three times as many long-range bombers as the Soviet Union and 7,000 nuclear weapons in Europe. Moreover, multiple independently targetable reentry vehicles (MIRVs) on top of Minuteman III ICBMs and Poseidon SLBMs had given the United States a two-to-one advantage in nuclear warheads which is expected to grow to four-to-one by the time the interim agreement expires in mid-1977. Viewed in a more realistic perspective, then, the agreement permitted the Soviet Union a temporary numerical advantage in missiles which was more than offset by the American technological and numerical lead in warheads. Without these ceilings, Kissinger estimated that the Soviet Union by 1977 would have been able to build 80 to 90 submarines and hundreds more ICBMs (Nixon's estimate was 1,000).

Talleyrand once observed: "An absolute equality of power between all the states, not only can never exist, but also is not necessary to the political equilibrium and would perhaps in some respects be hurtful to it." The unequal numbers in the offensive-arms agreement were the result of complex factors: an attempt to balance the American lead in warheads against the higher number of Soviet missiles as well as a reflection of the geopolitical reality which finds the Soviet Union with potential nuclear adversaries on its southern and western flanks while the United States enjoys secure borders. The military postures of each country reflected such factors, but the fact that the agreement permitted unequal numbers made it politically vulnerable to a simplistic attack. Jackson, who is no disciple of Talleyrand, was aware of this and soon shifted his attack away from the politically *in*vulnerable ABM treaty and aimed instead at the unequal numbers in the offensive-arms agreement. Once again, he charged that U.S. negotiators had "caved in," even though the chief delegate, Smith, explicitly informed Jackson that Nixon and Kissinger, not the SALT delegation, had personally negotiated these numbers.

Nixon was then heading for a landslide reelection, and Kissinger was widely respected. It would have taken considerable courage to attack them in public, but having recently and painfully discovered his own lack of popularity as a presidential candidate, Jackson was not about to take such an approach. So he aimed instead at the more vulnerable SALT delegation and ACDA itself.

General Royal B. Allison was in a delicate position. He wore, as the saying goes, two hats. He was the principal military delegate on the SALT team as well as assistant to the chairman of the Joint Chiefs of Staff for SALT and related matters. On one hand, he was responsible to Smith for negotiating arms-control measures; on the other, he was expected to protect the military's interests. By all accounts, he did creditably in both roles, and after most negotiating sessions called the JCS chairman, Admiral Thomas Moorer, on the secure, "scrambler" phones to tell him what had transpired and seek his guidance. Although Jackson would later charge that Allison did not diligently represent the JCS, Moorer was thoroughly pleased with the general's work.

Once the President signed the two SALT accords in Moscow, Allison conducted himself exactly as a military officer is supposed to: he supported the foreign policy of the Commander in Chief. This did not suit Jackson. He was looking for a way either to scuttle the agreements or to strip them of public support. From the senator's questioning of earlier witnesses, Allison had deduced what Jackson was up to and was prepared when he tried to get him to denigrate the agreements during the hearings. The following exchange reveals the trap Jackson tried to spring.

JACKSON: "Under this agreement, do you think that if the

Soviets take maximum advantage of the provisions of this agreement, that the United States can retain a survivable Minuteman force against a first strike?"

SMITH: "In what time period?"

JACKSON: "Within the agreement five-year time frame."

SMITH: "I am quite sure of that, yes."

JACKSON: "General Allison, do you agree with that statement?"

ALLISON: "I think a very meaningful percentage of Minuteman can survive, but I would like to expand on that if I may just slightly."

JACKSON: "Could you give me an indication of what you mean by meaningful?"

ALLISON: "I would prefer not to attempt to put a numerical figure on it because I don't think it will improve my answer.

"I do believe, Senator Jackson, that when one talks about survival of a deterrent one should not identify solely one element of the deterrent force. I think to talk about the vulnerability of Minuteman alone is not providing—"

JACKSON (interrupting): "Let's not stray from the subject. The administration can't have it both ways, General. . . . Now, the administration argued that an ABM was needed, since 5 percent of Minuteman surviving would not constitute a credible force.

"Is 5 percent of Minuteman a credible force? Do you subscribe to that formula or do you disagree with it?"

ALLISON: "Fifty surviving MIRVed Minuteman can be a meaningful addition to the rest of the strategic force."

JACKSON: "Is it creditable [*sic*]?"

ALLISON: "Is our total deterrent posture credible? Is that the question?"

JACKSON: "No. The question is whether 5 percent of the Minuteman surviving is credible. Now, if 5 percent of Minuteman is credible in 1972 when the administration is defending the SALT agreements, why was it not also credible in 1969 when the administration was defending ABM? . . ."

ALLISON: "You are asking me to make a judgment as to how the Soviets' strategist will apply his force and implicit in the question it seems to me is the estimate that all the Soviet force is going to be focused on striking one element of our strategic force and thus making it a very vulnerable force. I, on the other hand, think the Soviet would not devote his entire force to that kind of attack. That is an opinion, Senator, no more, no less. But I don't think his strategist would set out to do that with the force they have in the time period."

Jackson may have had a point about Nixon's switching his arguments, but Allison was correct when he later remarked, "Good strategy should not focus on a single fact." Yet that is precisely what Jackson had been doing in his attempt to trap Allison and other SALT delegates into criticizing the Moscow accords. When they would not play his game, he began to badger them. In fact, his treatment of Allison became so harsh that the committee chairman, Senator John Stennis of Mississippi, found it necessary to reproach him: "I think the gentleman [Allison] has made his position clear, that he recommended certain things. Those recommendations are here before us, and as I see it, he ought not to be pursued beyond that now. It is up to the Congress now, with the supposition that they might turn them down. But in the capacity he is here in, it seems to me he has gone about as far as he can, Senator."

Although Stennis found it necessary to admonish Jackson several more times, he was not deterred. Although Allison was simply being, in the words of a committee staff member, "a good soldier," Jackson thought otherwise and at some point became determined to destroy his career.

Jackson felt the administration had ignored him on SALT before the agreements were signed, and he was right. His suggestions on negotiating strategies, such as the four-for-one ABM gambit, had been politely received but never followed. The White House simply assumed the senator would go along with whatever agreements Nixon brought back from Moscow. After all, how could one legislator possibly thwart the combined force of Nixon and Kissinger in foreign affairs? They were soon to learn.

The military has always resisted arms control; so, in order to get the services to go along with the SALT accords, the administration felt it had to "bribe" them by accelerating spending on those weapons not prohibited by SALT I. The most important of these was the Trident ballistic-missile submarine.

In the fall of 1971 the Pentagon had made a tenfold increase in its request for funds to speed up development of the new boat and rationalized it as a "bargaining chip" to induce the Soviet Union to come to terms at SALT. But, when the agreements were signed in May, Trident was not returned to its original, more deliberate schedule. In late June the Senate Armed Services Subcommittee on Research and Development, led by Senator Lloyd Bentsen of Texas, recommended that the Trident request of nearly $1 billion be halved. To everyone's surprise Jackson voted with Bentsen when the motion came before the full committee, but it failed to carry on an 8-to-8 tie.

With this vote, however, Jackson had broken with the Defense Department on a major nuclear weapons program for the first time in anyone's memory; so Bentsen's chances of winning a fight on the Senate floor began to look good. The White House was greatly concerned because its witnesses had been testifying that they could not support the SALT accords without strong congressional support for Trident and other strategic weapons. Thus, Jackson and the colleagues he might sway now looked to be the margin of victory or defeat for Trident. The administration had argued itself into a box and found to its chagrin that it could not get out without Jackson's help.

During this same period Jackson also began drafting an amendment which called for "equality" in any future offensive-arms treaty. The initial drafts of this measure were clearly calculated to send a shiver through candidate Nixon and his national security adviser, and they did. The most chilling phrase was a threat that "Congress would consider action or deployment by the Soviet Union, having the effect of endangering the survivability of the strategic deterrent forces of the United States, whether or not such action or deployment was undertaken within the terms of the interim agreement . . . to be contrary to the supreme interests of the United States" and, therefore, grounds for abrogating the agreement. He quickly found a score of senators to cosponsor the measure.

These were palpable threats to SALT, the keystone of Nixon's policy toward the Soviet Union. Should Trident be returned by Congress to its original schedule, the half-billion-dollar cut might lead to the services' quietly undermining or even openly retracting their avowed support for the agreements. Should Jackson's language threatening abrogation of the offensive-arms accord be attached to the agreement, the Soviet Union could justifiably claim that the terms of the pact had been unilaterally altered and renounce the agreement. With the November election fast approaching, Nixon felt he had no choice but to come to terms with the junior senator from Washington State and did.

On July 27, Bentsen brought his Trident amendment to the Senate floor. Just before the vote, Jackson rose and announced he would now vote *against* the Bentsen amendment he had supported in committee four weeks before. It was defeated, 39 to 47. Jackson may well have been responsible for the administration's margin of victory.

On August 7, Jackson introduced a much softer version of his amendment to the offensive-arms agreement. Gone was the phrase which threatened American abrogation; what was left was an expression of the sense of Congress, which, if enacted, would not have the force of law. "Congress recognizes the principle of United States–Soviet Union equality reflected in the antiballistic missile treaty," began the key phrase, "and urges and requests the President to seek a future treaty that, *inter alia,* would not limit the United States to levels of intercontinental forces inferior to the limits provided for the Soviet Union."

Getting Jackson to soften his amendment took several weeks of hard bargaining. Kissinger and Jackson were on the phone as often as three and four times a day, while their assistants crisscrossed the city with proposals and counterproposals. At one point Jackson threatened to join forces with Representative F. Edward Hébert of Louisiana, the archconservative chairman of the House Armed Services Committee, to get both houses to pass a tough amendment. It was a threat the administration could not take lightly.

In public, however, Jackson discouraged his allies in the House from introducing his amendment there. Had the other chamber actually passed a tough measure, Jackson would have lost his "bargaining chip." Equally important, Kissinger would have had to split his negotiating effort between the House and Senate. Jackson did not want that to happen because then he would no longer be the focal point of the negotiations. Better to work out a compromise with Kissinger, have it pass the Senate, and then have it added by the House-Senate conference committee to the final measure, which was exactly what happened.

So, with Jackson's crucial assistance, the administration got everything it wanted: Trident, the ABM treaty, and offensive-arms agreement. Anyone who has closely followed the senator's career knows that he would not have engineered so major a confrontation with the White House and made important concessions unless he had a purpose. That there had been a "deal" was obvious. The only question was: what did Jackson get in return?

On September 30, there was an elaborate White House ceremony when the President signed the offensive-arms agreement in the company of congressional leaders. Reporters and photographers were trooped in to record the occasion and then trooped back out. Soon thereafter, Nixon and Jackson strolled into the Rose Garden and conferred alone for forty minutes. Unless Nixon bugged the rose bushes, the only record of what transpired exists in the memories of the two men. Individuals who were close to the events which followed, however, are convinced that from this tête-à-tête flowed the purge which over the next few months decimated the ranks of the Arms Control and Disarmament Agency and the SALT delegation as well.

Jackson apparently told the President he had been badly served by both ACDA and his SALT team. This was demonstrably untrue. As the hearing record makes plain, Jackson knew that the unequal numbers in the offensive-arms accord to which he took such sharp exception had been negotiated by Kissinger and Nixon himself in Moscow, not by the SALT delegation which was in Helsinki hammering out the *language* of the agreement. But Jackson shrewdly chose not to attack the President and his popular national security adviser even though they were responsible for the terms of the agreement: he aimed instead at ACDA and the SALT delegation.

That suited Nixon for several reasons. First and foremost, he would not have to suffer any public criticism from Jackson in the months before his reelection. Second, he would not have to confront whatever personal failings might have been responsible for a "bad" agreement; he could simply blame the SALT delegation as Jackson had. Finally, he hoped to restore his working relationship with Jackson, who had been so instrumental in splitting the Democrats to Nixon's advantage on ABM, Vietnam, and McGovern's presidential candidacy. Although Nixon demanded and received total loyalty from his subordinates, he regarded them as pawns to be expended in the great international chess match he was playing. If he was required to play Herod to Jackson's Salome and serve up the heads of some loyal assistants, he would not be deterred by any human feelings.

Jackson did not hide his hostility toward ACDA and the SALT delegation at the hearings that summer or in the months that followed. In a speech to the NATO military committee on November 21, for example, he asserted: "Now, minimum deterrence is the orthodoxy of the arms control community that planned and negotiated the American side of the Moscow accords. But it need not become the basis of our strategic doctrine and still less the strategic objective of our alliance partners. For that matter there is, in principle, no reason why minimum deterrence should persist as the central doctrine underlying SALT II."

Jackson defined minimum deterrence on this occasion as "a capability to destroy some finite percentage of the adversary's cities and industry in response to a direct nuclear attack." This described neither the nuclear posture of the United States nor the position taken by the SALT delegation. What's more, Jackson knew it. At the hearings, chief negotiator Gerard Smith acknowledged that while there were people in the United States who advocate minimum deterrence "they are not in the SALT delegation and they are not in the administration that I know of."

Jackson replied, "I know it is not your view." So, when he raised the canard of minimum deterrence in November and called it "the orthodoxy of the arms control community that planned and negotiated the American side of the Moscow accords," he was either deluding himself or dissembling.

Several weeks after his reelection, Nixon asked for the resignations of all appointed officials in the executive branch, retreated to the solitude of Camp David and began issuing ukases from the heights of the Catoctin Mountains. To White House Chief of Staff H. R. Haldeman fell the task of turning ACDA upside down, and he performed it with his customary zeal.

Gerard Smith was ACDA's director as well as chief delegate at the arms talks, He had announced his firm intention to resign after the agreements were signed in Moscow and left government service of his own volition in January of 1973.

Others who had submitted their *pro forma* resignations hoped to stay at ACDA and were greatly disturbed when their resignations were accepted. Says one: "I don't think I expected this after SALT was successfully completed. After the election, I still didn't think so. But after Smith's resignation, I thought it was possible. It evolved slowly but then came quickly."

Haldeman practically swept the place clean, as a glance at the agency's roster showed. Of the seventeen people who were in ACDA's top posts in 1972, only three were still assigned to the agency in 1974. Some left of their own accord, a few were reassigned but at least six were forced out of government service, according to knowledgeable sources.

Kissinger's role in the purge is hard to assess. If he went to bat for these officials in his private meetings with Nixon, he made no outward indication of the fact to his subordinates. The National Security Council, which he headed, was asked to recommend to the President those at ACDA who ought to be retained. Only one name, that of Deputy Director Philip Farley, was submitted. (Farley nonetheless left, reportedly of his own volition.) In short, there is no evidence to suggest Kissinger tried very hard, if at all, to save ACDA.

Nixon also moved to diminish ACDA's already limited influence in other ways. With a $10 million budget, ACDA is one of the smaller government agencies. By contrast, the Pentagon's budget is ten thousand times larger, which should tell you something about the relative importance government attaches to arms as distinct from arms control. Even so, ACDA had its budget cut by a third and lost 50 of its 230 employees.

On January 4, 1973, after Smith's resignation was accepted,

the White House announced that U. Alexis Johnson, the Under Secretary of State for Political Affairs, would be the new chief delegate for SALT II but would not concurrently hold the ACDA directorship. In fact, Johnson was assigned to State rather than ACDA in a move clearly aimed at reducing the agency's institutional role from that of central direction of the negotiations to secondary support.

ACDA had all but been destroyed, and it was no wonder the administration had a difficult time finding anyone willing to take the directorship of an agency which seemed to be going the way of the Office of Economic Opportunity. Several prospective candidates turned the post down, including Fred C. Iklé, the chairman of the social sciences department at the Rand Corporation, the government-financed think tank in Santa Monica. The office had been vacant more than three months when the administration finally talked Iklé into accepting the post. His appointment reportedly had Jackson's blessing.

Jackson was still infuriated at General Allison for having stood up to him at the hearings that summer. "Courageous and forthright" is the way a former ACDA official describes Allison's conduct under verbal fire, but to Jackson it was "arrogance." So, while Haldeman was doing his dirty work at ACDA, Jackson went directly to the JCS chairman, Admiral Moorer, and demanded that he relieve Allison of his SALT duties. Moorer resisted at first, but when Jackson threatened to block any promotion or assignment for Allison which required Senate action, the admiral capitulated.

Allison's wife was reportedly packing for their return to Europe for SALT II when the general learned that he had been summarily removed from the delegation. He was offered a new assignment, but because billets for three- and four-star generals are usually made a year or more in advance, he was not "in cycle." Thus, the assignment he was offered was considerably below what an officer of his rank and experience deserved. Generals are rarely cashiered; they are removed by more indirect tactics such as a bad assignment. They are then forced to decide whether to take the assignment or resign: there are no other choices. Thus, it was clear to Allison someone wanted him out of the military.

When he learned that Jackson had demanded and indeed received his removal, Allison asked the senator for an appointment. His purpose, reportedly, was not to plead for reinstatement but to see if Jackson would permit him a few months' grace so he might get "in cycle" and receive an appropriate assignment. Jackson was intransigent. In the course of their chilly, forty-five-minute meeting, it became clear to Allison that Jackson not only wanted him off the SALT delegation, he wanted him out of the Air Force as well. Allison's career was at an end—Jackson's political influence had seen to that—so the general chose to retire.

Raymond Garthoff was the delegation's executive secretary and one of its most valuable members. Thoroughly fluent in Russian, he often met with his opposite number on the Soviet delegation to work out differences in the texts of various proposals. He was supposed to return to SALT II as the State Department's representative—a promotion, in effect—but was subsequently called in by a senior State official and told that he would be reassigned to duties which did not involve SALT. Although Jackson's name did not arise then, an even more senior State official reportedly indicated to him that Jackson had asked for and received his removal.

Only two members of the original delegation survived: Harold Brown, the president of California Institute of Technology and former Secretary of the Air Force, and Paul Nitze, the Defense Department's delegate. Brown was somewhat immune from attack because his role was largely that of liaison to the scientific and academic community; indeed, his negotiating duties were so modest that he was not called upon to testify about the SALT accords before the Armed Services Committee. Nitze, a long-time Defense official (who resigned in 1974), had been close to Jackson for many years; so his position was secure.

In the early months of 1973, after Allison and Garthoff had been removed from the SALT delegation and ACDA was cleaned out, Jackson's assistant, Richard Perle, bragged to several people in Washington that he and Jackson were responsible for the purge. "I avoided Perle," says a former NSC staffer. "I was told he had a little list and that I was on it."

Later in the year, when the Watergate hearings produced revelations about a White House "enemies' list," Perle apparently switched tunes and began denying there was a list or that he and the senator were responsible in any way for the purge. To have continued his earlier bragging would have invited—heaven forbid—an invidious comparison of Jackson to Nixon.

In February the Navy announced that it would build its only Trident submarine base at Bangor, Washington, at a cost of $550 million. The new base would eventually create three thousand military and three thousand civilian jobs in that economically depressed area. The decision came as a complete surprise because the service had earlier indicated that the base would be built on the Southeast coast. Few took seriously the Pentagon official who now asserted that the decision represented "a victory for the strategists," because an Atlantic base made much more sense from a military point of view. The choice of Washington State was thought by many to have been politically motivated to keep Jackson solidly behind Trident so he could not use it again for a "bargaining chip" as he had in 1972. It might also have been part of the quid pro quo which passed between Nixon and Jackson.

There were news accounts at the time all these events took place, but they rarely penetrated the surface. Jackson's surreptitious role in the purge, while alluded to by some reporters, remained largely uncovered. Watergate was returning to the front pages, and the SALT accords had passed into ancient history as far as the daily press was concerned. Moreover, so many officials throughout the executive branch had been forced out over a period of several months that the ACDA and SALT reshuffling was barely noted. When Nixon had returned from Moscow with the SALT agreements, he had told Congress they would "forestall a major spiralling of the arms race." A year later, most of the officials who helped the President negotiate those accords had been removed from their posts. Nixon's sense of gratitude had left more victims than survivors.

Jackson, who had tried to kill ACDA when President Kennedy first proposed it in 1961, had finally succeeded in undermining the agency and received a SALT delegation more to his liking as well. The new Trident base back home must have made the taste of victory sweeter still. He had forced the Nixon administration to meet his terms, and his power in the Senate had never been greater. That the victims of the purge were not responsible for the specific facets of the arms agreement to which he had objected troubled him not at all. If a few careers had to be destroyed to increase his power, he would not shrink from the deed. Power was what mattered, not the scars it left on others.

CHAPTER

15

The Roots of Power

"IF YOU had asked me in 1967 or '68 who were the most effective senators, I would not have named Jackson in the top ten," says one of Washington's "superlawyers," who was also a high official in the Johnson administration. "He was not a Senate titan back in those days. In fact, for years he was a loner and one of the less-effective senators. Most of his power he acquired under Nixon. As Nixon's Democratic senator, the administration gives him authority he would not have in a good Democratic or Republican administration. He is the creature of the Nixon administration. . . . Nixon made him what he is today."

These remarks were made two months before Nixon's resignation in one of the many "not-for-attribution" interviews I had with present or former government officials and members of Congress who have observed Jackson at close hand. The superlawyer just quoted expressed it more pointedly than most, but his was by no means an isolated view. Even those who contend that Jackson's power stems primarily from his institutional roles in the Senate alluded, explicitly or implicity, to his unique relationship with the former President.

One Democratic senator suggested "seniority is the key" to Jackson's power and cited as evidence his chairmanship of the Interior Committee and Permanent Investigations Subcommittee and prominence on the Armed Services Committee. "He moves forward in his areas of discipline," this senator said, and with his committee posts it is "not hard for him to find a vehicle. His power is of the establishment type."

This is a straightforward, almost textbooklike interpretation of power in the Senate, but it hardly explains Jackson's preeminence in so many areas. Indeed, when his colleague and I were talking about how Jackson got such strong support from fellow senators, the Nixon factor came out. In describing the favors Jackson would do for colleagues, he cited a personal example: "He brokered a meeting for me with Nixon at the White House." What other Democrats—or Republicans, for that matter—enjoyed such entrée to the isolated inner sanctum of Richard Nixon? Not many.

A senator often loses influence when his party gains control of the White House. During the final Eisenhower years, Jackson began an inquiry into the ways in which national security policy is made and carried out: the procedures as distinct from the substance of policy. His work came to fruition during Kennedy's Presidency, but it seemed to have little impact on Robert McNamara's Pentagon and Dean Rusk's State Department. Although Jackson was disappointed by this lack of attention, he personally gained an intimate understanding of how high- and mid-level policy makers were selected and, most important, *who* had control of *which* aspects of foreign and military policy.

Although Lyndon Johnson often turned to Jackson in times of stress, it may have been less for his advice than his loyalty. Jackson was gung-ho for fighting communism in Southeast Asia—or anywhere else, for that matter—and a call to Jackson would always reassure Johnson that he was pursuing a firm and noble course in Vietnam. Because Jackson had so closely tied himself to Johnson's policies, there was little more he could do for the beleaguered President than continue to be a sympathetic listener and loyal partisan on Capitol Hill. Thus, his influence and ability to shape substantive matters were practically nonexistent.

Seven-tenths of one percent was the margin of Richard Nixon's popular-vote plurality over Hubert Humphrey in 1968, and his mandate was even further circumscribed by the Democrats' control of both houses of Congress. If Nixon was going to be an activist President, he had to have congressional support, or at least acquiescence, for his foreign and military policies. With anti-war sentiment growing in the country, he needed to neutralize congressional opposition to the war and the possible spillover of this sentiment, which could threaten his plans for increased military spending in other areas. The tactic he chose was an old one: divide and conquer.

Jackson was visiting Hawaii for the Thanksgiving holidays when the President-elect called. Jackson had been hearing rumors that he would be asked to be Secretary of Defense, and Nixon now confirmed them by formally offering him the post. Jackson asked for a few days to think about it and during that time telephoned Senate colleagues, friends, and the outgoing President Johnson. They confirmed his judgment that becoming Nixon's Secretary of Defense would be a good way to cap his political career if, at age fifty-six, he was ready for what might well be his final government assignment. He ultimately concluded that the risks involved in losing the independence of his Senate seat far outweighed whatever benefits there might be in heading the Pentagon for a Republican President during the terminal stages of an unpopular war. It was obviously a wise decision.

The Supreme Court in the 1930s overturned key economic legislation of FDR's New Deal, and a Southern-dominated Congress killed important civil rights bills until the 1960s; thus liberals tended to base their hopes and programs on legislation which would transfer power from these more conservative branches of government to an activist Presidency. In this regard Jackson has always been an orthodox liberal, albeit of a 1950s' vintage. He believes in concentrating power in the executive branch, and most of the legislation he has spearheaded—from the National Environmental Policy Act to the Safeguard ABM—was premised on the need for greater presidential power. He has long believed this country can afford both "guns and butter": indeed, one of his staffers once bragged that he could not recall a single appropriations bill Jackson had voted against.

Such profligacy with the public treasury has led to annual federal budgets in excess of $300 billion (about a fourth of the gross national product) and deficits which require heavy borrowing and thus dry up money needed for housing and business expansion in general. Jackson, however, seems to understand little about economics; his recent interest in the subject stems entirely from the present necessity for presidential candidates to promise us out of our economic malaise. But, by being so generous in voting public funds, Jackson has made many friends in the executive departments and on Capitol Hill among the sponsors of various spending measures. So he has usually been in a good position to ask Senate colleagues to support his pet programs.

This may explain some of his attractiveness to Richard Nixon. Jackson, like Nixon, was a hawk, and his standing in the Senate had potentially great value to the new administration if he would use it to win Senate approval for Nixon's national security programs. Nixon's offer of the Defense and (later) State posts understandably flattered Jackson, and a strong rapport developed between the two erstwhile antagonists. According to the scrupulously impartial *Congressional Quarterly*, Jackson supported Nixon's position on foreign policy in every recorded Senate vote but one in 1969 and 1970. (The sole exception was the 1970 Cooper-Church amendment which cut off funds for military operations in Cambodia: a largely symbolic measure because Nixon had already pledged that he would withdraw all American troops by the amendment's stipulated date.)

Nixon agreed with Jackson's belief in concentrating power in the Presidency and, equally important, regularly sought his advice and assistance. Jackson's prestige and influence in the Senate, particularly with members of his own party, grew considerably as a result of this relationship. Democratic senators who wanted something for their constituents from the Defense Department's gargantuan budget naturally turned to him for help, and his administration connections often got results. When he later needed votes for Nixon's Safeguard ABM or to block anti-war legislation, he was always certain of sympathetic listeners when he called in his IOUs. Wittingly or not, Jackson became the instrument of Nixon's strategy to divide and conquer Democratic opposition in the Senate to his foreign and military policies.

What did Jackson get from this arrangement? In a word,

plenty. He had always had substantial Republican support in his reelection campaigns, but his visible proximity to Nixon made his 1970 race an incredibly lopsided affair. C. Montgomery (Gummie) Johnson, who was then chairman of the Washington State Republican party, learned just how lopsided when he went to a GOP state chairmen's meeting in Washington. "I met Nixon in the Oval Room at the White House, and his first comment to me was: 'Well, Gummie, I hope you're not going to defeat Scoop.' Later I met Ehrlichman, also in the White House, and he said the same thing."

Senator John Tower of Texas was then chairman of the Republican Senatorial Campaign Committee. "He came to the chairmen's meeting in a downtown hotel," recalls Johnson, "and he was very candid about the whole thing. 'Hey, he's one of ours, a member of the club,' is the way Tower put it."

The Republican anointing of Jackson was also conducted in public. Senator Barry Goldwater of Arizona praised him on the floor of the Senate and obliquely endorsed his reelection when he said he hoped Jackson would be "around for many years to give us the kind of backing and assurance we need." John Ehrlichman, who had been a zoning lawyer in Seattle before going to the White House, told a reporter that Jackson was his idea of an "ideal" Democrat. The greatest blessing of all came once again from Nixon himself. At a Veterans of Foreign Wars convention he praised Jackson as "a man who understands the threat to peace and freedom in the world as well as any man I know."

Nixon bestowed other favors on Jackson. In 1970 people in the Pacific Northwest were greatly disturbed about a shipment of lethal nerve gas which was scheduled to pass through the region before it was destroyed. The Republican governors of Oregon and Washington State, Tom McCall and Daniel Evans, and Senator Warren Magnuson had spoken against the shipment, but Jackson remained silent. When Nixon finally decided to stop the shipment, he informed only Jackson, who naturally announced it and grabbed all the glory. A spokesman for an infuriated Governor Evans gave this account to a reporter for the Seattle *Post-Intelligencer*: "Gov. McCall, who led the fight against the gas, could not find out about the decision until Sen. Jackson had held a press conference and announced it. In fact, Gov. McCall, in phoning the White House, couldn't even get the decision confirmed *after* Jackson's press conference." The aide described his own boss, Evans, as "irked" by Nixon's relationship with Jackson.

A week before Jackson's big fund-raising dinner in Seattle, Gummie Johnson was meeting with the state Republican finance committee when, according to the Seattle *P-I*, "somebody noticed the $50,000 . . . item for a GOP Senate candidate against Jackson. They balked. 'Hell, Gummie . . . everyone of us has bought a ticket to Jackson's dinner. Most of us are raising money for his campaign.' " Outraged, Johnson fired "his" finance committee. With justifiable pique, he called Jackson's liaison with Nixon an "illicit love affair."

The relationship remained close until late in 1971, when Jackson began his overt campaign for the Presidency. They disagreed about the SALT accords in the summer of 1972, and Jackson wisely put as much distance as he could between himself and the discredited President when Watergate began to dominate the news in 1973. But by that time Jackson's power in the Senate had become secure; he no longer needed his White House patron.

One tactic Jackson uses to maintain his power is to undercut rivals. In the summer of 1974 Warren Magnuson was preparing to run for reelection to the Senate. He faced a potentially tough race if his Republican opponent turned out to be Slade Gorton, Washington State's popular attorney general. Gorton ultimately decided not to run, and when he bowed out, he had complimentary things to say about Magnuson but only harsh words for Jackson. Relieved at not having to face Gorton in the general election and being a gentlemanly sort, Magnuson returned the compliment and said a few nice things about Gorton. When the news reports reached him, Jackson was furious at both men, and some of his staff insinuated to newsmen—off the record, of course—that Gorton's remarks might have been written by Magnuson's staff. There was no truth in the accusation, but Jackson's rage and his staff's rumor mongering revealed much about the way the man and his associates react to potential or actual rivals for power.

Gorton, who hints that he may seek Jackson's Senate seat, could give the senator his first serious race since 1952, and it is apparent Gorton has been closely watching his quarry: "One of the more disturbing things about Jackson is his tendency to whine. He hasn't even pretended to say nice things. When Ford was appointed vice-president, he sounded like a kid whose cookies were taken. Whenever the fortunes of an opponent go up, he whines. He has an emotional and negative reaction to any setback."

Others have made similar observations. Although Jackson is generally cordial to his colleagues, he is easily provoked to anger by a rival for power in the Senate or, more recently, the Presidency. His frequent clashes with former Senator J. William Fulbright of Arkansas provided some colorful examples.

Once, in 1967, when Fulbright remarked in the course of a debate on the supersonic transport that he had recently returned from his home state in a Boeing 747, Jackson quickly corrected him. "The 747 is yet to be built," he said. It was a 727.

"I apologize," intoned Fulbright in his mellifluous baritone voice. "There are so many of these planes with fancy numbers that no one can keep them straight except those who are closely associated with Boeing."

Jackson was infuriated. "What does the Senator mean by that?" he demanded.

"It is obvious," said the Arkansan in the same courtly tone. "Boeing is located in the Senator's state. It is the largest employer in the State of Washington. . . . There is no secret about it. I did not know the Senator was so sensitive about that."

"I am not sensitive about it," replied Jackson, irate at any implication that he was "the senator from Boeing."

The two senators often collided on foreign policy: Jackson favoring a hard line with the Soviet Union and Fulbright generally supporting Kissinger's concept of détente. So there were often substantive reasons for their clashes, but I suspect that personal jealousy may also have been a factor. Fulbright was an outstanding athlete in college, a Rhodes Scholar, and a national legislator from his earliest days in Congress, whereas Jackson was a provincial politician whose personal accomplishments were meager by comparison. While Fulbright was establishing the international scholarship program that bears his name, Jackson was answering constituents' letters, struggling to build more post offices, and losing sleep on late-night, propeller-driven airplanes called "red-eye specials" so he could speak to a handful of people at an Odd Fellows' hall back home. Fulbright was a Senate "show horse" who spoke with authority on international affairs, while Jackson, a "workhorse," moved mundane legislation and received little public acclaim. If Jackson, as some friends indicate, had an inferiority complex early in his career, a man of Fulbright's accomplishments must have heightened his feelings of inadequacy.

The rivalry intensified in later years, and one Fulbright aide told me that Jackson's staff would usually be among the first in line to pick up advance copies of Fulbright's speeches so their boss could prepare for battle. One particularly bitter clash occurred in 1972 during the debate over Jackson's amendment to the offensive-arms limitation agreement. Jackson wanted to delay the vote for a few days because some of his supporters were out of town; so he read his speeches *very* slowly and was plainly stalling for time. Fulbright accurately accused him of delaying tactics and said, "That kind of arrogance, I think, is not acceptable."

"Mr. President, that is ridiculous," Jackson retorted. "That is the height of arrogance on the part of the senator from Arkansas. I have never been involved in filibusters. My record on issues of civil rights—a frequent subject of filibusters— and other matters speaks for itself. I am talking about an amendment that will make it possible for the United States to be on an equal basis with the Soviet Union. I am for equality at home as well as abroad, and I am proud of that record."

Fulbright was probably goading Jackson in both these instances and succeeded in eliciting an emotional and somewhat irrational response. After all, of what relevance was Fulbright's civil rights record to the matter at hand: limiting nuclear arms?

Calm, cool, and analytical is the image Jackson would like to project: "a steady hand in a very unsteady world" is the way he indirectly referred to himself on CBS's "60 Minutes." As these outbursts indicate, he sometimes is not. Moreover, his rivalry with Fulbright is not an isolated case. He has clashed bitterly with Senator Stuart Symington of Missouri, his one-time rival for the unofficial title of "Mr. Defense," and with Senator Edmund Muskie of Maine on environmental issues. Secretary of State Henry Kissinger has become another target. Again, there are substantive issues involved in most of these collisions, but Jackson also seems to personalize the dispute, treating a difference of opinion as a personal affront.

This hostility toward rivals has been adopted by some on his staff. A particularly vicious example occurred in the summer of 1974. On "Meet the Press" on Sunday, July 14, Jackson had charged that Americans firms "are going to sell—get this—to the Russians police equipment that will help the KGB [Soviet secret police] to hold the dissidents even under tighter control." It was a matter that deserved looking into, and the next day the chief counsel of Jackson's Permanent Investigations Subcommittee sought to make the exportation of crime equipment an agenda item at the panel's executive (closed) session on Wednesday, with an eye to holding a public hearing on Friday.

At the Wednesday meeting, Senator Charles Percy of Illinois (then a dark-horse presidential contender), objected to the addition of so important an agenda item on such short notice. Subcommittee rules stipulate that the ranking minority member (Percy) must be kept "fully apprised" of panel investigations; a purpose of this rule is to permit members enough time to study the matter being investigated and arrange their schedule so they can be on hand for important hearings. Although this investigation had been under way for several weeks, Percy had not been "fully apprised"; indeed, he was completely unaware of it. Moreover, he and the other Republican members of the subcommittee were already scheduled to be out of town that Friday; so the request for a few days' delay in the public hearing was quite reasonable. The subcommittee ultimately agreed to discuss the matter on Friday and hear witnesses but only in executive session: a fair compromise. Jackson, however, was very angry because he had, on his own initiative, already announced there would be a public hearing. This anger was shared by his staff, and Richard Perle decided to retaliate against Percy.

Later that day a reporter approached Percy and asked him if there was any substance to a story he had heard about the Illinois senator having "blocked" the subcommittee's investigation "because there was a Chicago firm involved." Percy went through the roof and asked the reporter where he had gotten such a story. "A confidential source" was the reply. Within the next few hours Percy was deluged by calls from the wire services and Chicago newspaper correspondents asking him to confirm or deny the same story. Although there was a small (seven- or eight-person) firm involved in exporting police equipment, Percy did not even know of its existence. The story was a complete fabrication and a deliberate attempt to defame Percy.

It took very little detective work to trace the story back to Perle. (Few reporters feel obliged to protect an anonymous source who lies to them, particularly if the lie is a vicious smear, as it was in this case.) Percy wrote Jackson a letter asking for an explanation and an apology from the staff member responsible for spreading the false story. Jackson did not respond; instead, Perle wrote a lengthy letter denying his culpability.

At the executive session that Friday the minority counsel, speaking for the absent Percy, told Jackson he hoped "that the chairman will take such action as is appropriate to prevent that from happening in the future."

Jackson replied: "I, of course, know nothing about it. I didn't talk to any of these reporters about the matter you refer to." Indeed, there was no indication he had any knowledge of Perle's dirty work. Yet, later in the hearing, when the minority counsel voiced his concern that certain subcommittee subpoenas might have been issued in violation of the rules—thus raising the possibility that any evidence obtained with them might be "tainted"—Jackson angrily shot back: "If the minority wants to take the position here of covering up this whole thing, I think—" He did not finish the sentence, which was probably just as well because he seemed to be raising the same false charge that his assistant had tried to spread.

If we learned one thing from Watergate, it is that the man at the top is largely responsible for the attitudes of his personal staff. One cannot help but remember former Attorney General John Mitchell's lamenting before the Senate Watergate Committee that he did not throw G. Gordon Liddy out the window of his Justice Department office when Liddy presented his million-dollar plan for sabotaging the 1972 Democratic campaign. Jackson, alas, seems not to have learned from Mitchell's mistake.

A politician's choice of staff often reveals something of the man himself. A self-assured legislator wants the most intelligent people he can find, even if they outshine him, whereas a hack looks first for obedience in his subordinates and is most comfortable when surrounded by mediocrity. Looking at four of the most important members of Jackson's staff one finds a curious blend of characteristics and one dominant trait common to all: total loyalty to the senator.

For sheer brainpower, Richard Perle stands out. Although his name appears on the payroll of the Permanent Investigations Subcommittee, he is Jackson's principal aide on military issues in general, Israel, and strategic affairs in particular. He often represents the senator at academic or institutional seminars to argue the Jackson case against Kissinger's concept of détente. Even those who disagree completely with his point of view usually come away impressed with his intellect and the skill with which he presents his case. His major flaw seems to be a combination of ambition and loyalty. "Scoop got him brand new, and he's grown up there," says a former Senate aide who had extensive dealings with Perle. "He's now a true believer, and it's reinforced because he wants the senator to use his input and speeches." His assistance to Jackson in the purge of the SALT delegation and crude defamation of Senator Percy reveal a propensity for Machiavellian tactics which, because he is really not very adept at it, could ultimately prove to be his (or Jackson's) undoing.

Dorothy Fosdick is Jackson's foreign-affairs specialist and Perle's nominal superior on the subcommittee staff; however, reports one former aide, when Perle speaks, "she'll pick up on what he's been saying." In other words, she tacitly acknowledges Perle as her intellectual superior. Fosdick has been working for Jackson for two decades and still seems awed in his presence. At hearings she has been known to change seats so she can get an unobstructed view of the senator, and observers report that she sometimes sits on the edge of her chair when she is talking to Jackson in his office and seems to hang on his every word. If he raises a particular subject, rather than offer her own ideas, she is likely to recall a relevant passage from a speech he gave eight or ten years before. Although she has a doctorate, she seems to relish doing even menial chores for Jackson, such as delivering news releases to the various press galleries in the Capitol. After one closed Senate session in which Jackson used secret Pentagon charts to sell that body on the Trident submarine, I saw the diminutive Fosdick with the giant charts tucked under her arm, listing slightly to starboard but walking with grim resolution back to her office. No task is too small, none demeaning, if it will advance her man and his cause. Although some believe Fosdick's rigid cold war outlook is the prism that distorts Jackson's perspective, she is, in truth, but a loyal servitor: a Rose Mary Woods with a Ph.D.

S. Sterling Munro is Jackson's administrative assistant, the highest-ranking aide in his Senate office. "He's the ideal AA for Jackson," says a former Capitol Hill associate. "The paper moves; the work gets done. He protects Jackson and reinforces him. He can guess what his position will be. . . . He's almost a mechanical man. Very proper. When he's upset, you'll not hear a word. No feedback. He's cool and tight; he's made a profession of guarding his emotions. When he's really upset, you simply don't hear from him. He's not a very secure man because he's got nowhere else to go. He started in the Capitol as an elevator operator under Jackson's patronage."

In 1961 Jackson rescued Brian Corcoran from the obscurity of the Everett *Herald*, where he was a sportswriter, and made him press secretary. "Corcoran is one of the stupidest people I've ever met—obnoxious and insensitive," says a former Senate aide, who nonetheless admits, "but Scoop gets a lot of press." Corcoran regularly grinds out press releases and maintains close contact with friendly reporters and editors but reacts to journalists critical of Jackson the way a bull does a waving red flag. His favorite tactic is a call, not to the offending journalist but to his editor or publisher. For example, during the 1972 Florida primary campaign, a television commentator criticized Jackson for his anti-busing amendment. When Corcoran heard about it, he called the man's boss and pointed out: "This is Florida; it's not America." The implication was that the commentator was naïve not to realize such political ploys are part of the game. Reporters are generally angered by back-door tactics such as these and rightly describe Corcoran as "heavy-handed." Moreover, his tactics often backfire because reporters are more likely to intensify their criticism rather than abandon it if only to convince their colleagues they have not been intimidated. Still, Corcoran does get his boss a lot of publicity.

Jackson, like Nixon, does not want thinkers on his staff so much as loyal operatives, but unlike Nixon, loyalty is a two-way street with Jackson. He takes a paternal interest in his employees and goes out of his way to help them even after they leave his office. A senator worried about schisms within the ranks of his staff inevitably loses some of his effectiveness. With loyal assistants such as Perle, Fosdick, Munro, and Corcoran, Jackson has no such worries. Helping him maintain and increase his power and prestige is their full-time occupation.

Legislative power at its root is the power to say no. Bills can be pigeonholed by hostile committee chairmen, watered down by opponents, filibustered by a determined minority or simply defeated by a majority: the forms a legislative veto can take are limited only by the imagination, influence, and parliamentary skill of an antagonist. On the other hand, there is essentially just one way to get a bill enacted, and a senator's mastery of the legislative process in the upper chamber will be to no avail if his measure is vetoed by the House.

Jackson's effectiveness in the Senate stems in part from his willingness to threaten and use the legislative veto. In 1963, for example, he raised objections to the partial test-ban treaty in the month and a half between its signing in Moscow and the Senate vote consenting to its ratification. Although he ultimately voted for it, his threatened obstruction contained an implicit message for President Kennedy and his successors:

either heed my counsel before you conclude another arms agreement or face the risk that I will obstruct it in the Senate.

Individual legislators deliver such ultimatums every time they speak against a presidential proposal, but they can reasonably be ignored when the only vote at stake is their own. Presidents become concerned only when a legislator's standing is such that he might attract significant support among his colleagues. Jackson's committee assignments and expertise on military affairs and natural resources enhance his influence in those areas, but because he has never been a leader on economic or human issues, such as consumer protection or health care, any speech he might make on those subjects will have a predictably small audience in the Senate. So Jackson's modest support (48 percent) for President Nixon's domestic policies, as compared to his strong support (93 percent) for Nixon's foreign policies, in Senate votes in 1969 and 1970 probably caused Nixon no concern because Jackson's standing among his colleagues on domestic affairs was slight to nonexistent. In foreign affairs, the one area that really mattered to Nixon, Jackson was a sure and steady ally for several years.

Jackson's influence in national security affairs during the Johnson era was modest at best, but his close working relationship with the Nixon administration catapulted him to prominence. Democratic senators concerned about the loss of defense contracts or the closing of military bases back home turned increasingly to him as a channel to the White House and the Defense Department. He also used his position to manipulate those of his colleagues who could be swayed by the specter of further base closings or the lure of the Pentagon's pork barrel. From what he learned of the national security decision-making process in the early 1960s, he knew which generals and bureaucrats at Defense and State were formulating policy options. They were receptive to him in the first place because he had always been sympathetic to their establishmentarian point of view; Nixon's anointing of Jackson made them even more receptive. Thus, when he sought information in advance about major policy options or more mundane matters such as base closings, he was certain to get cooperation.

Like Dr. Frankenstein, however, Nixon saw his creature turn into a monster. Power on Capitol Hill is essentially the ability to influence others, and once a legislator has gained significant power, he can often maintain it independent of his sponsor if, like Jackson, he has rewards and punishments to dole out. In the early days of the Nixon administration Democratic senators who approached it in search of a favor might be told to "clear it with Scoop." They did and continued the practice long after Jackson's own presidential ambitions and Watergate convinced him that being perceived as close to Nixon was as sure a path to political oblivion as being photographed on stage with a stripper. Moreover, Jackson was now in a position where he no longer needed Nixon's help because he could increase his power even more by turning into an adversary and threatening the President's policies with a legislative veto, as he did after SALT I.

Jackson is no legislative craftsman. For example, he has often had to introduce what is called "an amendment in the nature of a substitute" to his own bills because they have been poorly or hastily drafted and rushed by him through the Interior Committee, over which he has nearly total control. On the other hand, he is an extremely cunning parliamentary tactician, particularly when he is threatening to obstruct a bill unless its authors accede to his demands. He can often frame a complicated issue in such stark, simplistic terms that the Senate feels compelled to go along for fear of appearing to be against God, Flag, and Motherhood. This favorite Jackson tactic is what I call the "Godfather Gambit": I'll make them an amendment they couldn't possibly refuse.

Jackson's amendment to the SALT agreement limiting offensive arms was of this type. After all, how many senators would feel comfortable opposing "equality" in strategic arms? Not many. But what does the term actually mean? The Soviet Union has heavier missiles; the United States has three times as many warheads. Their warheads are larger, but ours are more accurate. They have potential adversaries armed with thousands of intermediate-range nuclear weapons on their western and southern borders; with our borders secure, we are threatened by intercontinental forces but not those of intermediate range. Given such asymmetries the term "equality" can have no precise meaning. Yet, as we saw in the preceding chapter, Jackson convinced so many of his fellow senators to accept this meaningless abstraction that the Nixon administration felt compelled to come to terms with him.

Senators generally lose influence on Capitol Hill when they run for the Presidency; and in spite of Jackson's prominence in military affairs, Soviet relations, and energy matters, his power in the Senate seems to be diminishing. The Percy incident, mentioned earlier, indicates how much his presidential ambitions have influenced his conduct. In other years, when his only business was the Senate, he would probably have acceded to Percy's request for a few days' delay in the subcommittee's hearing and kept the ranking Republican informed of the panel's investigation. Instead, he kept the information to himself so he could spring it on the media and get all the publicity. This is not the behavior of a serious legislator, and it does not go unnoticed—nor will it long be tolerated—in the clubbish Senate.

In the fall of 1973, Jackson was voted the "most effective" senator in a poll of Senate legislative assistants conducted by Ralph Nader's Capitol Hill News Service. Since then, however, he has suffered a number of reversals at the hands of his colleagues. One indication of how much he has slipped occurred on June 11, 1974.

Jackson had introduced an amendment to the military authorization bill which would have given the Secretary of Defense the power to "disapprove any request for the export of any goods or technology to any controlled country [*i.e.*, the Soviet Union or Eastern Europe] if he determines that the export of such goods or technology will significantly increase the military capability of such country." In other words, the Pentagon would have had primacy in trade, and the President would have been put in the politically untenable position of having to overrule, publicly, a cabinet officer if his Secretary of Defense decided that an American computer destined for, say, a Soviet tire factory had the potential to guide missiles.

The amendment was really unnecessary because the Pentagon already had an input to the Commerce Department, which handles export matters. Although the White House opposed it, Jackson got sub rosa support from Pentagon officials, such as Deputy Secretary of Defense William

Clements. Like Jackson's amendment calling for "equality" in future arms accords, the new measure seemed the sort of amendment the Senate couldn't possibly refuse. Yet this time the "Godfather Gambit" failed. Jackson's amendment was defeated in a parliamentary manuever which replaced it with a watered-down version. Close Senate observers agreed that Jackson could easily have won passage of his measure a few years ago, but now that he was perceived as a grandstander using the Senate for presidential campaign publicity, his colleagues were beginning to look more skeptically at defense proposals they might once have accepted on his sponsorship alone.

Jackson still has important committee posts and is capable of wielding the legislative veto; so he is by no means in danger of completely losing his power in the Senate. Still the signs are clear that it has been diminishing in proportion to his rising presidential ambitions.

The key to Jackson's rise to power was Richard Nixon, but he shrewdly ended his close relationship with the former President well before Watergate engulfed him. Jackson cannot escape the fact, however, that of all the Democrats in the Senate he alone was singled out by Nixon and invited to be Secretary of Defense or Secretary of State. Should Jackson win his party's presidential nomination in 1976, his likely opponent would be President Ford, Nixon's hand-picked successor. Such a race would, indeed, be ironic because no matter which man won he could properly be called Nixon's choice.

Index

ABM. *See* Antiballistic missiles
Adams, Brock, 35, 78–79
AFL-CIO, 13, 72
Agnew, Spiro T., 108, 114
Agriculture, Department of, 139–40
Allen, William (Bill), 74, 105
Allison, Royal B., 205–07, 213–14
America and Palestine, 188–90
American Gypsum Corp., 129
American Jewish Committee, 195
Anderson, Clinton, 107–09, 111, 128, 129, 134
Anderson, John Z., 58–59
Anderson, Konrad, 31
Anderson, Robert, 75–76
Andreas, Dwayne, 24
Antiballistic missiles, 108–09, 111, 144, 161, 199–203, 205–07, 210–11, 219–20
Anti-busing amendment. *See Busing*
Appropriations, House Committee on, 49
Arabs, 193–94
Arafat, Yasser, 189
Argus magazine, 167
Armed Services, House Committee on, 150, 209
Armed Services, Senate Committee on, 98, 162, 183, 202, 207–08, 217
Arms Control and Disarmament Agency, 118, 199–216 *passim*
Aspinall, Wayne, 137
Associated Press (AP), 188
Atomic Energy Commission (AEC), 71, 103, 146. *See also* Hanford (Nuclear) Works
Atomic Energy, Joint Committee on, 99, 155
Atwood, Marilyn, 126

"Ballastic blackmail" (1956 speech), 155–57
Bantz, William ("Big Bill"), 77–78, 114
Baroody, Jamil, 183–84
Beeks, William, 67, 73
Bellingham Normal College, 33
Bentsen, Lloyd, 161–63, 165, 208–09
Black, Lloyd, 41, 44
"Blanket primary," 75
Boeing Corp., 24, 72, 74, 95, 109, 159–60
Bouchard, Edward L., 46–48, 52
Bremerton *Sun,* 166
Brezhnev, Leonid, 161, 199–201
Brown, Harold, 214
Bryant, Alice Franklin, 80
Buchenwald, 152–53, 187–88, 190, 194
Budget, Bureau of the, 140
Budget, Senate Committee on, 145
Busing, 19–20, 194, 228
Byrd, Robert, 121

C-5A transport plane, 158
Cain, Harry P., 56, 61, 73, 77, 95–96, 154
Caldwell, Lynton, 141–42
Campaign financing, 23–25, 73, 77, 139, 194–95, 221–22
Campbell, Clyde, 128
Cannon, Howard, 164
Chamberlain, Neville, 175
Chaney, Neale, 66–67, 90–91
Chase, Maralyn, 82
Chevy Chase (Maryland) Club, 75, 79, 193
China, People's Republic of, 105, 130, 175–78, 179, 180–81, 201
Churchill, Winston, 175, 181
Clarke, Irving M. Jr., 71
Clements, William, 232–33
Cohn, Roy, 96–97
Commerce, Department of, 140

Congressional Directory, 39, 67
Congressional Quarterly, 114, 115, 220
Congressional Record, 50, 141, 187, 190, 193
Corcoran, Brian, 228–29
Corps of Engineers, Army, 144, 146
Cox, Patricia (Tricia) Nixon, 129
Culp, Gordon, 16–17, 67, 72
Custer Died for Your Sins, 134

Daley, Richard, 116
Davis, Walter R., 24
Defense, Department of, 100, 103, 150–68 *passim,* 201, 203, 205, 208, 212, 214, 218, 220, 230–33
Deloria, Vine, 134
Delta Chi fraternity, 38
Democratic National Convention: (1960), 81–82, 113–17, 122, 128; (1968), 82, 85; (1972) 22–23, 85–86, 90
Devine, Ed, 70
DeWitt, John L., 59–60
Dickson, Tom, 86–88
Domino theory, 170–71, 175–76, 178, 180–81
Dootson, Jack, 29–32, 36, 123, 150

Earth Day, 143
Ehrlichman, John, 110, 144, 221
Eisenhower, Dwight D., 95, 114, 171, 218
Elicker, Charles, 78
Elks club, 75, 98
Environmental impact statements, 146–48
Environmental Quality Council (EQC), 143–44
Equal Rights Amendment (ERA), 125, 194
Ervin, Sam, 23
Escalation theory, 170–71, 173–74, 180–81
Eskimos. *See* Native Americans
Evans, Daniel, 221–22
Everett, 29–48 *passim,* 64–65, 74, 75, 127, 184, 185–86
Everett *Daily Herald,* 31, 32, 42, 43, 46, 48, 74, 184
"Everett Massacre," 37
Everett Pulp and Paper Co., 36

F-111 fighter plane, 158
Farley, James A., 39
Farley, Philip, 212
Fink, Reuben, 188–89
Finn, Terence, 140, 146
Ford, Gerald, 233
Foreign Affairs, 165
Foreign Relations, Senate Committee on, 120
Forest Service, 137, 139
Fosdick, Dorothy, 112, 124, 188, 227–28, 229
Fulbright, J. William, 169, 183, 224–25
Fuller, Frederick W., 129

Garner, John Nance, 113
Garthoff, Raymond, 214
Gavin, John, 38, 40
General Accounting Office (GAO), 25
Glacier Peak Wilderness Area, 137–38
Goldsworthy, Patrick, 137–38
Goldwater, Barry, 221
Golub, Stanley, 14, 23, 152, 180, 184
Gorton, Slade, 112, 222–23
Grant, Ulysses, 199
Gulf Oil Corp., 24

Haldeman, H. R., 212
Hanford (Nuclear) Works, 51, 71, 74, 95, 99
Hardin, Helen Eugenia. *See* Helen Jackson
Harding, Warren, 199
Harvey Aluminum Corp., 25
Hébert, F. Edward, 150, 209
Hempelmann, John, 76–77
Hess, Leon, 24
Hiroshima, 157
Hiss, Alger, 96
Hoeck, Gerald, 21, 25, 65
Hoff, Irvin, 68, 115
Hoffman, Abbie, 22
HUAC. *See* Un-American Activities, House Committee on

Humphrey, Hubert, 13, 21, 82, 125, 218

"I Love Lucy" television show, 126
Iklé, Fred C., 213
Indians. *See* Native Americans
Inouye, Daniel Ken, 59
Interior, Senate Committee on, 16, 25, 98, 102, 107, 133–49, 217, 230
International Labor Organization (ILO), 68
Investigations, Senate Permanent Subcommittee on, 95–98, 116, 217, 225–26, 227–28, 232
Isaacs, Stephen, 195
Israel, 182–95 *passim*
"Issues and Answers," 179

Jackson, Agnes, 30–31
Jackson, Arthur, 33–36
Jackson, Gertrude, 30–32, 33, 44, 122
Jackson, Helen, 122, 128–30
Jackson, Henry M.: and 1972 presidential race, 13–26, 80–92 *passim;* approach to state political campaigns, 16–17, 41, 63–79 *passim;* and Senate Interior Committee, 16, 25, 98, 102, 107, 133–49, 217, 230; and "busing," 19–20, 194, 228; and George McGovern, 21–23, 163; and campaign financing, 23–25, 73, 74–75, 76, 80, 101; and military affairs *(see also specific headings),* 26, 52–53, 72, 73–74, 118–20, 152–53, 153–68 *passim;* as ombudsman, 26, 70–71, 111; and growing up in Everett, 29–49; and family, 29–40 *passim,* 53, 122–23; and nickname "Scoop," 31; and personal frugality, 32, 125–26, 127; at the University of Washington, 38–40; as welfare worker, 40–41; as private attorney, 41; as prosecuting attorney of Snohomish County, 41–45, 46–49; and first House race (1940), 48–49, 63–65; early years in the House, 49–61, 123–24; maiden House speech, 49–50, 52; House committee assignments, 51; and Pearl Harbor attack, 53, 150–51, 177; speech to Norway (1942), 53–54; attitude toward Japanese-Americans, 54–62; first Senate race (1952), 61–62, 63, 95–96 and membership in discriminatory clubs, 75, 79, 193; and Washington State liberals, 80–92; and the Vietnam war, 77, 79, 121, 169–81 and 1972 state caucus vote dispute, 85–92; and Joseph McCarthy, 96–98, 114; and Warren Magnuson, 101–12; and Richard Nixon, 110, 144, 163, 170, 179, 200–33; and the 1960 Democratic Convention, 114–17, 128; and vice presidential ambitions, 114–17, 194; and John F. Kennedy, 115–21 *passim,* 160, 169, 170, 171–73, 178–79, 200, 218, 229; and Arms Control and Disarmament Agency, 118, 199–216 *passim;* and United Nations, 118–19, 154, 192; and attitudes and relationships with women, 122–30; and marriage, 122, 128–30; and Native Americans, 133–35; and North Cascades Act of 1968, 136–39; and National Environmental Policy Act (NEPA) of 1969, 139–49; and military service, 150–53; and the U.S.S.R., 92, 101, 153–68 *passim;* and China, 175–78; and Jews and Israel, 182–95; and the "Silver Shirts," 184–87, 194; and Buchenwald, 187–88, 190, 194; attitude toward Arabs, 193–94; and SALT, 199–216; and J. William Fulbright, 223-24; and his staff, 227–29
Jackson, Marie, 30, 33, 122
Jackson, Marine Anderson, 30–31, 34, 53, 104, 122
Jackson, Peter (Gresseth), 30–31, 33–34, 37, 53
Japanese Americans, 54–62
Jefferson, Thomas, 10
Jewish Daily Forward, 184
Jews, 75, 182–95
Jim, Robert B., 133
Johnson, C. Montgomery ("Gummie"), 221–22

Johnson, Lyndon B., 115, 151, 169–70, 178, 201, 217, 218
Johnson, U. Alexis, 212–13

Kennedy, Edward M., 77, 121, 195
Kennedy, John F., 16, 82, 115–21, 138, 160, 169, 170, 171–73, 178–79, 200, 218, 229
Kennedy, Robert F., 71–72, 82, 97, 116–17, 120–21
Khrushchev, Nikita S., 200
Kissinger, Henry A., 204–05, 207, 209–10, 212, 225, 227
Koenig, Vern, 78, 84–85

Laird, Melvin, 161
Lake Chelan National Recreation Area, 138
Langer, Helen, 126–28
Langer, William, 127
League for Industrial Democracy, 38
LeMay, Curtis, 120
Lend-Lease Act (1941), 49
Liddy, G. Gordon, 227
Lincoln, Abraham, 15, 63
Loeb, William, 18
Lombardi, Vince, 107

MacArthur, Douglas, 61
McCall, Tom, 221–22
McCarran Act of 1950, 69
McCarthy, Eugene, 82
McCarthy, Joseph, 96–98, 114
McCarthy, Thomas, 87, 88, 90–91
McClellan, John, 97
McGovern, George, 17, 21–23, 78, 80, 84, 86–92 *passim*, 125, 211
McIntyre, Thomas, 153, 163, 165
McNamara, Robert S., 118, 174, 218
Madison, James, 135, 139
Magnuson, Warren, 68, 78, 101–12 *passim*, 115–16, 151, 221–22
Manchester *Union-Leader*, 18
Mankiewicz, Frank, 90
Mansfield, Mike, 114, 125
Mao Tse-tung, 166
Martin, Clarence D., 29, 44
Masons, 20, 37
Maxey, Carl, 35, 73, 83–84, 89
Mayo Clinic, 34
"Meet the Press," 177, 200, 225
Merchant Marine and Fisheries, House Committee on, 49, 50, 51, 53
Metcalf, Lee, 164
Metropolitan Democratic Club (Seattle), 81
Meyner, Robert B., 115
Milford *Cabinet*, 193-94
Military service, 150-53
Mills, Wilbur, 23
Mines, Bureau of, 144
Minuteman ICBM, 201–04, 206
"Mr. Smith Goes to Washington," 105
Mitchell, Hugh B., 51, 96
Mitchell, John, 227
Montoya, Joseph, 164
Moorer, Thomas, 205, 213
Moss, Frank, 136
Multiple independently targetable reentry vehicles (MIRVs), 204, 206
Munro, S. Sterling, 17, 228–29
Muskie, Edmund, 18, 21, 125, 141–49 *passim*, 225
Myers, Vic, 66

Nader, Ralph, 101–02, 232
Nagasaki, 157
Nasser, Gamal Abdel, 191
National Environmental Policy Act of 1969, 136–37, 139–49, 219
National Security Council, 100, 143
Native Americans, 133–35
NEPA. *See* National Environmental Policy Act of 1969
Neuberger, Richard, 73
New Republic, 73
New York Times, 119–20, 157–58, 192, 193
1984, 165
Nitze, Paul, 214
Nixon, Patricia. *See* Cox, Patricia (Tricia) Nixon
Nixon, Richard M., 19, 24, 68, 99, 103, 106, 112, 114, 143, 148, 160, 161, 170, 178, 195, 199; and Henry M. Jackson: 110, 144, 163, 170, 179, 200–33 *passim*
Nixon, Thelma Ryan (Pat), 129

North Cascades Act of 1968, 136–39
Northrop Corp., 24
Norway, 30–31, 49, 53–54, 153, 200
Nuclear test-ban treaty (1963), 119–20, 160, 200, 229

O'Brien, Lawrence, 117–18
Orwell, George, 165, 186

Pacific Car and Foundry, 34
Palestine Liberation Organization, 189
Pauling, Linus, 81
Peale, Norman Vincent, 117
Pearl Harbor, 53, 150–51, 177
Pearson, Drew, 151
Pedersen, Paul, 78, 87
Percy, Charles, 225–27, 232
Perle, Richard, 111, 188, 214, 226–29
Peterson, Payson, 48–49, 151
Petit, Mrs. Vern, 88
"Point of Order," 97
Polaris ballistic-missile submarine, 160, 164, 168
Public Works, Senate Committee on, 141, 142, 144, 147
Pueblo, 150, 166–67

Rand Corporation, 213
Randolph, Jennings, 145
Rapid-American Corp., 24
Real Majority, The, 18–19
Reed, William, 74
Revelle, Randy, 91
Ribicoff, Abraham, 191
Rickover, Hyman G., 158, 162, 164
Riklis, Meshulam, 24
Rochester, Al, 81
Roosevelt, Franklin D., 22, 44, 49, 64, 151–52, 184, 186, 219
Rosellini, Albert, 116
Ross Lake National Recreation Area, 138
Rubin, Jerry, 22
Rusk, Dean, 218
Ryherd, Mike, 83–85

Safeguard ABM. *See* Antiballistic missiles
Salter, John, 16, 32, 33, 34, 38, 40–41, 42, 44, 46, 48, 50, 53, 67, 68, 72, 84, 87, 96–97, 115, 116–18, 123, 125, 127, 150, 152–53, 186
Scammon, Richard, 18
Schine, G. David, 97–98
"Scoop," source of nickname, 31
Scott, Hugh, 22
Seattle magazine, 69, 134
Seattle Pacific College, 33
Seattle *Post-Intelligencer,* 60, 85, 89, 102, 151, 159, 191, 193, 221–22
Seattle *Times,* 84, 89, 179, 188
Seidel, Henry, 68–89, 78–79, 81
Seven Days in May, 156
Sheridan, Phil, 34, 42–43, 46, 48, 65, 70, 185–86
Shriners, 75
Sierra Club, 137
"Silver Shirts," 184–87, 194
Simpson Timber Company, 74
"60 Minutes," 169, 225
Smith, Gerard, 203, 206, 211, 212
Smith, Margaret Chase, 108
Soviet Union. *See* Union of Soviet Socialist Republics
SS-9 (Soviet) ICBM, 202
Stalin, Joseph, 22, 155
"star system" in state politics, 76, 101
Starbuck, Kathy, 193–94
Stennis, John, 207
Stern, Bernice, 129
Stevenson, Adlai, 114, 116
Stewart, James, 106
Stiley, Pat, 89
Strategic Arms Limitation Talks (SALT), 161, 199–216 *passim,* 227
Subversive Activities Control Board, 69
Swanson, Al, 41–42
Sylvester, Jack, 40, 44
Symington, Stuart, 97, 115, 117, 225

Talleyrand, Charles Maurice de, 204
Tanner, Jack, 87–88, 90
Taylor, Glenn, 96
Thant, U, 192
Thieu, Nguyen Van, 179–80
Thomas, Norman, 38
Time magazine, 73

Time Oil Company, 24
Tonkin Gulf Resolution, 169
Tower, John, 221
Trident ballistic-missile submarine, 160, 161, 168, 207–09, 210, 215–16, 228
Truman, Harry S, 51, 69, 154, 172, 189

Un-American Activities, House Committee on, 69, 72
Union of Soviet Socialist Republics, 22, 62, 98, 153–62 *passim,* 177, 182, 191, 195, 199–200, 201–04, 205–09, 232
United Nations, 118–19, 154, 192
United Press International (UPI), 13
University Club (Seattle), 74, 75, 79, 193
University of Washington, 38–40, 76, 106, 137
Unruh, Jesse, 23
Urban Affairs Council, 143

Van Ness, William, 140–41
Veterans of Foreign Wars, 221
Vietnam, war in, 71–72, 77, 79, 82, 83, 111, 169–81

Wallace, George C., 13, 19–21
Wallace, Henry A., 22
Wallace, Mike, 169, 170, 174
Wallgren, Monrad (Mon), 46, 64
Warren, Earl, 119
Washington *Post,* 193, 195
Watergate Committee, 23–24, 215
Waters, Lyle, 31, 37
Wattenberg, Ben J., 18–21, 25
Welch, Joseph, 97
Western Washington State University, 33
Westmoreland, William, 174
Whittaker, James, 71–72
Wild, Claude, 24
Wilson, John F., 82, 86, 130
Wohlberg, Mitchell, 182

Yankelovich, Daniel, 195
Yorty, Sam, 18
Young Socialists' League, 38
"Youth Wants to Know," 74

Ziegler, Ron, 188